A Man Like Him
Portrait of the Burmese Journalist, Journal Kyaw U Chit Maung

T0349767

Cornell University

Wedding day of U Chit Maung and Daw Ma Ma Lay

Journal Kyaw Ma Ma Lay
Ma Thanegi, translator

A Man Like Him
Portrait of the Burmese Journalist, Journal Kyaw U Chit Maung

SOUTHEAST ASIA PROGRAM PUBLICATIONS
Southeast Asia Program
Cornell University
Ithaca, New York
2008

Cornell Southeast Asia Program Publications
640 Stewart Avenue, Ithaca, NY 14850-3857

Studies on Southeast Asia No. 47

Printed in the United States of America

ISBN: hc – 978-0-87727-777-4
ISBN: pb – 978-0-87727-747-7

Cover Design: Maureen Viele, Ithaca, NY

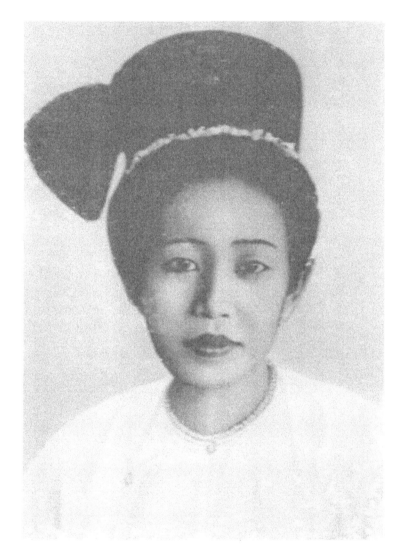

Daw Ma Ma Lay, with the high chignon fashionable in the 1930s

Portrait of Journal Kyaw U Chit Maung

Portrait of Journal Kyaw Ma Ma Lay
as a young widow

TABLE OF CONTENTS

TRANSLATOR'S NOTE

Ma Thanegi

Thu-lo Lu (A Man Like Him), is the story of the last eight years of Journal Kyaw U Chit Maung's life. This account was written ten months after his death in 1946 by his twenty-nine-year-old widow, Journal Kyaw Ma Ma Lay. It was first published in May 1947 and went through three printings in the same year. The tenth edition was published in 2003.

This young couple had published the prestigious *Journal Kyaw* weekly, and thus their names are forever associated with the paper. U Chit Maung was a great editor and committed patriot, and a brilliant, self-educated man who served his country well and who was deeply involved in politics from behind the scenes during the colonial period and the Japanese Occupation. He was a man who had no desire for power, position, or fame.

The eight short years of their union, from 1938 to 1946, covered a period of great change in the country, with the nationalist movement rising to the height of its fervor against British rule, followed by the Second World War and the Japanese Occupation.

Thu-lo Lu provides an insight into the politics and economy of Myanmar, as well as into the traditional relationships between parents and children, where personal pride has to give way in the face of love.

It is interesting to note the women's issues of that period, which are illuminated by this narrative, while at the same time learning about this unlikely romance between two very different personalities. Each word of this book shows how intensely they loved each other and how she supported him at all times. Theirs was a marriage of destiny. However, Journal Kyaw Ma Ma Lay herself was a much respected writer who achieved success in her own right and retained her identity and independence.

It is my privilege to translate this book, and the work has been a labor of love.

I am indebted to Dr. Daw Khin Lay Myint, professor of French, the daughter of U Chit Maung and Ma Ma Lay, and to the poet U Moe Hein, their son, for reading over the manuscript and making thoughtful suggestions.

I am also deeply grateful to Robert Taylor, who, busy as his schedule is, kindly took the time to write the introduction and edit my manuscript.

As I worked, my thoughts dwelt on my late uncle, journalist and editor Tetkatho Htin Gyi, who as a college newspaper reporter covered the 1938 students' demonstration, and who regaled me with stories of those times throughout my childhood. I am also indebted to my late friend Kyi Kyi Yin, known to many as "Ma," who introduced me to Journal Kyaw Ma Ma Lay's works when we were students at the Institute of Economics. She and I are among the thousands of Myanmar women to whom Journal Kyaw Ma Ma Lay gave the strength to face life with courage. With this work, I am but repaying a minute amount of the debt that my friends and I owe to the writer.

In this translation, I have added footnotes to explain some Burmese terms, to provide biographical and geographical data, or to clarify historical facts. The name "Burma" was coined by the British through hearing the word "Bama," the name of the majority race. I have used the word "Myanmar" for the name of our country, since for centuries "Myanmar" has been its local name, a name first recorded on a stone inscription in 1235 AD and in use since that time. Also, I have used the original name "Yangon," which means "End of Strife," instead of "Rangoon." Some anglicized names remain unchanged where relevant.

A note for the reader: Myanmar proper names for an adult man are prefixed with the honorific, "U," pronounced "Oo," and for a woman, "Daw." When addressing a young man, one uses the prefix "Ko," or "Maung," and for a young woman, one uses "Ma." Sometimes "Maung" or "Ma" may be adopted as part of a person's pen name or performing name. Very close friends or family members may ignore the use of prefixes in addressing or referring to those younger than themselves, but it is never acceptable to address or refer to a person who is older without using the honorific prefix. In the text, a particular character may be identified with different prefixes; for instance, in one situation U Chit Maung refers to U Ba Hnin as "Ko Ba Hnin" when speaking informally.

"Thakin" for men and "Thakin-ma" for women were nationalist prefixes meaning "Master," used by Myanmar politicians during their fight for independence.

The Burmese do not take on family names. Each person has his or her own given name, and the same names recur frequently throughout the population. Also, a person can change his or her name to reflect his or her experiences, as noted above.

FOREWORD
Moe Hein

Thu-lo Lu, what a blessing that you have come out in an English version! My long-awaited desire now becomes a reality, though not of my making. I wanted so fervently to translate you myself ... who else would be as eager? Whenever I am introduced as my parents' child, the first word uttered by anyone having read you would be your name: *Thu-lo Lu*.

To all readers, you are an inspiration and role model, as they so often tell me. So what then held me back from translating? Two things. First, my head knew it was not competent to take up the task and, second, my heart feared the flood of feelings that would be unleashed, for within you both my parents are embodied. My mind would be laden with memories and feelings. In such a position, I cannot trust my hand. Sentimental—subjective—one may call me. But truly, I would be at a loss and the work a failure. You are far beyond my reach.

Now, fate has been so good as to provide a hand capable of mastering the task. With a strong spirit driving hard to fulfill its aim, this hand has transformed you, *Thu-lo Lu*, into a work for international presentation, thereby enabling you to cross all frontiers. The skilled work of the translator exactly reflects the tone and tempo of the original writer, and many more readers can now enjoy you. Moreover, footnotes and explanations are provided to give a fuller picture. What more could be expected? With heart and soul, the hand has painstakingly labored. It is a work of dedication and no less a work of art. Even if I had attempted to translate, I could not have done better.

When my eyes first fell upon the translated manuscript, I was reawakened. As before, *Thu-lo Lu*, you have brought back to life the ones I love. I see them, hear them, and feel them. Reborn am I! A man over sixty is simply reduced to a child of six. Tears of joy and sadness well up as I see my parents again in this translation.

Thu-lo Lu, in the same way that you have inspired many a reader in the past, so will you in the future. Your characters died long ago, but they are not dead, for in you they live. They continue to strengthen the morale and morals of readers through you.

What a blessing! Fate honors you with a translation, fate honors the hand that accomplished the work. As for me, I feel I do not even deserve this page, even though kindly offered. All in all, the two hands, one that first brought you to life and another that led you further, will leave a lasting imprint upon your readers.

"To Serve and Sacrifice"

Moe Hein
Son of Journal Kyaw
April 2006

Preface to the First Edition

by Journal Kyaw Ma Ma Lay

In the preparation of this book, I did not have the ease that I had with my earlier works. This book was begun in the month of Tabaung, ten months after the death of its central character, my husband, Journal Kyaw U Chit Maung. In the actual writing of it, I found that I could hardly continue from one paragraph to the next. As I began to write it after U Chit Maung was no more with me, my heart felt as if it were burning, and this hampered my writing and delayed the completion of the book.

When I had previously advertised in the *Journal Kyaw* an upcoming book titled "A Man like Him," I had not meant this particular one. Instead, the title had been chosen for a novel intended to be a guide for young women in the choosing of marriage partners. Ultimately, if it had not been for someone who persuaded and entreated me to write about U Chit Maung, this book using the same title would not have been written.

Out of love and respect for my husband who had been his mentor, Tetkatho Ko Myo Thant repeatedly exhorted me to write this story about him—to show that someone of his stamp had lived and breathed, and to title it "A Man Like Him." There are other reasons, as Ko Myo Thant explained to me: in the recently published *Diary of U Chit Maung*, there is a poem in which he spoke of the extraordinary way in which he met me, the person destined to one day become his wife—

"*Coming to know you, through what fate ordained from times past ...*"—surely, Ko Myo Thant said, those who read this poem would wish to know the details of this first encounter.

Then, he said that, U Chit Maung having been a veritable storehouse of knowledge, his biography would have been full of illuminating and noteworthy facts. As he had been so uncomfortably shy in the presence of women as to earn the moniker of "monk," his "love story" would certainly be out of the ordinary, something that people would be exceedingly curious to know about. Ko Myo Thant also repeatedly argued that such vignettes from his life—from the time he met his destined wife to his last moments—would be of interest to his children and to other readers.

Therefore, since Ko Myo Thant was very persistent, and as I myself believed that my husband's biography should be written, this book has been produced and presented to my readers.

Innumerable biographies and autobiographies of prominent people have existed in the West since ages past. However, such works have not emerged in Myanmar, and I wondered whether I might not be too far ahead of the times in penning something like this. I also had to weigh the benefits of revealing a late person's private affairs to the reading public.

However, it so happened that when U Chit Maung was alive, the two of us had promised each other that one day we would present each other with our life stories titled "My Husband" and "My Wife," respectively, and this really was the main reason for this book. Ever since that promise, every single day I had recorded all that I could about U Chit Maung with the writing of such a book in mind. However, the files of those records, meticulously maintained since our marriage, were partially lost when the house where we had been living during the Japanese Occupation, opposite the Teachers' Training College on Pyay Road, was heavily bombed shortly before the British reoccupation of Myanmar towards the end of World War II. I was heartbroken after this destruction of the fruits of nine years of laborious record keeping, and I despaired of ever producing the book in mind. But now, although it is not a full biography, this volume has come into being, and my initial objective has been fulfilled, although not in full, as I had hoped to do.

This work is not one of fiction written purely to arouse a reader's interest but is about real events. After the readers have gone through both volumes I and II[1] of this work, it is for them to decide if they have in fact found it interesting.

1309, Fifth Waning Moon Day of Kason
May 9, 1947

---

[1] The original edition of *Thu-lo Lu* was published in two volumes.

BIOGRAPHY OF
JOURNAL KYAW U CHIT MAUNG

U Chit Maung was born in 1912 in Oke Po, central Myanmar, to U Mya and Daw Saw Yu. When U Chit Maung finished high school, he was three years too young to be eligible for college. During the wait to attend college, he worked as a teacher at his own school and read all he could independently. While in his late teens, he moved to Yangon, applied for an opening at *Nawrahta* newspaper, and was hired as soon as he applied, even at such a tender age. When this paper folded, he went to work for *Myanmar Alin,* where he became chief editor, a post he held for many years without using the title. However, in 1940 he fell out with the publishers, who he felt were infringing on his rights as a journalist, and he left the paper, although he would still speak out on its behalf when necessary.

Thereafter, along with his wife, Daw Tin Hlaing (also called Ma Ma Lay), whom he had married in 1938, he published a weekly paper called *Journal Kyaw,* or *The Weekly Thunderer.* The paper became highly popular, as it was strongly supportive of the nationalistic movement and the rights of the poor. From that time, he became known as Journal Kyaw U Chit Maung and his wife as Journal Kyaw Ma Ma Lay.

U Chit Maung wrote several novels and a few nonfiction political works. His novel *Thu* (He) became an instant bestseller and is regarded as a classic of Myanmar literature. It was made into a feature movie that enjoyed box-office success.

During the Japanese Occupation, his intelligence work was unknown to others apart from a very few. He later joined the executive committee of the Anti-Fascist People's Freedom League party (AFPFL), formed under General Aung San, and was active in the fight for independence. Many of his suggestions were used in the demands submitted to the British. All his life, his goal was to serve his country without any wish for a political role or recognition. His diary entries and his last satirical poem were testaments, among many other works, of his lifelong disgust with the corruption that so often results from power.

He passed away on April 3, 1946, at the age of thirty-four, after a short illness, one year and nine months before Myanmar gained independence. He remains a highly respected figure and role model for generations of men and women of Myanmar.

BIOGRAPHY OF
JOURNAL KYAW MA MA LAY

Journal Kyaw Ma Ma Lay, the fourth child of Dawson Bank manager U Pyar Cho and Daw Kwi, was born on April 13, 1917, in Kamar Kalu, a village of the Bogalay township. Her given name was Ma Tin Hlaing. She finished middle school in Bogalay, where her father worked, and then studied up to the ninth grade (1932) at Yangon's Myoma Girls' High School. In 1938 she married U Chit Maung, chief editor of *Myanmar Alin.*

In 1946, U Chit Maung passed away, leaving behind his wife, a daughter, and two sons.

In 1959, Ma Ma Lay married U Aung Zeya, who took care of her the way she had taken care of U Chit Maung.

As a young girl, Ma Tin Hlaing was active in nationalistic activities in Bogalay, experiences from which she drew for her famous novel *Mon-yway Mahu* (which was translated into English as "Not Out of Hate"). The same book was also translated into French by her daughter, Daw Khin Lay Myint, who was a professor of French, under the title *La mal Aimée.*

Ma Ma Lay was the co-publisher of *Journal Kyaw* and editor for both the *Journal Kyaw* and *Pyi-thu hit-taing* papers (1939), vice chair of the Women's Pen Club and editor of *Writers' Magazine* (1947), chair of the Union of Myanmar Journalists Association (1948–49), and secretary of the Union of Myanmar Writers' Club (1961–62). Besides her novels, Ma Ma Lay wrote many short stories. She used the pen name Journal Kyaw Ma Ma Lay, adopting the title of the journal that she helped publish, in the same way that her first husband was known as Journal Kyaw U Chit Maung. She was also a renowned and successful indigenous medicine healer.

In spite of her well-to-do background, she often wrote about poverty-stricken urban workers or peasants. For those pieces she did extensive research, and few other writers managed to capture and convey the details that make her subjects seem to come to life. Almost all of her writings addressed the role of women in society and the workplace. In her time, the majority of writings were "Pyin nyar pay," that is, "educational" works to teach the young about issues of morality, and *A Man Like Him* is no different.

While Ma Ma Lay supported the traditional social norms of decorous behavior for women and thought that women should fulfill their "housewifely" duties, she nevertheless made a strong call for women to value intelligence and independence, and to have successful careers. She stood out among the other educated, gracious, and well-bred Burmese women of her day as a great writer and role model for many.

She passed away in Yangon on April 6, 1982.

Journal Kyaw U Chit Maung and Myanmar's Late-Colonial Politics

by Robert H. Taylor

The decade prior to the death of Journal Kyaw U Chit Maung, in 1946, including the eight or so years described so effectively by his widow Journal Kyaw Ma Ma Lay in the book *Thu-lo Lu*, were among the most significant of Myanmar's turbulent twentieth century. The seeds then planted helped bring forth the British colony's tortured post-independence civil strife and the eventual rise of socialist autarky and military rule. These years witnessed the administrative separation of the Province of Burma from India; the introduction of a system of limited parliamentary democracy for the majority of the population; the growth of student and left-wing ideological ferment and radical nationalist agitation, international intrigue, and war; and, finally, the rise of armed resistance and multi-sided, mass political struggle verging on revolution. Whereas Myanmar commenced this period as an effective and outwardly prosperous colonial economy, it ended the era with its major industries and their markets devastated and its people suffering extreme economic deprivation. The legacy of those eventful years is still apparent in the first decade of the twenty-first century.

U Chit Maung and Daw Ma Ma Lay were at the center of those developments, as *Thu-lo Lu* makes clear, both chronicling events and attempting to guide them. The hugely different social and economic backgrounds of this unusual couple highlight one of the fascinating aspects of late-colonial Myanmar. While Daw Ma Ma Lay came from a prosperous family—her father worked for the only Myanmar-based, but British-owned, bank in the country, a major supplier of agricultural credit to the country's farmers—U Chit Maung was from a relatively impoverished small town in the central dry zone of the country. Their small-town origins, fierce independence, and keen intellects, as well as their mastery of English and desire to see an end to Myanmar's colonial status, were perhaps the only things this couple initially shared. As Daw Ma Ma Lay lived without want or care, reading books and magazines from

England in the midst of Myanmar's rice-growing Ayeyarwaddy delta, her lush environment stands in marked contrast to the arid circumstances of U Chit Maung's boyhood in Myanmar's dry-zone cultural heartland. While both came to develop a deep apprehension of the contemporary world and its challenges and opportunities, both never forgot their diverse Myanmar origins.

The complexity of the years described in the book is obvious from the tale itself. For those who are unfamiliar with the saga of Myanmar's late-colonial political economy and social history, it may well seem incredibly perplexing. It was a colony full of contradictions and conundrums. Despite the country's colonial status, the press was relatively free, and censorship of books and other published material did not become onerous until the beginning of the Second World War and the introduction of the Defense of Burma Act and Rules after 1939. The British were so confident of their power and the stability of their empire that the existence in Burma of a free nationalist press and the development of political parties, some with their own "private armies" of unarmed supporters, was not seen as a major threat. The introduction of electoral politics in the early 1920s and the expansion of elected ministers' powers in a Westminster-style cabinet government following the introduction of the Government of Burma Act on April 1, 1937, were seen as steps in Myanmar's inevitable, but still distant, evolution as a self-governing dominion of the British Empire. As long as the British- and Indian-dominated civil service "held the ring," and the British governor maintained sole authority over defense, finance, and the separate administration of the Shan States and the frontier areas in the north of the country, Myanmar politicians were allowed to play the parliamentary game with as much bravado and money as they could muster. The massive peasant revolt known as the Saya San rebellion (1930–32) was the only event prior to the Second World War to raise doubts about the perpetuity of British rule. When the British suppressed that huge outpouring of peasant discontent, they suggested agrarian reforms, but Myanmar nationalists drew very different and much more radical lessons from that violent episode.

Similarly, the University of Yangon, though viewed by the business community and other conservative groups as a hotbed of subversion, enjoyed relative academic freedom, a situation that encouraged its students to debate widely on the ideological and political issues of the day. Their British and Indian teachers watched with a benign tolerance, which was only occasionally challenged by the most vociferous nationalists, as the students organized themselves in the student union and published newspapers critical of their education. The faculty's benign tolerance merely served to increase the radical energies of those Myanmar students who had come from provincial towns to what was in many ways an alien city, an alien university, and an alien existence. The education offered to them they described as a "slave" education, designed to entrap their spirits rather than liberate their minds and their country. Journal Kyaw U Chit Maung's reference to G. E. Harvey's widely read *History of Burma*[1] reflected this situation. Harvey claimed that the British had "saved Burma," evoking the question, "saved the colony from what and for whom?" The answer was sought not in the classroom but in the books and magazines of British, Indian, and Burmese left-wing writers, which were readily available and

---

[1] G. E. Harvey, *History of Burma: From the Earliest Times to 10 March 1824, the Beginning of the English Conquest* (London: Longmans, Green, and Co., 1925).

which intellectuals like U Chit Maung knew well. The 1930s was an ideological age all the world over, and Myanmar fully shared in its debates.

Imagine the impression on a late adolescent who, having gained admission to his country's most prestigious educational institution, discovered that most of his or her teachers were Indians or British. To suffer the apparent disdain of sophisticated urbanites might be difficult for a country lad or lass to bear. To be told that one's ancestors were incapable of preserving their own civilization without foreign rule must have been unbearable. Imagine the anger that would rise in one when most of the officials one dealt with on a daily basis in one's capital city were foreigners. Even the language spoken in its major market city was foreign—Hindi rather than Burmese—and the language of government was foreign—English, not Burmese. In the 1930s, half of Yangon's population was composed of Hindus and Muslims of South Asian descent, now called Indians, Pakistanis, and Bangladeshis, who had come to live among the Theravada Buddhists of Myanmar. Yangon at that time was the second busiest port in the world for immigration, as thousands of South Asians entered and left the colony each year, with increasing numbers settling permanently and competing for the jobs and land that the indigenous population considered theirs. The resulting economic and social competition fueled the racial and religious riots that are described so graphically in *Thu-lo Lu.*

The mixture of student radicalism, feeding on nationalist and Marxist publications, and racial conflict, fueled by religious discord and economic competition, provided a volatile source of support for politicians playing the parliamentary game that the British declared open to all who agreed to stay within the rules. The two politicians who dominated that game until the Japanese declared it over in 1942 were Dr. Ba Maw and U Saw. These two rivals, and their maneuverings, are part of the backdrop to the early political events that Daw Ma Ma Lay describes U Chit Maung attempting to mastermind and criticize, both in his journalism and in his capacity as a political advisor. The parliament elected Ba Maw the country's first premier in 1937. U Saw, who lacked Ba Maw's intellectual finesse and stylish manners, nevertheless possessed an instinct for grasping a political opportunity, creating a political force, and remaking the balance of power in his own interest. He soon set out to do so.

These two rivals made and broke alliances with nationalist youths such as Thakin Aung San and other leaders of the Yangon University Students' Union and the Do Bama Asi-ayon (We Burmans Association) in order to unseat their rivals and gain power for themselves. When Dr. Ba Maw dominated the parliament, U Saw plotted to bring him down with the assistance of students who despised them both—and made that clear rhetorically—for playing the British parliamentary game and seemingly being their willing stooges. When U Saw strode to power on the backs of the students, and with a little help from his Japanese, Chinese, and Myanmar financial backers, he watched Dr. Ba Maw form an alliance with the students known as the Freedom Bloc. Happy to work with the British whom he had previously denounced so forcefully with Thakin Aung San at his elbow, U Saw, when he reached the top job, embraced the Defense of Burma Rules that the Governor handed him to suppress his political opponents and erstwhile allies, eventually even canceling scheduled parliamentary elections. These events and many others like them took place during the first half of the decade that *Thu-lo Lu* documents.

The second half of that decade commenced with the bombing of Yangon by the Japanese in December 1941 and January 1942. The confidence of the colonial state in its ability to keep in check the nationalist energies and racial antagonisms was part of the same self-satisfaction that created the complacent belief that there was no possibility that international conflict could disrupt their world. The speed with which the Second World War engulfed Myanmar was not only unexpected but also unprecedented. The British were completely incapable of defending their colony, and thousands of persons, British and South Asians, were forced to flee ignominiously in the first four months of 1942—by sea if lucky, on foot if not—to India. Thousands died along the way. Three years later, in 1945, the British returned to a different country, one in which they could no longer preside with moral and military self-confidence, but where they were instead overwhelmed by the radical nationalism that they had so indifferently ignored in the first half of Daw Ma Ma Lay's and U Chit Maung's exciting decade together.

How did this quick turnabout occur? Again, the story is complex. Before the Japanese invaded British Myanmar, they prepared a means to undermine the British short of war. Primarily this was through providing military training to a small group, eventually thirty individuals, nationalist youths from the larger "leftist" Kodaw Hmaing faction of the Do Bama Asi-ayon and the smaller, anti-socialist Ba Sein faction of the organization. This was done by spiriting individuals such as Thakin Aung San, Thakin Ye Htut, Thakin Hla Pe, Thakin Hla Maung, and Thakin Shu Maung (later Bo Gyoke or General Ne Win) to Hainan Island for specialized training. When the Japanese war in South East Asia proceeded far more easily than expected, and the Japanese decided to take the war to the Indian border, the Thirty Comrades, as they became known, became the nucleus of an indigenous army that was raised on the march from Bangkok into Myanmar via Tanintharyi (Tenasserim) in the first months of 1942. The Tatmadaw, Myanmar's armed forces, were thus born.

Promised independence by their Japanese mentors, the Burma Independence Army (BIA), led by Thakin, then Bo Gyoke Aung San, assumed they had the right to rule. The Japanese thought otherwise, and they soon had to rein in the force they had unleashed by imposing an indigenous government of their choosing on the country. Thakin Tun Oke, one of the Thirty Comrades, was the first to head this imposed government but he was soon replaced by the irrepressible Dr. Ba Maw. Ba Maw's nemesis, U Saw, spent the war in a British prison in Uganda, having been caught promising the Japanese that he would raise his own army to assist them. He had relayed this promise through the Japanese embassy in Lisbon on his way home from a failed mission to London and Washington, DC, during which he had demanded a promise of dominion status for his country when the war was over.

The BIA, soon greatly reduced in size and renamed the Burma National Army (BNA), became a new factor in Myanmar's overt political and institutional life. During this same time, the Communist Party of Burma (BCP) arose, also born in the midst of the defeat of the British and the victory of the Japanese. The BCP, founded in 1939 by Aung San, had several other figures who aspired to lead it with their own ideological and programmatic policies. With Aung San now in charge of the budding Myanmar military, one Communist faction, led by Thakin Than Tun, who served as Minister of Agriculture during the Japanese era, organized the country's restive agrarian population as a potential political force. Than Tun also became Aung San's brother-in-law, the two men marrying sisters in the midst of the Japanese-sponsored interlude when Dr. Ba Maw presided as the Adipati Ashin Mingyi. The other faction was led by the irrepressible Thakin Soe. Soe, the originator of many of the Marxist-cum-Buddhist concepts that formed the heart of Myanmar socialist rhetoric for years after his political demise, refused to ally himself with the "Fascist Japanese." At the start of the war, he and his followers went underground and began organizing a resistance movement against the Japanese. His group also dispatched Thakin Thein Pe (Myint), U Chit Maung's interlocutor at several points in *Thu-lo Lu*, to India, where he joined up with British military intelligence to lay the groundwork for an eventual temporary alliance between these diverse Myanmar nationalist forces and the British against the Japanese.

After independence came to Myanmar just six years after the Japanese invasion, all of these young men were to be involved in leading one or another of the major political forces of the country's incipient civil war that Daw Ma Ma Lay anticipates in the months prior to U Chit Maung's premature death. In the first half of the 1940s, they were all still in their late twenties and early thirties, having led the Students Union and the Do Bama Asi-ayon in street protests against the British and in support of various older established political figures such as U Saw and Dr. Ba Maw just a few years before. Myanmar's politics was in the midst of a revolution that resulted in the replacement of an older generation of political leaders and thrust remarkably young men into positions of authority for which they admitted they were poorly prepared. The generation they replaced, whose members had collaborated with the British and come to be perceived as largely unworthy of respect in the new nationalist Myanmar, was discarded in the rush to independence. The official and unofficial historiography of Myanmar has tended to reflect this view.

Among the many events that Daw Ma Ma Lay describes in *Thu-lo Lu*, three stand out as deserving fuller consideration. One is the 1938 Revolution, or Ayeidawbon; the second is the move of their family to Bogalay and the arrival of the BIA to the town in the wake of the British withdrawal; the third is the return of the British to Yangon and the maneuverings within the Anti-Fascist People's Freedom League (AFPFL) that she so ambiguously describes. Each of these events highlights an aspect of history that both fiction and honest memoir of the kind represented by *Thu-lo Lu* are much better at capturing than formal academic analysis would be. Historians and political scientists look for patterns and categories into which political actors can be slotted in order to create a narrative order out of the chaos of events. Official and unofficial hagiography uses this same device to justify praise for one party or individual and condemnation of all others. That heroes lead parties and armies, and villains organize plots and sabotage, is easier to believe if you were not in the midst of the human drama of the kind that rapid political change creates. Journal Kyaw Ma Ma Lay makes it clear that this kind of historical analysis denies the complexity of actual events, and she reminds us of the human factor in any historical occurrence. Friendships and personal interests usually outrank ideologies and policies in conditions where there are no established rules nor clear codes of procedure.

The 1938 Ayeidawbon is recorded in the annals of Myanmar's prewar politics as a somewhat less significant event than either the 1920 Students Strike over the allegedly elitist nature of the Yangon University Act or the 1936 student strike over the expulsion of student journalists Nu and Aung San for refusing to reveal the author of a potentially libelous article in the Student Union magazine critical of the personal behavior of a university teacher. Though few of the future rulers of Myanmar took leading roles in the 1938 Ayeidawbon, it was an important development, as it brought together student nationalists with worker politics in a broad coalition, creating the illusion of being a broad revolutionary force. It was also an object lesson and a model for future student and worker protests into the 1990s. U

Chit Maung was a role model for many political aspirants who viewed him as a smart politician and journalist. *Thu-lo Lu* was on the reading lists for discussion by many of the leftist, usually Communist-affiliated, reading circles that persisted in socialist Myanmar during the 1970s and 1980s. Journal Kyaw U Chit Maung continues to be a role model for young people, many of whom are political aspirants who view him as a sensible politician and journalist.

During the course of 1938, students led by Yangon University Students' Union Chairman Thakin Hla Pe, the future Bo Let Yar, traveled to Yeinanchaung, the heart of the Myanmar oil industry, and joined striking oil field workers in a march on Yangon that terminated at the Shwedagon Pagoda, the center of the country's protest politics. The inability of the government to control the situation led to the eventual rise of U Saw as premier, but the turmoil also led to a split in the Do Bama Asi-ayon just as it replaced the Students' Union at the heart of youthful political organization. Being part of a movement that helped change a government, but did not undermine British control, forced the leaders of the Do Bama Asi-ayon to rethink their political strategies. This lesson gave rise to the conspiratorial politics that resulted in the founding of the Communist Party by Aung San and others in 1939 and the Freedom Block by Dr. Ba Maw and his new youthful allies in 1940, and eventually to the BIA. Ideological positions were of little importance to individuals as they sought allies and strategies for ending colonial rule in whatever role it adopted, benign or not. *Thu-lo Lu* captures some of the fluid alliances to which U Chit Maung's younger associates were drawn and concerning which he advised them.

At the end of the volume, one finds described a similar period of plotting and scheming for position and power in the country's final effort to end the grip of imperialism on Myanmar. That complex period would require a lengthy essay to describe at all adequately or objectively. Allies and associates from prewar and wartime politics now came together in one great national coalition, the Anti-Fascist People's Freedom League (AFPFL), to force out the British. The leaders of the disparate forces that had been born in student and Do Bama Asi-ayon politics and factionalism in the late 1930s and in the formation of the Burma Independence Army and the fissiparous Communist movement during the war years realized that they were on the cusp of independence if only they could remain united against the British.

At the same time, they all also realized that if the AFPFL succeeded in its nationalist quest, some of them would become the nation's first post independence leaders and shapers. Relationships of trust and animosity that had been established, broken, and reestablished in the previous decade of student union and covert politicking now became the basis on which coalitions were built and future positions established. The premature death of Bo Gyoke Aung San, killed by an assassin's bullets just fourteen months after he delivered U Chit Maung's funeral eulogy in April 1946, has elevated him to a position of preeminence in that period that his rivals at the time would not have recognized. Daw Ma Ma Lay only hints at these conflicts, but the hints are clear enough to draw our attention to the intrigues of the period.

The 1938 Ayeidawpon and the 1945–47 AFPFL independence struggle provided dramatic scenes of intrigue and conflict connected to well-known events in Myanmar's political history. The struggle for physical security that occurred in Bogalay during the 1942 invasion, though little known but repeated in towns across the country, better reveals the underlying sociopolitical reality of the times. Here the personal and the familial replace sweeping ideological categories like the "workers and the peasants," "the capitalists and the landlords." Though U Chit Maung considered himself both a Buddhist and a Communist, he was also an admirer of good government and sound administration, which he thought ought to insure the protection of personal property. As it became apparent that the British administration was about to collapse in the face of the joint Japanese-BIA rout of the British Indian army, U Chit Maung took steps to insure that the lives and property of the residents of Bogalay were protected from potential attack by "men from the surrounding villages and those across the river [who] gathered like flies and came into town holding knives and swords, bent on robbing the richer townspeople." "The sons of good families" rallied to protect those who had benefited from colonial rule from potentially losing their property to the underclass that had felt a spot of looting was justifiable as it would rebalance the wealth of the community.

U Chit Maung also dreaded the coming to power of his friends and advisees from the Do Bama Asi-ayon as they marched into Bogalay wearing the uniforms of the BIA and brandishing their guns with the bravado of the victorious. When Bo Yan Naing, the soon-to-be son-in-law of Dr. Ba Maw, ordered the "sons of the good families" to surrender their arms to a new BIA-dominated administration, U Chit Maung sensed danger. He reveals his fears when he tells Daw Ma Ma Lay:

> We need some sort of administration set up for the town. The Thakin are not going to allow the officials of the previous government to take any posts, they will want to form it amongst themselves. If they form an administration with people of little or no ability, the town will suffer. The administration must be entrusted to these officials, with the Thakins holding the strings, and that's the only way to have a stable and strong administration. If these men of experience are left out altogether all over the country, they will have no place to go, if they have not left with the British. Or they may well side with the Japanese. Then the country will continue to suffer without able men in places where they are needed. What a great shame that nothing was prepared for a situation like this!

His recognition of the need for competent and stable administration, even if tainted by prior contact with the colonial power, and his despair at the lack of preparations to provide such a government in the wake of the invasion, heralds one of the tragedies of modern Myanmar's history. The effort to find a system of rule that provides for the well-being of the population and provides them with the day-to-day security and protection that are required to live a productive and satisfying life has yet to be fully resolved. This is a lesson that can be drawn from *Thu-lo Lu* by those living more than half a century after the book was written. The advantage of hindsight was, of course, not available to the individuals caught up in the drama of events that Daw Ma Ma Lay describes in these pages. They had more pressing and immediate issues to face.

Robert H. Taylor
Yangon
July 19, 2008

A Man Like Him

(Thu-lo Lu)

CHAPTER 1

REPLY FROM *MYANMAR ALIN*[1]

The day was May 18, 1936.

I was returning with my family by boat from the monastery of Dhamma Thuka Village after taking the Buddhist precepts in the presence of the Sayadaw.[2]

On both sides of the riverbank we would frequently pass by huddles of decrepit bamboo huts. The land stretched as far as the eye could see with *danni*[3] and bamboo thickets and wild weeds growing all over. The dwellings for human habitation could not make any use of this space: the huts, constructed out of bamboo and *danni*, were just large enough for a few people to crawl in. I saw none that was strongly built: the huts were all ramshackle and leaning sideways in decay. These homes were not in the wilds of the country, nor were the villages on the far borders. They were homes for the poor of Myanmar living not too far from the towns. Their living conditions were barely of human standards; only because they had been born human could they be considered such, for they did not enjoy a life worthy of humans, nor did they have any rights.

The wind carrying the scent of rain swept over us, and waves rose in the river to slap against the sides of the boat, which rolled and dipped. The man at the helm steered the boat closer to the bank as we continued our journey.

It was more heartbreaking to see these villagers up close. What wrenched my heart most was the children of six, eight, or ten years digging for crabs in the mud with their bare hands. Some were casting nets at the water's edge. None of them had any clothes on, and they were all covered with mud. We went past them, but their images remained in my mind. A life such as this in childhood and then, what sort of life would they face when they grew up? Their bodies might grow but not their circumstances, nor their skills ... why were they stuck hopelessly in such a life? How could they be saved?

I was twenty years old at the time and no longer had childish fancies. I was by then beginning to make use of my mind. I stared at the waves, unwilling to look towards the riverbanks. I felt confused and unhappy as my mind whirled with thoughts and my eyes stared at the churning waves. The idea I had seemed to slip out of my mind and to fall into the depths of the river; then I felt as if something inside me was trying to grasp the thought again so as not to let go of it completely.

My thought was that maybe the newspapers and the young politicians could somehow help to turn around the life of these people into one fit for human beings ... I have never forgotten my thoughts of that day, as it happened to be the very same day that my life, too, would completely change.

---

[1] A newspaper, "New Light of Myanmar."

[2] An abbot.

[3] A kind of reed, with leaves that are used as roofing.

We got back home about six in the evening to Bogalay.[4] Just as I was about to mount the steps to our house, the doorman handed me a letter that had come by post. I stared at the envelope and for a moment forgot to open it as my thoughts raced.

About five months ago, I had disagreed with something declared by a group of women in my town and had written an article explaining my views.[5] I had posted it off to the *Myanmar Alin* newspaper: it was the first article I had ever written and sent to a paper. I had no idea how to address the letter so I looked all over the paper and saw the title "Chief Editor: U[6] Sein" on the front cover and "Executive Publisher: Maung[7] Chit Maung" on the back. Still not sure to whom I should address it, I had written "To, U Editor" on both the envelope and at the beginning of the letter.

For about a week I kept my eyes out for the paper and the post to see if my article would appear, or if I would receive a reply by mail. When nothing happened, I assumed they did not want to publish my article or bother to reply, and I forgot all about it. But today ... I stared in fascination at the envelope printed with the newspaper's name, hesitating to open it immediately. Only when my family members began to ask "What's that? Where is it from?" did I come to my senses and, running up the stairs to my room, I flung myself on my bed and opened the letter.

> *To:*
> *Ma Tin Tin*[8]
> *Care of Dawson Bank*[9]
> *Bogalay*
>
> *Your letter of 22 January was mistakenly discarded with other letters and we came upon it only just now.*
> *We cannot decide if the contents of the article are still relevant but we felt that it might be too late. Only you can know and that is the reason we are writing to you for confirmation. If the said fifteen-member women's group still exists and if what you wrote is still relevant, we could publish this letter in the "Clarion" column. If however it is too late please let us know.*

---

[4] A town in the delta where the writer lived.

[5] An anonymous letter was sent to Ma Tin Hlaing, signed by "a group of fifteen women," condemning her for "unladylike behavior" for playing badminton with boys her age. This group had threatened that if she continued to be so "shameless," they would write about her in the *Myanmar Alin* to humiliate her, at which point she decided to write her view on sports and platonic friendship between opposite sexes and submit her response to the same newspaper.

[6] Equivalent to "Mr.," a polite prefix used for men's names. For women, it would be "Daw." Both are compulsory when addressing someone who is older and not on familiar terms. When speaking to someone older who is familiar, one would address that person as "Uncle" or "Aunt," or "Elder Brother" or "Elder Sister," as appropriate.

[7] Male prefix for a name used for the young or as a sign of modesty.

[8] As her legal name was Ma Tin Hlaing, it would be normal to use the diminutive "Tin Tin" in unofficial and informal situations.

[9] The British-owned bank where Ma Tin Hlaing's father worked owned about 60,000 acres of paddy land and gave loans to farmers. Dawson's Bank was the only alternative to the Indian Chettiar moneylenders for most farmers in colonial Myanmar.

Please forgive us that the assistant editors, thinking your letter unimportant, had discarded it.

Chit Maung
Editor–Myanmar Alin
May 17

The letter was clear enough to understand with one reading but I read it repeatedly, losing count of how many times I did so. I was wondering why a letter sent in January and discarded by an assistant editor was nearly five months later discovered by this editor and why he would want to reply to it at all.

I replied that the subject was no longer relevant, but to my own surprise I somehow knew the editor would write to me again. As I thought, nearly three months later another letter came.

I reply to Ma Tin Tin,[10]
In your reply to us, you wrote that you would write another article to promote women's issues to be published in the newspaper, and we were hoping to receive the said article. However, since we did not hear from you, we felt it might be due to our fault in not replying sooner.

We are already planning to publish articles written by women on women's issues, and as you also said in your letter that you wanted to, we would like your article to be the first in the series. Please feel free to write on any subject. When you do, if it is longer than one and a half foolscap pages we would not be able to print it, so I would advise you to make your article short and to the point.

If you have no objection, please also include your photo so that if necessary we could use it.

When you post the article, please send it directly addressed to me.

Please stay healthy.

We wish you well.

Chit Maung
Editor–Myanmar Alin
August 16

---

[10] This is an old-fashioned, respectful form of salutation.

CHAPTER 2

ABOUT MYSELF

To tell you something about myself, I am the middle of five children, and after I left school, unlike my sisters who worked at the bank, I had more free time. I spent it reading newspapers and monthly magazines, all new fiction as well as classical prose and poetry.

My parents were not very wealthy, but if I were to describe our lifestyle without stating the actual expenditure, I could say that we lived with comfort and standards on a par with the British, with modern facilities in a well-set-up house. My father worked in a position usually filled by the British, and besides, we lived in the same building as the bank he worked at, so we existed in close proximity with the Westerners. As for housework, we had enough household staff so that there was nothing for us to do. My mother ministered to the needs of this big family in this big house, so we only had to comply with her rules of behavior and discipline in dress and for mealtimes; otherwise we were free to do what we wanted.

I enjoy wearing expensive clothes. Even if I were staying at home, I like to dress well. My cupboards were packed with clothes, and every day I would try to look my best in different fabrics and colors. My elder and younger sisters who worked with my father in the bank on the ground floor of our building also dressed well, so we shared this interest in fashion. However, our personalities and interests differed widely, as I am very active and outgoing, and so I was somewhat aloof from them. They are gentle of manner and soft of heart and reserved; they liked peace and harmony above all. As for me, if there is unfairness, I could not keep quiet about it. I must have my way in things I wanted to do, and I would not rest content until an unfair situation, big or small, had been justly resolved. I used to be stubbornly disdainful of what others say and had the grim patience to hold on to something even if I should suffer in the process. I made my own decisions and did exactly as I wanted, and such were the things that set me apart from my gentle sisters.

My mother could not condone some of my traits and would impose rules on me. I would carefully consider these rules decreed especially for my benefit, to see whether they were really necessary or fair. If any one of her rules was made out of anxiety for my sake, then, although not liking it, I would not rebel against it. I promised to myself that one day I would ease her mind concerning these anxieties. My vow to myself that one day she would be free of any worries for me gave me the strength I needed.

Some people gossiped that I would turn out badly if I were allowed so much freedom, in a way putting freedom in a bad light. Nevertheless, I wanted to lead my own life and be free to live, speak, and do as I wished. I could not even imagine living according to other people's wishes. They were only looking at what they saw on the surface, and, as I knew my own innermost thoughts full well, I was confident that I did not owe them any explanation. On the other hand, I had one personality trait that made me different from them: I am known throughout my extended family of distant relatives for my kindness and generosity in sharing what I have with others. I could not look at or speak with anyone, man or woman, who was stingy, and merely to hear about them would fill me with dismay at their mean-mindedness. This was my character, and my main interest, as mentioned above, was reading.

I enjoyed it so much that apart from talking my meals and taking baths I only wanted to sit and read. My parents did not like me reading fiction and would forbid it most strongly.[1]

According to traditions of respect, I did not want to rebel openly against my parents' wishes, so in their presence I did not touch the novels, but once out of their sight I devoured one book after another. At the same time, I looked into these books to find the reasons why novels were considered such a bad influence. When I came across passages describing vulgar behavior, I would reflect that such were the words my parents wished me not to see, but then, rather biased in favor of my own enjoyment, I would decide that, after all, the writer merely wanted to be realistic. After finishing a novel, I would consider carefully how it began and ended, the story line, the writing—in fact everything about it. In my mind, I would delete or add scenes, change things around, and analyze the merits of the story and the writer. So, actually, I was not reading novels merely to entertain myself but I was studying the art of writing, although unaware of what I was doing.

I especially liked the epic poems: I loved how the words were chosen with care and strung into rhymes! I felt such admiration for the old poets, and their words were embedded in my heart. In school, our Burmese language teacher, Saya[2] Tin, encouraged me a lot. Thanks to him, I grew to love Burmese literature.

I was spending all my leisure in reading when my parents decided it was time for me to get married. By then my elder sister had married, and only my younger sister continued to work at the bank. My father had the idea that, not knowing which of his children one day would be running businesses of their own, each should learn accounting, and that was the reason he had his children work in the bank under him. My brothers and sisters followed his advice, but I had refused, saying I did not wish to serve under the British. My parents had apparently decided that this lady of leisure should find security in a marriage.

Since I was sixteen, I had been friends with someone, and I had decided that when we grew up and he became a man with enough qualifications to impress my parents, we would marry. I supported and encouraged him in many ways so that he would make something of himself. I had formed my own ideals concerning marriage that I told no one but kept secret in a corner of my mind. Whenever the question of marriage came up, these ideals would surface. The nonexistent man of my dreams, with the qualities I desired and the personality I admired, would loom in my mind whenever my marriage was mentioned.

I did try with the above-mentioned boy of my youth to turn him into the type of man I wanted: one with a good education, a generous and noble heart, integrity, and

---

[1] Fiction available in Myanmar at the time was mostly romantic novels and was considered damaging to the morals of young girls.

[2] "Teacher," also a term of respect or politeness used when addressing men. "Saya" is the male form, "Sayama" the female. Both can be used as honorific titles for nurses, doctors, or superiors, and so forth, or as a polite form for manual laborers, such as for trishaw drivers and mechanics.

one who was as successful as any man could be, but to no avail: he did not live up to my expectations.

He, poor boy, had no idea of what sort of a person I was nor had he any inkling of my personality, but, merely blinded with love, he asked me to elope with him when he heard of the marriage plans my parents had for me. I felt deeply saddened that he did not consider how unlikely it was that a girl like me would disregard my parents' wishes and elope with him instead. I was dismayed that he had not tried to understand me and that he would think I would so easily agree to a husband of my parents' choosing.

After I told him that my marriage partner would have to please both my parents and myself, he gave up his efforts to marry me. I should say this was good for both of us: if our minds were not alike in the future, there would be serious problems. By giving me up, he also rid himself of further responsibilities, and I felt that for me, too, it was a wise turn in my life.

None of the men my parents proposed as candidates were anything like the partner of my imagination. They were wealthy, they were educated, they had looks and prestige, but I saw nothing out of the ordinary in them. None of them stood out as having a nobler personality or a more worthy nature that I could love. I refused all of them, telling my parents that if I married any of them, I would be spending my life wondering what I liked about my husband. My parents were completely at a loss. They did not know what to do with me, especially when they realized they could never force me into anything. They became increasingly anxious that I might do something rash, but they did not force my hand. They reasoned with me gently and said they would wait until I came to a decision, but at the same time they kept a close watch on me.

I could not begin to say how grateful I was to my parents at the time for not forcing me into something that would surely make me miserable. In gratitude, I vowed that I would only marry with my parents' approval.

CHAPTER 3

"WHAT DO YOU THINK OF IT?"

As I neared the age of twenty, my parents gave up any hope of getting me married off, and I continued to enjoy my freedom, reading books and learning much from them. From dawn till dusk I had no other work and nothing to worry about: it was a comfortable life, buying the clothes I wanted, eating what I liked, and traveling where I wanted to go. I had no problems with getting whatever I wanted, and all my wishes were easily fulfilled.

The second letter from the newspaper asking for an article as well as my photo placed me in a quandary. I was an avid reader, but no writer, and I was faced with a dilemma. I could not think of what to write. To send a photo was a great embarrassment for me, as I took it to mean sending it to a man, moreover, a total stranger. I did not believe I could write anything worthwhile, so without replying to the letter I let the matter drop. However, it was surprising that although I did not reply I felt certain that another letter would come, and my suspicion proved correct.

> *I write to you, Ma Tin Tin,*
>
> *As there was no reply to my letter, I sent another enquiry after it. However, I still did not receive a reply, so I was worried that you might be ill or away on a trip or feel reluctant to reply. I am praying the last be not the reason, and I also pray that the first is not true.*
>
> *My letters may be lacking in tact, or maybe they were too demanding: if due to their lack of anything you had no desire to reply, or if they were so demanding that you were upset, I can only apologize. Please at least reply to state the reason for your silence.*
>
> *May I tell you of the high regard I have for you? I believe that it is not only the work of men to help enlighten the masses but that we will reach our goal of uplifting their lives when the women take part in this endeavor. The problems facing our country can be eased when women help to solve them. Men would try harder when women also change their attitudes. I would say so quite unabashedly that only with the support and encouragement of women do men go forth to conquer all.*
>
> *So, as I am planning to have women write articles for our paper, it is a lucky chance to know you, albeit through the mail, and I am hoping to have a reply from you on this matter. I hope to awaken new thoughts among women through your writings. We do publish works by women writers when they are sent to us, but they are not as many as we hope to get, and they do not contain any trace of encouraging women to think for themselves, so I must keep on urging you to send us an article.*
>
> *Through the article you sent us refuting the accusations of the fifteen-member women's committee, I could see that you have the wish to help your*

country prosper and that you have the sharp intellect for it. This is the reason I am writing to you, and you can imagine how anxious I am when I receive no reply to my entreaties. I know very well that I have no right to compel you to write anything. I know I shall receive the article only when you decide to write it, but I am writing to you now to tell you how eager I am to have you write for us. Not only I but anyone who has a love for his country would want to depend upon someone like you who so clearly has the good of the people at heart.

At present, the Burmese are concentrating on politics to the detriment of their financial affairs, and it is up to the women who are capable of handling business issues to come to their rescue. I can only urge you to decide for yourself where you stand on this.

As for our country …
"Have pity on the people I would not dare to say,
But why with saddened look do you keep hidden all you write?
How strange that your thoughts should be cloaked
With such dark clouds. I cannot think the reason …
Do you still not forgive?
Please let me know, I urge with these sweet words …"

Chit Maung
December 8

Because of this letter, I could no longer put it off, and I went over to my desk to prepare myself to write. The *Myanmar Alin* was the paper with the highest circulation [in the country], and the thought so terrified me that I could not think of a single thing. Not only that, but whatever I already had in my brain deserted me, and I could not begin to think of where to start.

Finally, I put the paper's importance out of my head and pretended I was just writing an essay for school, and only then did my brain begin to function. When I got past the difficult first sentence, I found that others followed easily. As he had warned I should not go beyond one and a half pages if I wanted it published, and as I was not used to this sort of limitation, it caused me great stress. Worse than that, when the article was done I had to consider under what name I should send it in.[1] The next day, I mailed off the article titled "To Have Brains with a Capital B" and wrote the writer's name as Yaway Hlaing. Each day I got up early to check on the paper before anyone got up; after two days it appeared in the paper, and I proudly kept looking at my words in print over and over again.

From that time onwards, every time he asked I would send off one or more articles. Each time when he wrote asking for more, and each time that I replied, we would exchange long letters, but so far we had no idea what the other looked like. We only wrote intense discussions on politics, education, and the like. We wrote modestly about ourselves and with respect for the other. In his letters there were always new things for me to learn, sometimes in the form of poems, and so for someone like me who was eager to learn, he served as a great library.

Whether he thought about me at all after reading my letters was not known to me, but his letters made me think about him. His letters were always thought provoking.

---

[1] The majority of writers used pen names during that period.

I reply to you ...

In your letter number two, I could see the brilliance of your mind more clearly than ever before. In letter number one, I see your wit and in two I see your wisdom. So ... I feel a bit apprehensive about how I can continue writing to you ...

Men like to think that they are brighter than women but they dare not match wits if they meet a brilliant woman. Someone wrote once that men run to avoid meeting such a woman if they spot her even ten streets away!

There are many instances of men who have lost after challenging women to match instant rhymes.[2] Now that I have encountered such a woman, I must reflect deeply on whether I should run at once or pretend to be of equal intellect and continue with my pose of being clever enough for her.

> *Chit Maung*
> *February 16*

The whole letter honored me and humbled him, but I was rather of the mind that it was I who should be running away in fear. It seemed he pretended to be ignorant of things he really knew about. But then at times I could not make out his intentions clearly and felt as if I were reading too much into his words.

Dear Ma Tin Tin,

To my delight the political situation, by sheer accident, got better. In taking advantage of this state of affairs, I joyfully gave sound and sharp advice on how things should continue. For my pains, I have been condemned by someone as being part of a subversive act plotted by Dr. Ba Maw, and even taken to task that I had not said anything before.

The country seems unable to make up its mind. For just once, I stepped in and spoke out with nothing but sincere intentions and without any ulterior motive to heal the present political malaise and for that I am accused of malice! I am deeply saddened that these misunderstandings should arise.

I so wish to hear your political views. Before the window of opportunity passes, may I beg you to write for us something on the situation? If, however, you have no wish to write on it but would be willing to tell us your views, it would be of great value to someone who is involved in the matter.

In your letter, Ma Tin Tin, you said, "As you wrote that a woman who wants to better herself will surely succeed if she is as beautiful as she is intelligent, I take it to mean that a woman who is not beautiful could not go far with only her brains, and is there any hope for an intelligent woman without looks of ever succeeding?"

Seeing your photo in the special New Year edition of the paper, let me say that the classical poet Taungthaman U Hpay Nge has already judged you. There is a very elegant piece of poetry that to my knowledge had not appeared in print. U Hpay Nge's writings are quite exquisite: "In elegance, your manner pierces the soul of one who sees. Comparable to Ohnmar Dandi,[3] your beauty knows no

---

[2] Many examples are given, but they are impossible to translate as they are puns in verse.

[3] A legendary beauty.

bounds. *Soft gold is your skin, [you are] someone who is as priceless as a precious ruby."*

Now, I felt like trying to outdo this poet, but hours passed but not a sentence came to my mind, so I finally threw down my pen. But eventually a poem emerged that one could say is no equal with the one above. Nevertheless, just to show you how bad it is ... "In all the great forests, this rare orchid blooms, with a beauty no other flowers can hope to share. So noble and glorious, none would dare pluck it to wear. From afar to revere, this beautiful flower is so rare that it is fitting to dwell only in golden palaces, but often one yearns to own it."

What do you think of it?

Chit Maung

He asked, "What do you think of it?," but the poem was written as if not addressed directly to me, but rather as if it were just his challenge to U Hpay Nge in a contest of poetic skill.

In thinking over his query, "What do you think of it?" I could not very well say, "What's there about it?" and if someone were to ask me, "What do you mean?" I would have had to admit my utter confusion. In the end, I finally decided there was nothing personal in his poem, because at the time I was studying the Kogan Pyo, a very difficult epic poem, and he had been helping me with it. So I merely noted this latest development as a lesson in the art of turning poetry into clear prose and, disregarding the "What do you think of it?" continued simply to respect him as my teacher.

My gratitude and admiration for someone teaching me thus from a distance grew day by day. In other letters, too, it became very clear how earnest he was in wanting to spread knowledge to others.

CHAPTER 4

FIRST MEETING

It was surprising that we came to know each other with mutual respect and admiration through letters, and yet we had no desire to meet. After all, why should a writer for a newspaper need to meet the editor? The writer would only want to see the work in print, and the editor would only be interested in getting the article sent to him. Whenever I went to Yangon, I never thought of meeting him and regarded our relationship as something based on common interests.

Then the *Myanmar Alin* came out with a column on "Today's Thoughts" for which I sent off five short contributions just for fun, and they all appeared in the paper. A letter came asking for more, so off and on I would dash off something but could not send longer articles. By then I was working with a women's organization in my town and was busy with this work, and even my letters to him became sporadic. The "Do Bama Asi-ayon,"[1] a nationalist organization, opened a branch in our town, and, as a member of the women's representatives of that organization, I became busier. Political leaders, "Thakin,"[2] from Yangon often came to Bogalay, and I would be busy with arranging their public talks, even giving speeches myself, and so very often I failed to answer or write to him.

My father worked for the British, so his employers were quite upset that I should be so active in political work and gave him a hard time. My father did not forbid me, but hinted that it might be dangerous work. However, he was quite happy to see me spend my money in hosting many meals for the visiting politicians. I worked heart and soul to support those who were working with such sincerity for the sake of our country, and through my work of that period the political leaders of today came to know me well.

After the politicians left, they went to the *Myanmar Alin* offices to give their news, and some of them would mention my name to U Chit Maung and say how active I was. He wrote that since he learned of my involvement in politics, he had stopped asking me for regular contributions, and that he fully supported me. He said he was planning to translate the story of the Chinese girl revolutionary Shi Min for the paper, to encourage me.

In that letter, he wrote:

> The appeals of the [arrested] Thakin have reached the High Court. The people of our country still do not know that they should respect and admire political prisoners. Not only that, most of them blame and condemn them, so in order to change their minds and to encourage you, Ma Tin Tin, and to

---

[1] The "We Burmans Association," formed in 1935 by the student leaders.

[2] Politically dissident students adopted the form of address "Thakin," or "master," in front of their names in reaction against the British, who had insisted on being addressed as "Thakin."

strengthen your political views, I decided to translate the story of Shi Min, but so far I have done only the preface. But it should soon be finished to be published in the paper, and I hope it will encourage you to be more than ever active in politics. Also of course, I hope the readers will be moved by Shi Min's story so that men will learn to raise their fists with patriotic spirit and women to be inspired by nationalistic fervor.

But I wonder if I will be successful as I am bad at translating, worse with words, have no time to spare, and all around me my friends sleep and snore, and I, too, more than once or twice, have dozed off at my desk while pondering all this!

Chit Maung

As his letter was so supportive of my work, I sent a reply of thanks.

While I was caught up in the social welfare and political work of my town, suddenly Father began coughing up blood and was diagnosed with tuberculosis and rushed to the General Hospital in Yangon. The specialists there recommended that he be moved to Meikhtila in the dry zone, and I hurried to Yangon to see him before he left. After I had been in Yangon for about ten days, my family sent me the letters that had arrived for me in Bogalay. Among them was a letter from the paper urgently requesting an article for a special issue. I had no idea whether there was still time.

I often suffered dizzy spells, and after my father left for Meikhtila, I had stayed on in Yangon to be treated at the Indo Burma Clinic on Sule Pagoda Road, which happened to be next door to the *Myanmar Alin* office. Every morning I was going to the clinic, but so far felt no need to meet my editor friend. That morning, since I had his letter in my hand, I stood for a minute looking over at the paper's office before I went into the clinic. As I was sitting in the reception room, chatting to the young Japanese lady doctor, I noticed a telephone on the counter. I excused myself and immediately went to the counter and, after looking up the number in the telephone book, called *Myanmar Alin*.

"Who would you like to speak to?" the man answering the phone from the editorial desk asked.

"I would like to speak to the editor, U Chit Maung," I replied.

"This is he. Who is this speaking, please?"

"I'm Ma Tin Tin. I am in Yangon, and I received your letter only just now, the one asking for an article. I just wanted to know if there is still time and ..."

Before I could finish, he eagerly interrupted.

"Where are you calling from? When did you arrive in Yangon?"

"I'm calling from the Indo Burma Clinic. I got to Yangon ..."

"I was just about to go home for lunch and turned back to answer the phone ... I'm coming over, wait for me."

He hung up as soon as he said these words, so I went back to my chair. The doctor said goodbye to me and went upstairs. The reception area was deserted. I took up the *Rangoon Gazette* newspaper from the coffee table and idly glanced through it, waiting for him.

I had no idea he was standing behind me until the druggist working behind a far counter looked over at me and jerked his chin towards him. I turned and saw: a gaunt face with thick glasses, a worn and shapeless *taik-pon*[3] of rough *pinni*,[4] a faded silk *longyi*,[5] and a very thin body of a starving ascetic.

"So you are Ma Tin Tin?" he asked, and I realized it was U Chit Maung, editor.

Looking at his gaunt cheeks and grey hair, I decided he was someone in his late thirties, fast approaching his forties, but, at the same time, I reflected that the dignity and seriousness of his expression might also make him appear older. The penetrating eyes behind the thick glasses and the broad brow told of a high intellect and a brilliant mind. Those were the only things that saved him from looking entirely the religious recluse. His face held no keen expression whatsoever, and the gloomy look of it drove away all aspects of youth from him.

His clothes looked shabby, but he was dressed neatly; because of his worn cotton jacket and faded *longyi*, he seemed to be a man who cared nothing for his looks. If I were to judge by his clothes, I would have said that this was a man who could not afford to have even a five- or ten-*kyat*[6] note in his pockets. In his hand he held an old-fashioned Burmese parasol of cloth and bamboo, and he was wearing rough leather slippers, both normal items of use for monks. Indeed, who would believe this man to be educated in Western subjects, as he looked exactly like a Hpon-gyi Lu Dwet,[7] a monk who has returned to the secular life.

I looked at him for a moment and then offered him a seat. I quickly noted the look of surprise on his face at my fashionable attire and make-up, as if I were dressed for a special occasion.

"I am very happy to meet you, U Chit Maung. I have been in Yangon for some time, and I'm staying with a nurse of this clinic. I've been consulting a doctor here, and I only got your letter today sent on by my family, and so I rang to ask if it were too late for the article you wanted."

He did not look at me but stared at the cement floor. He sat very still as if he were lost in thought.

"The special issue has been done, thank you. Do please look after your health and rest well. I did not know you were coming to Yangon, and when I did not receive a reply, I was worried that you might be ill. So, since you have finished studying the *Kogan Pyo* and the sixty *Sutras Pyo*, what do you plan to study now?"

I had never heard such a gentle and gracious voice before. By his voice alone, you could judge him to be a man without anger, greed, or vanity, a man of integrity and peace.

"I thought I'd study the *Thanwa Ya Pyo*, but I don't have the book yet, I thought I'd buy it today. Is that more difficult than the *Kogan*?"

"Yes, it's equally hard. May I request you, don't buy this book, I would like to give it to you."

"Do you have an extra copy?"

"No, but it's easy enough to get. Are there any other books you want?"

---

[3] A long-sleeved, collarless jacket open at the front and with simple cloth buttons.

[4] A reddish or brown unbleached, hand-woven cotton worn by nationalists.

[5] Unisex word for "waist garment," a tube of fabric knotted at the waist. A woman's waist garment is called a *htamein*, and the man's is *pasoe*.

[6] Burmese currency. One hundred *pya* make one *kyat*.

[7] Misfits in society.

"I have no idea which books to buy. I thought I'd go to the bookshops like Hanthawaddy, Pyi Gyi Mandaing, and Zabu Meikswe to look for some Burmese titles."

"Where are you staying now?"

"Number 145, Fiftieth Street."

"On behalf of the country and *Myanmar Alin,* may I tell you how much we are indebted to you for the articles you have contributed?"

I was so shocked I thought I would fall from my chair. I was the one who should be thanking him: I have files at home thick with his letters in both Burmese and English, telling me about literature, poetry, and the classics, and these had been written even while he had a busy career. Only I knew how much I owed him, and now, hearing him thank me, I felt very uncomfortable.

"If the articles did some good for the country, it is not the writer who should be thanked: you, U Chit Maung, you urged me to write, and you supported me, taught me, and it's only because of your kindness that my articles were ever written. If anyone should thank you, it is I. I should be the one to be grateful."

He sat unmoving and silent as if he had nothing to say, still staring at the floor. Time passed, and he sat there for nearly half an hour without saying a word. I felt *ah-nar*[8] to be using the clinic's reception room like this, as if it were my private sitting room, but he sat rooted to his chair. I racked my brains trying to think of something to say to him, but to no avail. Besides, I wanted to go home, but felt I could not just get up and leave. I worried what the people of the clinic would think of us sitting there together in complete silence. He acted as if there were no need to speak to me, a person who was sitting right next to him, so I was hesitant to continue talking to him.

Nearly one hour passed, and he still sat there without a word. I made up my mind that even though he might think me rude, I had better make moves as if I were leaving, so I clicked my handbag open and shut a couple of times and, shifting in my seat as if about to get up, I said, "So, I'll get to this clinic about ten tomorrow morning. You can leave the book here, thank you so much."

"I'll come over and give it to you," he said, and still sat there as if he did not notice my body language.

For me to get up first would be very impolite since I was not the person who had come to see him. I should leave only after him, or we should leave together. As the minutes passed, I began to wonder what sort of a man this was. The doctors were all back in their offices, having returned from lunch, and as they walked past they had glanced out of the corners of their eyes at the two of us still sitting silently in our chairs. By the minute, I became more uneasy. The words I longed to say, "May I go?" would not leave my lips. I kept wishing desperately for him to leave. As time went on, he still did not give any sign of moving, sitting there with quiet dignity while staring now at the tabletop. The footsteps of the doctors as they went about their work sounded as if they were telling me to go. If it were my house, he could sit there the whole day if he wanted to, but finally I had to do something I had never done before: to be rude enough to dismiss a visitor.

"So, U Chit Maung, let's meet again tomorrow, my friends are waiting for lunch at home so please excuse me. And you, too ... "

---

[8] To feel badly about taking advantage of or upsetting others.

At this, he said, "All right," and swiftly led the way out of the clinic. I was still feeling embarrassed to have been so rude, but what I could not understand was that he had got up and left with an air of sudden and welcome release.

Luckily, the next morning I saw him right at the entrance to the clinic. He was dressed exactly as he had been yesterday, and even after just two meetings he had become a familiar figure to me. I did not ask him in but stood a few minutes thanking him for the book he had handed to me. He hung his head and stood there without a word, so I went on to say that, as the book looked new, did he buy it and could I pay the cost? In response to which he still stayed silent, so I dared not ask again, but saying "thank you" a few times more, I made as if to go into the clinic. Only then he asked if I had bought any more books. I said no, and he said that he would make a list of books I should have and bring it the next morning to this place. I said thank you again and, firmly saying goodbye, went into the clinic. Even this exchange took about half an hour.

The next day I arrived early at the clinic with my nurse friend as she had something to do in the morning. After getting my injection,[9] I was free to go home, but as he had said he would bring the book list, I sat down to wait for him. Later, to give up my seat to new arrivals, I went to stand by the entrance. He turned up a few minutes later.

"How are you, Ma Tin Tin?"

"I'm better, thank you."

"Here's the list ... when will you go to the bookshops?"

"I'm waiting for a horse cab; I think I'll go right now."

"Are you going alone? Isn't there anyone with you?"

"No, I don't need to bring along anyone, I can go on my own."

"That's not right, I don't believe a girl on her own is safe in Yangon."

"Is that so?"

"I would like to come with you to the bookshops, I'm always happy to go there. I want to choose myself the books you should read ... "

He hesitated and did not say anything more.

I had no doubt that he really wanted to make sure that I was safe, and his saying he wanted to choose the books himself was truly because of his desire to help, and so I naturally thought he wanted to come with me. He sounded kind, and to go about with such a dignified man as him was not a problem for me, but if anyone should see us, people might gossip, and I did not want that. Moreover, what would the doctors think if they saw us climb into the same cab together? I did not know what to say. Since I had come to know him, he had been encouraging me and teaching me so much that, although I felt uncomfortable, I thought I should not refuse his kind offer regardless of what people might say. So I said, "If you can come with me, U Chit Maung, please do so. I would be most grateful."

"No please, I cannot come with you, it won't do."

"Excuse me?"

"It's bad enough that I'm standing here talking to you. I have never been on such friendly terms with any woman, and my friends know this, so if they see me with you they will tease me and laugh at me. It would damage my good name if they do that. I've never had anything to do with women, and so I think it would be impossible for me to come ... "

---

[9] In Myanmar, getting an injection is considered the best treatment for all ills.

"You ...? What ...?"

"So, I was going to say how sorry I am that I can't come with you."

"Right, then, U Chit Maung, why did you say you wanted to come with me if you felt that to be seen with a person like me would damage your well-earned reputation? I understand perfectly now that you have explained your problem, but rest assured there is nothing to be sorry about for not coming with me. Only I can know how relieved I am that you could not accompany me. Thank you so very much, U Chit Maung ... please excuse me."

With that I climbed into the cab that had stopped for me and left him standing there. I felt icy cold all over and had to try hard to remember what I had said to him as a parting shot. I had acceded to what I thought was a request to come with me, in spite of feeling uncomfortable about it. It should have made me happy to have that issue resolved, but the way he had explained his views on *his* reputation without thinking about mine made me furious. I simmered all the way home.

When he had said he wanted to come with me to the bookshops and had paused, he was in fact thinking about his own difficulty, while I had thought that he was hesitating about asking my permission, and so, wanting to be nice, I had asked him to come. Even if I had been the one to first beg him to come with me, he could have given a dozen polite reasons not to do so. What happened had not made me think well of him, for it showed him as a man who had no female relationships of any kind[10] and who implied I should admire and respect him for this. I only thought him a strange man but could not imagine exactly what *sort* of a strange man he was.

---

[10] It is a point of honor for men, and to a much higher degree for women, that they not be familiar with unrelated members of the opposite sex.

CHAPTER 5

WHAT SORT OF STRANGE MAN WAS HE?

I stayed home for three days because it was not necessary for me to be given another treatment until the fourth day after my injection. On the evening of the third day, at about 7:00, while I was resting on my bed, my hostess called me from the front room. I was astounded to see him sitting with great dignity in the parlor.

"Oh, it's you, U Chit Maung," I greeted him while trying to recover my composure, and then sat down in a chair. During the past three days he seemed to have become more haggard, his cheeks even more sunken, and he looked visibly upset, all of which I noticed as soon as I saw him. To break the silence, I asked, "Did you come by cab?"

"I came on foot, Ma Tin Tin. I did not see you come to the clinic, so I thought you might have left for home."

"Oh, really? Did you go to the clinic?"

"Yes, I kept going there to ask, but they just said you didn't come."

"Actually, I don't need to go until tomorrow, as I get my treatment every four days."

"I wrote a letter for you," he said, and, taking it from his pocket, handed it to me.

> Ma Tin Tin,
>
> What a blunder I have made, Ma Tin Tin, what a horrible blunder. My dilemma is one I alone knew about, and I could have kept silent and not have been so inconsiderate as to blurt it out to you, thus upsetting you so much. I only realized it when it was too late; there is a proverb, isn't there, that fools repent only when it is too late?
>
> I did so want to accompany you, but as I could not, I should have had the brains to give an excuse and thus avoid upsetting you. And I, I would not have to bear this great burden of despair as a result of having seen how I have upset you …
>
> It is my fault, Ma Tin Tin, entirely my fault. I have been suffering from the pain of my guilt since you drove away that day, and until I learn from you that you have forgotten and forgiven … until I know it, I will continue to suffer.
>
> Can you ever forgive me, Ma Tin Tin?
>
> Chit Maung

I finished reading the letter, put it on the table, and placed the key I was holding on it. He wore an expression of such despair and guilt, as if he deeply regretted everything. I could see how desperate he felt by the look on his face.

"Well, U Chit Maung, when you said you wanted to accompany me, I did not want to refuse, and so I told you to come with me. When you blurted out the real reason, I felt that you should at least have said something else, so I impulsively retorted with anger. Only when I got back here did I realize that you were simply being honest with me, and I no longer hold any grudge against you. Please forgive me if I was too harsh with you."

"I was wrong. As soon as I realized I had said something I should not have uttered, I could not forgive myself. I feel I could not allow myself to go unpunished, and that is why I continued with the letter on the back of the page. Please read it, too. Only if you accept what I have written can I believe you have forgiven me and feel easy in my mind."

I felt badly that he should still be apologizing. I turned his letter over and on the back found the following:

> *Since I did not see you come to the clinic and you sent no word, I could only imagine one thing. Need I tell you, Ma Tin Tin?*
>
> *If you do forgive me, then please let me invite you and two companions of your choice to watch the talkie film* Hpoo Zar Shin[1] *this Thursday at the 6:30 PM show. There will be four seats for us. Please inform me tomorrow at the clinic if you can accept it or not. If you can come, you and your companions can wait for me at the clinic or meet me at the cinema.*
>
> *Please be assured that in no way would I do anything to smear your honor.*
>
> Chit Maung

The way he had insisted on punishing himself by having me accept his invitation made me realize that he was prepared to be laughed at and teased by his friends, or maybe by the whole audience, for being seen with me; and was I supposed to go with him for that reason? So, he would punish himself by allowing his reputation to be damaged by accompanying me in public, and did this also mean that I was to be the instrument of punishment?

"If I say I forgive you, U Chit Maung, do you still need me to come with you to the cinema and for you to become a laughing stock?"

"It's not you who's punishing me, Ma Tin Tin, it's me punishing myself. Otherwise I would still feel badly about the whole thing."

If I had not known what an honest person he was, I would have retorted angrily, "If your friends gossip about you for being seen with me, do you imagine my friends would cheer me on for it? Would you please think over what you are saying: that you would sacrifice yourself at my expense?"

Only because I knew of his honesty did I not lose my temper again. This was just as well, for if I were once again angry with him, surely the poor man would run for his life every time he saw a woman.

In addition, so that he could also protect me in this fiasco, he was actually urging me to bring companions! I stared fixedly at him and thought that he would surely lack a great many more social graces. I felt a great tenderness for him, and only because of that did I decide to accept his invitation, and I am sure he had no inkling at all of the reason behind it. He was simply not that type of man.

---

[1] Partner of Destiny.

"There's nothing to forgive, and if you will be happy only if I accept your invitation, there's no reason why I cannot accept. But I must say I'm not happy that you should apologize in this manner."

"I know that you are good hearted, Ma Tin Tin, and that you have compassion, and I feel great admiration and respect for you. That is why I need to apologize this way."

I had been wondering what sort of a man he was; finally, I had my answer. He was a man who so fully deserved my compassion.

From that day, he visited me almost every evening. Every time, he would bring me interesting books, and he would also bring one for himself to read. He kept a finger between the pages to mark the place when we were talking, but if I got up to do something, he would lower his head to the book, reading even two lines if he could in that short space of time.

We spoke little of our personal affairs, but we discussed all sorts of things about politics and education. When we ran out of words, I would sit there looking at his face, but he, he sat with downcast eyes and the dignity of an abbot. I never saw him in new-looking clothes, but he was always neat. He only wore homespun fabrics, and his shirt would be buttoned up to the neck. In the breast pocket of his jacket, I would always see two pens and a red and blue pencil. His hair was cut so short that he need not bother with combing or oiling his hair. He certainly did not care to make himself look good. His complexion was neither dark nor fair, but tanned. Judging by his large frame and height, one could say he came from a family of big men. He had a sharply defined nose and large features, so I wondered if he were close kin to the old Burmese race. His way of speaking, his way of moving, and his body language all marked him as a gentle and decent man, and his words were equally gentle, but full of insight.

He seemed very well versed in Burmese literature. He would explain clearly anything that I did not understand in astrology, medicine, prose, and poetry, together with quotes from various texts. I wondered sometimes if he had indeed been a scholar monk. Some of the English words were difficult for me to understand when he spoke on history, economics, and Western literature or poetry, and about Western countries. In fact, he knew so much about England, France, and Ireland that it almost seemed as if he had been to those places.

When he spoke of personal things, he used the pronoun "I," but when he spoke in general, he used "we." When he talked of affairs concerning newspapers, he never spoke as if he knew all, or said that he did so-and-so. He was always modest in how he presented his knowledge, and in spite of it I knew that he had a brilliant mind.

I wanted to know where he had studied all this.

"U Chit Maung, when did you finish college?"

"I never went to college; I passed the tenth grade because they saw fit to allow me to pass."

I was dumbfounded.

"But why didn't you go on to college after passing the tenth grade?"

"Well, I was too young, so I would have had to wait about three years to be eligible. At the time, I didn't think much of college education,[2] and so I became a teacher at my own school while I studied independently by reading."

---

[2] Many students did not like the curriculum offered at the British-run colleges and universities, as the professors would inevitably insist that Britain had "saved" Myanmar.

"Were you interested in teaching?"

"Not really, but I had nowhere to live, and the principal loved me like a son. I was doing a lot of reading then, so I took his advice and became a teacher."

"And how did you become an editor?"

"Actually, it was my goal right from the start. While still in school, I often sent off articles to the English-language paper *The New Burma*. Since then, I had made up my mind that one day I would become an editor. I also gave private lessons to some students, and one summer holiday I came down to Yangon to buy some books for them. There was an opening for an editor at the *Nawrahta* paper, so I applied and did not go back at all."

"And from there, how did you get to *Myanmar Alin*?"

"The *Nawrahta* folded. During the time that I was working there, we even had to pawn our clothes to buy paper! We couldn't afford two meals a day: for dinner we would just wash down one pice[3] worth of Bayagyaw[4] with lots of water, but the paper went broke anyway. As for *Myanmar Alin*, chief editor U Sein was not well and wanted U Tin Gyi, who came back from Germany, to take his place, but U Tin Gyi's family did not approve, so he urged me to take the job instead, and I became the night editor of *Myanmar Alin*."

"So chief editor U Sein was overseeing the whole process of publication?"

"Yes, that's right."

"I really like the *Myanmar Alin* editorials. The language is so good, and it gets to the point clearly, and people who want to write can really learn from it. U Sein is so great, to have made this paper outstanding, and with such a high circulation. His talent in writing is brilliant. Every time I read the editorials, I cannot help but feel gratitude for him."

"Yes, that's right."

"Considering editors among all the people who want to serve our country, I never before realized what a big role they played, and how hard it is to become one and to have such a noble attitude. Only when I came to know you did I realize it, and U Chit Maung, your work is truly noble and valuable in spite of all the hardships."

He made no comment in response to my praise of editors, but sat with downcast eyes as if I were mocking him, his head hanging lower and lower with each word. He looked so strange that I wondered if he were somehow ashamed.

Each time he came he stayed until late. If there was nothing to say, he sat there like a stone with his head down. As I was not in my own home, I felt embarrassed this might inconvenience my hosts and, at the same time, could not bring myself to be rude enough to tell him to go. When he arrived, I would be delighted, but as it grew late, I would inevitably begin to feel miserable. I always had to remind him that it was getting late, and I was getting tired of having to be so rude. I felt resentful that he should be so inconsiderate.

That night, as he sat with his head down after I praised the work of editors, as it was getting late I thought I would teach him some manners.

"When I first met you at the clinic, U Chit Maung, remember I was in a hurry and I had to say goodbye first and leave you? I felt so embarrassed at the time, and it was because it wasn't my own home, you know. You must have thought me so rude."

---

[3] Smallest denomination of coin in Myanmar.

[4] Chickpea fritters.

"No, no, not at all, I didn't think you rude. Then I also wanted to leave, as I had a lot of work back at the paper, but I felt too embarrassed towards you to excuse myself and go, so I just sat there."

"What …? But … but … and now?"

"Actually, right now they are waiting for me back at the paper."

"Oh my goodness, U Chit Maung, please, you should leave at once, in that case. If you are waiting for the hostess to tell you to leave, why, it would be so rude of her to tell you to go!"

"Really? I've never called on anyone before so I had no idea, I always thought it would be rude for the visitor to say goodbye first. Well then, I'd better be off."

This man, this strange, naive man, this *barbarian*, this *simpleton* … what a man.

CHAPTER 6

IN YANGON

This trip to Yangon had dragged on for some time as I was hoping to clear up my ailment for good. He came almost every night, and from what he had said previously, I began to wonder if he was just being polite in calling on me so often.

Before, when I had not yet met him, I never thought so much about him, but now my mind seemed almost all the time to dwell on him. I noticed so many aspects of his personality, of which he himself seemed completely unaware. He was always one to put others before himself and did so with such a will that he disregarded his own well-being. I could say that, with all his caring for others, he was at the same time being too hard on himself.

One day, as we sat talking, I learned that he was not yet twenty-six years old, and I could see he was embarrassed and hung his head in discomfort when I stared at his face in utter amazement. I had thought him in his late thirties! He told me that others also thought him older than his years and that, even so, he couldn't care less about it and that he felt his only mission was to work as hard as he could. I sternly told him that it was not a good thing to look so aged and that it was not something to be proud of.

He replied that he was quite happy to be thought older, as it would lend weight to whatever he said. He smiled and told me, as proof of it, that when he talked to people from his hometown who knew his real age, none of them would believe his views, and that to have them accepted, he always had to say they were the views of older literary and political figures. Laughingly he told me that once he began to look older his words were easily accepted as wisdom. Since I had met him, this was the first time I had seen him laugh.

His workload was heavy; all through the day he received visitors, and they would talk politics. Then he had to write the editorial, the lead story, etc., for the next day. He had to read over about one hundred reports sent in by correspondents from villages and towns and edit their stories. At night, he read all the other newspapers, more books, and, to make ends meet, had to write various stories and columns for other publications in both English and Burmese. For each twenty-four hours of the day, he slept from four in the morning to six, so daily he only got two hours' rest. I could understand now why his hair was grey before he was twenty-six and the reason he looked so haggard. I worried that he would drop dead before he reached his goals and feared that he would die young.

I wanted to warn him to be careful, so I teasingly said to him, "Now, don't you honor what the Lord Buddha said about good health being good fortune?"

"My health is sound," he replied confidently, in English.

I also replied in English,

"Can't I look at you and see with my own eyes? You are committing slow suicide by overwork, that's what it is."

"I've been working exactly this way for over eight years!" he said in English.

I sharply scolded him, saying that anyone working with only two hours' sleep for eight years was bound to fall ill one day, just so that he would begin to worry about his health.

With exchanges such as this, we became closer to each other. My long stay in Yangon allowed me to know more of him. He had no mother, but his father was still living. He had six brothers and sisters, but he was not close to any member of his family, and it was not because he was physically far from them, but emotionally he held himself quite aloof. He had lived most of his childhood in school, and when he became an adult, his life was wrapped up in his newspaper work. He had no relationships, no fun, and even for relaxation he did not smoke. His head was forever sunk in books, and his life was quite a thing apart from the normal life of men.

Whatever he did or thought or believed, these actions and convictions were as strong as solid rock. In situations where one needed to be flexible and gracious, not knowing at all how to be so, he stood there unmoving like a rough-hewn boulder. Male companions could not change him into a person of grace; he surely needed some feminine influences. I thought that if he did not get married, he would surely face many problems. I tried to imagine what sort of a home life he had, and found I was not at all wrong when I saw where he lived.

One day some friends who lived in Kyeemyindine asked me to spend the night with them, so I needed to let him know that I would not be home in the evening. I did not want to go to his office, nor had I the time to go to the clinic to use the phone, and I thought I would drop off a note to him where he lived on my way to my friends' house. I wrote a note telling him not to visit me that night and got down from the bus at the Thirty-Fourth Street stop. I looked for the house number he had given me and went up the stairs. If I did not see him, I could just leave the note with someone.

I had to knock three or four times before the door opened. When it did, I saw several pairs of slippers lying untidily at the entrance.[1] As I had assumed, he did not live alone. In the narrow room beyond, dust and rubbish lay thick, and it was dirty and messy everywhere I looked. Clothes both newly washed and dirty hung from hooks on the walls. Bedrolls were not rolled and stacked neatly, but just piled up in a corner. It was as if a bunch of coolies lived here. I could guess at the nature of men living like this.

"What is it?" The man who opened the door seemed to think I had come to the wrong address.

"Is U Chit Maung here?"

"Oh … he just left."

"What time does he get back … does he usually come home in the early evening?"

"Yes, he does."

"If so I would like to leave a note … please tell him when he comes."

Not placing the note in his hands but in the letterbox attached to the top of the stairs, I left. Seeing that letterbox, I thought at least one among this lot had some idea of neatness and smiled to myself. They would eat their meals or take tea wherever it was convenient, that was for sure.

The next time I saw him, I gave him advice as I would to a brother.

---

[1] Footwear is removed on entering a Myanmar house.

"I used to think you might die young and now I'm sure of it. Are you trying to, U Chit Maung?"

"Why do you say that?"

"Well, I feel *ah-nar* [embarrassed] to say so, but I should tell you straight out if I must advise you on what to do. The place you live in, it's like a coolie's quarters. Working with your head is maybe harder than manual labor. For that you need to eat well and live well, sleep well and, even if one cannot be happy at all times, at least there must be peace of mind. Only if you look after yourself well could you work for a long time. You work with your head, and didn't you ever think how important a good environment is for that sort of person?"

"I never did, actually. I never thought of needing pleasant surroundings, but then, I never thought of my place as unpleasant. What good would it do for someone like me? What difference would it make? I go home only to bathe; I live and sleep at the office. I just clear papers off a desk and that's my bed. I never thought one way or the other about how I live; how I work is more important."

"So if you feel you must work hard for the sake of the country, do you think you will have many years to do your work if you continue living like this? You don't care about what you eat, your lifestyle is a mess, you don't get enough sleep, no exercise at all, and one day you'll be seriously ill. That sort of illness is something from which you don't recover easily, so please take care of yourself. Only when you are healthy can you be happy, and only when you are happy can you work as hard as you want. Any man who wants to reach his goals should have brains and a strong will, and you have these already. But remember that your health is not yours alone, it's for the sake of the country. For the sake of people who worry I beg you to take better care of yourself."

"Sometimes I feel as if I'm coming down with flu, but then if I resist I can to some extent keep it at bay."

"You can keep flu at bay … ?"

"You may think me mad, but it's true."

"You'll die pretty soon, I warn you, if you keep on like this."

That night I talked late into the night, trying to get some sense into him.

The next day, early in the morning when I got to the clinic there was a letter waiting for me. Presumably he had written it the previous night after he went back and had left it early this morning at the clinic.

> *I promise not to delay looking after my health, as you repeatedly tell me, Ma Tin Tin.*
>
> *In all the times we talked, I was the most happy last night. I felt strengthened and grateful. When you remarked that your stay in Yangon seemed as if for the sole purpose of harassing me, I must say I disagree with you. The happiness of looking forward to seeing you, the joy of seeing you, the contentment of talking to you, the pleasure of listening to you, the delight in the memories of our meetings and talks … these are the pleasures I enjoy through your stay in Yangon, Ma Tin Tin. Not satisfied with only that, I also asked you to write down your daily thoughts for me.*
>
> *Before, I had kept to myself the knowledge that you are a person of high intellect and good heart and that the patriotic spirit in you is strong. Now I*

cannot help but tell all this to people such as Thakin Thein Maung,[2] *and even if you refuse to acknowledge these praises, you do deserve them, Ma Tin Tin.*

It is my great fortune to have met someone like you. Your articles have made people think about our country and they showed people how to reason. It is so important for our enslaved country that all women should have these views, this pride, this intellect, and this strength. When you are completely well, I hope more of your works will shake our country to its foundations.

I was so happy to be talking to you that it became very late last night. It was cruel of me not to have considered your health.

I reflected on what you said about looking after my health before I collapse, and your words are so true that I now promise, Ma Tin Tin, to look after myself as much as possible.

Chit Maung

I was right in thinking he needed women friends. I felt that *I* was indebted to *him* through having him no longer try to "keep flu at bay," so I hurriedly wrote a letter to thank him and sent it around by messenger that very evening.

---

[2] A prominent politician who already knew Ma Tin Tin.

CHAPTER 7

AN UNFORGETTABLE NIGHT

One day I received an urgent message to return to Bogalay, and that night, as I was packing my things to leave by boat the next evening, U Chit Maung came around just before nine, but I was still tidying up so he had to wait awhile. As soon as I sat down, I told him the news. He had an expression on his face as if he were looking his last at someone who would never return to this life.

"I may come back in Tabaung,"[1] I reassured him, but it did not raise his spirits.

Tonight was the thirteenth time we had sat talking in this parlor, and every night I was never once bored. Some nights he would talk, some nights I would, and there were nights of heated exchange. But tonight he said nothing, and I sat silent. Before I left, I wanted only to hear his words, but had no desire to tell him anything; but I waited in vain. So we sat in silence without a word, as still and motionless as if we were in meditation. The sound of the big clock in the parlor chiming the hours seemed to be marking our very breaths.

We could hear noises of the night from around us, rising from the street. Our voices that had rung in this room every night for the past twelve nights were stilled, and a heavy silence fell on us. I would always remember that night.

Around about midnight, he said, "I'll see you off tomorrow at the jetty," and left.

After he was gone, I felt uneasy. He had not said a word for nearly four hours. I was frantic to know why and what he was thinking the whole time. I was not sure if we would have the chance to talk at the jetty or even if we would talk at all, so I wrote a letter, mostly urging him to look after his health, to give him the next day.

Early the next morning, I went to the Shwedagon Pagoda with my aunt and then to Scott Market,[2] where I shopped at one stall after the other. My aunt went back with the shopping to pack the things while I continued on my own to the clinic. I gave my doctor the present I had bought for her at Scott's, and then I called *Myanmar Alin* to tell him that I would be leaving early for the jetty. He told me to wait, so I did, but he did not appear for some time. I was getting impatient, so I went to wait by the front entrance. He came, not alone, but with a few companions.

"So you're leaving today?" he asked. His friends stopped a moment and then strolled on after excusing themselves.

I said yes and told him I would give him my letter at the jetty.

He asked, "Are you going back now? Where are you going?" and I said yes, I was going back. I thought he would ask me if I were going back alone, and when he did, I smiled and teased, "Yes, I'm going back alone, now do you want to come with me?"

He said yes, he did, and made as if to walk off with me, saying, "Let's go."

---

[1] From mid-March to mid-April.

[2] Now Bo Gyoke Aung San Market but to this day often called Scott.

"But U Chit Maung, don't you think … "

He did not allow me to finish but said firmly, "Yes, I will see you home. The first time I met you here I did not and now that it's your last day here I again have the chance to do so. Come."

I found it hard to refuse, and we came back by tram to Fiftieth Street. We got down at the top of the street, and saying, "I'll come down early to the jetty," he climbed back on the same tram.

CHAPTER 8

WHAT FATE ORDAINED FROM TIMES PAST

Thakin Thein Maung escorted my aunt and me to the jetty. "He" turned up only after we had stored away our baggage in our cabin. U Chit Maung spoke a few words to Thakin Thein Maung and then handed me a pile of books and a letter. Saying I would write him when I got home, I handed him the letter I had written the night before. He looked composed but his eyes could not hide what he was feeling in his heart. I, too, felt miserable to go back. I thought that there could be no one else but me who would so brutally point out his faults and I felt sorry for him. He did not say a word to me before my departure. As soon as the boat left the jetty, I opened his letter. It was written in simple but beautiful English. I found it very thought-provoking.

> *My Dear Tin Ga-lay,[1]*
>
> *I had thought that our meeting last night was our very last as far as this visit of yours is concerned. Fortunately I was deceived, for you have the kindness to give me this afternoon yet another opportunity ... the happy memory of which I should not easily forget. The "new" experience has given me both pain and pleasure, but, let me confess, it is so thrilling that I have not been able to stop to think whether I should be sorry or glad for it. Still, I must admit that in the end I should be glad and grateful.*
>
> *I have already told you that you have changed me. The change is so rapid — oh, so surprisingly rapid — that I am still suffering its sweet and tender shock. You are right when you said that you have worked miracles. Nor am I at all wrong when I state that I should be more miserable for the loss of those miracles. Misery will be mine but this misery is peculiar; it is mixed with happy memories and therefore should be bearable. If after your departure I should feel desolate — and I certainly will — I shall seek relief in the hope that you are coming back — back to Yangon, back to Paradise that you have built — the Paradise to which you alone can put life.*
>
> *I shall also seek relief in the belief that you have been kind and you shall continue to be kind to me. As I have already told you, you have exposed to me that part of myself which I have not discovered myself earlier. I had thought that I was strong, but alas, I wasn't. I had believed that I was unselfish, but you have seen how grossly selfish I have been! I had told myself that I did not care for*

---

[1] *Ga-lay* or *Lay*, meaning small or little, is an affectionate and intimate addition to the name of a woman or of someone younger. Translator's note: In the original letter, her name here was written in the numbered code that he liked to use sometimes, perhaps because he was shy about writing this intimate term openly. This letter was written in English by U Chit Maung.

myself, but you have shown myself to me; I cared more for my own honor than
that of a lady!

Such then are my weaknesses. You have revealed me to myself as no one has
revealed. I am very thankful to you for it. All my supposed knowledge of
psychology is hollow: your shrewd observation and keen sense of judgment has
[sic] revealed what the pages of psychology have not been able to reveal.

Now let me discuss your letter. However hurriedly written, it has not failed
to strike home. You write not only to my head but to my heart. You talk even so
cleverly, and you write as you talk. Small wonder, then, that you write well. I
have [sic] at one time no high opinion of women as a rule. Now I must alter my
opinion. I must confess that you have answered — and answered most
admirably — for the whole of womankind. I have perhaps been too harsh; I must
apologize now.

And there's one thing that strikes me as strange. No two people think alike,
goes the saying. But our conversations have disclosed the fact that there are
things which we have in common. I do hope that we shall if possible take
advantage of this common outlook and, if you are willing, strengthen our
friendship. "Like draws the like" and "Love begets love" are sayings that have
never been challenged since they were uttered by the ancient sages.

I believe that this friendship will do me an immense good. Our acquaintance
has already done me good. I mean, you have led me to walk the way of all men
without fear. I have always held the idea that it is improper to be seen with a
young lady if she is not one's own. People asked me who my beautiful
companion was. They asked out of curiosity but I could not tell them. I could not
tell them the truth. Nor could I tell them a lie. I have wrapped myself up in such
a rigid and tense atmosphere before that when this surprising experience
encountered me, I did not know what to do or say. I was unhappy and yet very
happy. I could not explain, actually, how I felt. My feelings, dear lady, are too
sacred to be expressed in man's tongue. If you think we are all happy for being
relieved of your company, you will be grossly mistaken. We are already very
sorry, and if you go away carrying the impression, we all shall be sorrier. You
have impressed me very, very deeply. The impression will last as long as I live. It
is indeed no exaggeration to say that as you are the only lady who has walked
into my heart so shall you be the only lady whom I care for and remember and
love. I hesitate to write this, but have not great men before me cared,
remembered, and loved intelligent women? I do hope I am not alone in paying
Woman this compliment.

So dear Lady, please be sure of our affection for you and admiration for your
tastes and talents. Just as I will seek your advice when I am in dire need, so
would I request you to seek mine — whenever necessary. And, give me strength
that I may give you only sound advice.

Yours very faithfully,
Chit Maung

I kept reading his letter again and again, thinking over from every angle what he
had written, but I came to no concrete conclusion at the end. The boat docked at
Bogalay at four in the morning, and I had not slept the whole night; I was rereading
his letter. I went to bed as soon as I got home and got up only at eight. As usual,

without even washing my face I took up the newspaper. It was the issue of March 22, a Saturday. I glanced at "Today's Thoughts." It was numbered seventy-four.

"When people part, some are happy and some are not. The happy ones would have felt relief and the unhappy ones, despair, to be parted. 'Parting' is just one situation but the reactions could be quite different. Think about it for today."

It seemed meant for me alone, this advice to ponder. I remembered about writing to him as promised, yet I could not, not because I did not want to and not because I was bored about it, I just felt unsettled. His letter arrived three days later.

> On Friday evening I left the boat with heavy steps and my thoughts were left at the jetty. I felt burdened with sadness, and if Mr. Rush[2] had not been with me, I would have stood there until the boat sailed out of sight. I parted with him with my head low, and he took the tram from Strand Road after telling me that if he was certain to leave for Bogalay on the twenty-seventh, he would let me know. I wanted desperately to read the letter you handed personally to me and I was going to take a rickshaw back to the office. But then I ran into Ko Hla Pe, Ko Nu, and also Ko Thein Pe,[3] who just returned from Calcutta, and they had been seeing off someone on the same ship, so I had to walk back along Dalhousie[4] Street with them. Ko Thein Pe said he wanted a faluda,[5] so all four of us had to have one.
>
> The dear little letter was still in my pocket ... I haven't had faluda for about eight years and it was tasteless in my mouth, but I thought I would taste immeasurable pleasure in reading your letter and longed to do so.
>
> I opened it as soon as I got back to the office and read your advice. If I had not done so I would have refused to look after myself and continued living my life like a vagabond, because no one would have cared if something happened to me. Now, here's one who has firm control over my life and death, and when this person warned that I might decline into devastation if I did not take care of myself, and added, please could she be free of worry, I am determined not for my sake but for hers to live better in the future.
>
> The words "work hard, too, for to earn well and to succeed is also one of life's fortunes" are well worth listening to, so I must confirm to you Ma Tin Tin that I will without fail and at once comply with your advice.
>
> I could not sleep a wink on Friday night thinking of the one who so cared for my well-being. As you said you might go to the country on Saturday, I spent the whole day and the night until daybreak, thinking and imagining: now she is there, now she is here, now she is like this. You said you would send a letter as soon as you got home so I was expecting one on Sunday and sent our doorman to the post several times. I thought for sure it would come by the second mail but when at half past eleven the doorman brought the mail, the letter I had been waiting for, for a night and day, had not arrived. I felt such emptiness. I felt such despair. The whole night and morning I lived to see the letter. As it was

---

[2] A British friend of Ma Tin Tin's family.

[3] All well-known politicians. Ko Nu later became Thakin Nu and then U Nu, premier of independent Myanmar. Ko Hla Pe, U Chit Maung's closest friend, became Bo Let Yar of the Thirty Comrades. Ko Thein Pe became a famous writer, Thein Pe Myint.

[4] Now Maha Bandoola Street.

[5] Indian-style dessert of cream, milk, rose syrup, ice cream, pudding, nuts, and sago pearls.

said in the Kogan Pyo, *one burns with suffering and you cannot know how painful it is. When others[6] could be careless about it while others[7] feel as if the universe has been shaken, those others do not seem to notice. So is that why "they" are so calm about it?*

I tried to console myself but when I could not read what I desired to so badly, I found no peace. The March 22 issue of Myanmar Alin's *"Daily Thoughts" would have no meaning for those who have not endured parting, but for those who do, they would know what a tragedy it could be. The writer perhaps sent it in without due concern, but for some it wounds the heart like a sharp knife. People who knew the* Dhamma *may console themselves with the wisdom of these teachings of Buddha, but for others there is no cure for a wounded mind. The mind will dwell on this the whole time, night and day. I never realized the intensity of the mind before and once disdained those who dwelt in their thoughts and were forgetful of anything else. But now that I am likewise inflicted, I felt* ah-nar *for these others for having disdained them once and fear greatly for myself. This intensity of the mind has a torturous hold on this fear for myself and embarrassment for the future. Although one deems oneself wise, one is but a fool, after all.*

> *Coming to know you,*
> *Through what fate ordained from times past,*
> *What prayers of my last life answered.*
> *If Lord Buddha were here,*
> *Would I fain beg of Him*
> *What of the past and what of now:*
> *And Lord, let me know what the future has in store.*

Chit Maung
March 21

I tried not to think of what he had written but rather what was between the lines. I also reflected on how he had sat silent for four hours on learning of my imminent departure. I kept thinking of him. I kept thinking of the future I could not see. I soon knew by heart the verse he wrote at the end. Was there anything in there that I should decide upon? I felt confused, as if I, too, wanted to ask of the Buddha to clarify our future. But in fact I did not feel there was anything concrete I could hold onto in his letters. I could not be sure if my interpretations were correct.[8] I felt hot and bothered by the tone of his letter.

That evening I went for a walk along the river. The bridge leaning over the water was always a good spot to stop for a rest, to think. The breeze blew briskly and there were few people about. My mind felt at peace again, to watch the boats and sampans on the far bank. The wide, bright sky was filled with clouds that floated one after the other, red and orange strips that merged into the massive white piles. My confused mind became clear and my spirits lifted.

---

[6] Meaning Ma Tin Tin.

[7] Meaning himself.

[8] Until a man openly declares his love, no decent woman would take it for granted.

As soon as I got home, I penned a letter telling him I was well and that I pray every day for his good health. Letters kept coming and I replied to them. Now, his words became livelier and in each letter there was always a bit of his own verse. Some longer verses were so good that I thought it would be enough to publish a book of "Poems by U Chit Maung in His Youth." To think of his demeanor of a monk and then to read his letters full of romance and joy—could it be him? I was seeing two sides of his personality.

Chapter 9

Strange Words

Three months passed after my return to Bogalay. I received a message from my father to come see him in Meikhtila, and I wrote to U Chit Maung saying when I would arrive in Yangon.

He came to the jetty. I saw him standing on the bank well before the boat docked, a book held in place under his arm, a monk's umbrella in his hand, and with his other hand holding up his *pasoe*[1] to keep it off the mud. So I was seeing him again! But this time my stay in Yangon was short as I would be leaving the same night by train for Meikhtila.

As soon as he came on board, I told him I would be leaving that night. His face fell, and he begged me to rest a day in Yangon. My aunt who was with me also added her pleas for me to stay. I agreed, and we parted at the jetty.

That night he came to where we were staying with as serious an expression as ever, although he looked happy. We sat in the parlor without a word and I thought fleetingly of the night when we had sat like this for four hours. He did not look upset but he did not look as if he were overjoyed to see me, so I could not make him out.

I began the conversation by saying I had received the novel he had written titled *Shwe Lin Yone*,[2] and thanked him. He sat there smiling as I analyzed his other novels, pointing out where they were weak. I told him that, as for the novel *Hmaing Hmon Hmon*,[3] I did not like the story but the writing was so good that after I finished the book I felt as if I had eaten a hearty meal. At that he stopped smiling and hung his head in embarrassment. He always became uneasy when praised—not only uneasy but acutely uncomfortable. Only when I teased him about his satirical book *Shar Shar Hpwe Hpwe*,[4] where he poked fun at women, did he smile once again.

When our talk turned to politics, he said more parties like the Thakin Party[5] needed to emerge. However, the name "Thakin," meaning master, also sounded unpleasant, he said. He thought that the party needed young members and told me he planned to campaign for more students to join. When I asked why he did not join the party if he supported it so much, he explained in detail that as an editor he should not be part of a political party. He said in politics one must be flexible and be able to change strategies as one goes along, like maneuvering a boat in swift currents. He predicted that someday the Thakin Party would grow into a strong one.

---

[1] Waist garment for men.

[2] Golden Eagle.

[3] Misty.

[4] Strange Odds and Ends.

[5] Meaning the Do Bama Asi-ayon (We Burmans Association).

I tackled him about his health and learnt that he had changed his habits: now he ate at regular hours, although he admitted to not having managed to do the same with sleep. He walked regularly for exercise, and he was following my advice.

I asked him what his friends thought of our exchange of letters. He replied that not only his friends, but he himself, at first sight of me, had been astonished at how fashionable I was. I had been very modern not only in dress but also in my looks and deportment, although not in the same way as other society girls. He commented that only because he had read so many books in English could he judge exactly in what way I was "modern." He repeated that I was "modern" in a much different way from other society women.

We then talked of women's issues, and I told him all I had on my mind. I said I thought of humans as such and not as men or women. We are what we are, I told him, not because of our sex but our minds. It depended entirely on the mind which religious meditative level one could achieve, I said. I told him quite bluntly that I would not think myself a lesser being because I am a woman,[6] which fact laid bare the very essence of my personality.

We discussed religion and science. He was well-versed in Buddhist scriptures and said he so admired the Buddha's words that every single day he remembered the gratitude we owe to the Lord. He carefully explained every important factor in the Buddha's philosophy.

Speaking of history, he praised the strength of King Anawrahta's reign.[7] Regarding Western history, he said he admired Napoleon and that as a student he had Napoleon's picture in his room. He said he once began to translate Napoleon's biography but nearing the end found out someone else had already done it, so he had burnt his manuscript.

We sat late into the night, absorbed in our conversation. I later wrote down in full what we said that night in a diary, but it was destroyed during the Japanese Occupation.

The next evening he saw me off to the station and on the way gave me books to read on the train. "I wish you would come back quickly," he said, and asked me to write. As soon as I arrived in Meikhtila, I sent off a letter saying I had arrived safely.

In the evenings, I would sit by the calm Meikhtila Lake and read his letters. In one he wrote with a tiny hand, filling nearly forty pages. I was never more engrossed in any book the way I was in his letters, written out of his vast experience of books he had read and from life. I doubt if anyone else apart from me ever found out how much he knew.

Reading his letters calmed my spirit, but on thinking over them, the contents caused a raging storm in my heart. When I returned from Meikhtila he was waiting at the station. He said he would come to see me in the evening and left. That night he asked me a question he had never asked before, apropos of nothing.

"Ma Tin Tin, how much do you spend a month?"

"I don't have a fixed allowance so I have no idea. Why?"

"I think it must be at least a hundred kyat."[8]

---

[6] A belief erroneously thought to be a Buddhist concept but accepted in very conservative circles.

[7] Founder of the first Myanmar Empire, 1044–1287, Bagan era.

[8] The lowest-level civil servant would earn about ten kyat a month at that time.

"I can't say for sure ... some months it might be less, sometimes more, according to the situation."

I also put a question to him, in my turn, apropos of nothing as well.

"U Chit Maung, what quality do you think is the most important in a person's character and one that you yourself try to practice?"

"Honesty. I think we Burmese need this, we have a good religion but there's a lack of good character. I think that the most wonderful thing in life is to strive to be honest. I know it's not easy to uphold, but it's not impossible, so I feel I should try. I don't know if I will succeed at all, but my life will testify to it. Someone like you, Ma Tin Tin, must be the judge."

I liked his answer so much that I wrote it down and underlined it in red.

I stayed about three days in Yangon, and every night he came to see me. One night my host's family asked me to go with them to the night bazaar. I told them I would prefer to stay home, and when he came I told him that I did not go out because he would be visiting.

"I don't know how to tell you how grateful I am for your kindness," he said.

I looked up at him, and he wore such a dignified look on his face I was hard pressed to realize it was him who had just spoken those words.

Our talk turned to poetry. "I remember my mother writing a verse when I was young," he said, "where she wrote that in times past we had poetry carried by birds, as the writers sent birds as messengers, then we had prayerful poetry where the writer prays to win his sweetheart. Then people sang to the moon to pass on their messages. Then they had friends carry letters. Now, she said, we might as well write poetry about airplanes carrying love poems."

Asking me for a piece of paper, he wrote down this verse in full.

We talked of poetry, of magazines, of writers. At dinnertime, I asked him to go out and buy Byriani[9] rice, which I had to urge him to eat. After our meal, we again continued chatting. All of a sudden, he asked me,

"Do you have anyone you plan to marry?"

"No, I haven't."

"So what sort of plans do you have concerning marriage?"

"I don't really have any plans, but I do have conditions."

"Am I allowed to ask ... ?"

"First, my marriage partner must be one of my choice and, second, he must have my parents' approval; but I really don't have any plans to get married yet."

Then we both fell silent. I sat reading over the verse he had written. After a while he asked where I wanted to go the next morning. When I said I was going to Kamayut[10] to visit someone, he asked if he could come along, and left.

---

[9] A one-dish Indian meal of spicy rice and chicken.

[10] A suburb of Yangon, near the main university campus, north of downtown.

CHAPTER 10

A FALLEN MONK[1]

The next day we went to Kamayut, and as he was with me I did not bring along anyone else. On the way, we talked of our childhoods. I told him about the time I was ill as a child and a vendor selling pineapples passed in front of the house calling out, "Now here we have … pineapples!" So that I would not ask for something I should not eat, sick as I was, my parents made a lot of noise to drown out the vendor's call. However, I just heard the words "Now here we have" and thinking it a kind of snack, had cried a night and a day for some "Now here we have" cake.

He, too, said that he had been hyperactive, and his exhausted grandmother who had to look after him had written a note in numbered code to his mother, asking her to please take him back, and sent the note by him. On the way, he tried to read it but could not, and on delivering the note demanded to be taught the code. By now he knew it well, and when I asked him to teach me, he promised he would, that it was easy enough. We laughed at each other's stories.

He remarked that he could guess I was quick-minded, so I replied I have a quick temper as well.

"A fierce mind, too, isn't that right?" he asked. I smiled and said nothing.

On our way back, I told him I would be leaving the next day, and he begged me to come to the cinema with him that evening, and I agreed.

Whenever he came to see me, he always brought a letter for me and I, too, began to have a letter ready to give back. The letters he posted also did not miss a single day, so even if I were seeing him in person, I had on file letters for all days of each month. As for my replies, if I had been out the whole day while in Yangon, I had to write a reply even as we sat talking in the evening.

That evening, as I handed him the letter I just finished writing, he looked as if he wanted to say something. Then he put the letter into his pocket. We both never read each other's letters in front of the other.

"When are you back in Yangon?" he asked.

"I can't say for sure, maybe about January."

"I will miss you so much."

I said not a word.

"I'd like to add some more to what I said the other day," he continued. "I hope that if you think of marriage you would also consider me as a suitor. I have never before been interested in any woman and have never known any woman as intimately as now, as I know you. At all times I long to see you. At all times my thoughts revolve around you. When I saw something in a book, I realized my feelings have changed. In the book a young man was telling a matron about a girl: 'I

---

[1] Powerful monks are believed to be able to float in air, and a few stories made fun of such monks falling to earth at the sight of a lovely woman and losing their powers, felled by secular feelings of love.

want to be with her, I want to be close to her. I want to possess her and nobody else to approach her.' And the matron replied, 'Why, isn't that love? I see you are in love, deeply in love.'

"It's exactly like that with me. I have opened my heart to you, Ma Tin Tin. I think the man who marries you would be the luckiest man alive. The man you refused would be the unluckiest person on earth. My fate is in your hands ... please let me know."

He spoke so gently, so softly.

"U Chit Maung, the question of my marriage is not an easy one, I need to think on it and on you. We know about each other only from the short periods when we have seen each other, but later on we might discover new things. Then, if we should change our minds it would make us both miserable. You, too, U Chit Maung, please think more about it. Let me think, and please don't ask me to decide now. I will consider your words very seriously."

I did not want him to feel bad and had to choose my words carefully.

"On my part I don't need to think anymore on this," he said. "I only need to wait for your decision. Please, I beg you not to take too long."

"All right, I will write when I get home."

We both fell silent after this, but this time we were both lost in our own thoughts; it was not the same as what happened the first time we had sat silent.

He said he would come to the jetty the next day and left. At the door, he turned to ask what books I needed, and I told him I wanted a particular treatise on healing. He said he would bring it the next day, and we talked about traditional medicine books at the door for some time. I did not sleep a wink that night.

As soon as I arrived at the jetty, I saw him standing in front of the teashop, books and the monk's umbrella in one hand and the other hand holding up the edge of his *pasoe*, and still wearing his frayed monk's slippers. I hated the sight of these slippers, so I gave him the package of black velvet slippers I had brought in readiness. My host's family, who also came to the jetty, were talking and laughing with Mr. Rush, manager of Polson & Co., but U Chit Maung did not say a word: he stood there with his head hanging down. I told him repeatedly to look after himself and that I would write, as the boat was about to leave. As usual I read the letter he had handed me as soon as the boat left the jetty.

It said:

> Yesterday, I was the happiest of men but this day, I would be the saddest. Our visit to Kamayut together, the movie we saw together, and our talk together at night, and when I got up to go, being unable to bear it I stood at the door and talked some more ... those times have taken over my soul, Ma Tin Tin. I cannot help thinking over these times, and each time the memories rise anew and I can only hope for more of the same in the future. The way I lost control of myself, the way I thought ... thought ... thought ... only of you, I am beginning to feel rather foolish! My friends call me "monk" and in consideration for my shyness do not even talk of women in my presence, but here I am, all my thoughts wrapped up only around you, Ma Tin Tin. This monk has fallen to earth!
>
> After your departure, my mind will surely be in a turmoil: when you are here it's in a turmoil of joy and when you are not it's in a turmoil of despair. While I must depend upon your letters to ease my despair, when no letters arrive I feel so ... very ... empty.

I cannot help reading your letter over and over again. What a brilliant mind you have, I keep thinking in admiration. Before we even met, after reading your article I was so impressed I wrote to get to know you, remember? On our first meeting I was astonished to see someone so modern and fashionable, but getting to know you only increased my love. When you told me about that matter[2] I learned how far you would go to help others, and it made me love you even more. I have many faults and believe that you would be the one to make me a better man.

If we know each other and care for each other, I doubt if there could be any problems no matter whatever new things we discover about each other in the future. I have no doubt you will make sure I become a complete man. People already know I live like a sub-human, and so do you know it, Ma Tin Tin. I did try, but as nobody can hope to be perfect I gave up many attempts to better myself. Not that I don't know about perseverance, but knowing also of destiny, I gave up after many attempts, and you see me as I am now. If anyone were to advise me, yes, I would try again, and if that person would be the one I love, I would do so much better, don't you agree?

You should know by now how much I love you, why I love you. I am waiting with great hope for your answer. First I felt I should give it up, that I should not pester you more than once and that if you had no plans to marry I should not force anything on you. But I could not help myself and most rudely had to put forth my plea. If you only know that your decision is very important to me, as it is to you, I shall remain happy.

I will not tell you about the state I would be in after you left, because maybe you would not care …

Chit Maung
March 19

---

[2] U Chit Maung is apparently referring to a private matter, which he does not describe in his letter.

CHAPTER 11

THIS MAN

After reading U Chit Maung's letter, I thought back on how I first came to know him. There was nothing left to think over apart from whether I could marry him or not. I was also filled with anxiety about my future. I had formed the ideal in my mind of the type of man I would like to marry, considering age, education, and character, and now I compared him to this dream man who so far had loomed like a shadow over my life.

I never wanted to marry anyone younger, nor someone my own age … he was five years older than I. I wanted to marry someone older, not by many years, but five or ten to my mind was perfect. From a young age, I always had this great desire to be reborn in my next life as a man,[1] and according to our beliefs one of the ways of achieving this is to serve one's husband well. I could do this only if my husband were older than I was. In addition, his being superior in intellect meant that he could keep me on the right path. To marry someone younger could lead to petty and childish quarrels and to marry someone much older is a matter of some shame in Myanmar. When people marry just for love, later on in life those people encounter situations that have little to do with whether they love each other or not, and this love often flies out the window. To ensure that love remained intact as we progressed in life together, I thought an older man would be the best partner.

As for education, although he had not graduated or attended college, his knowledge far surpassed what one could have learned in university. As for character, this is the most important aspect of a good marriage. It was rare to meet someone who strived to have integrity. Many men have, according to their station in life, in one way or the other, some looseness in character. I had wanted a man of unblemished character and that was why I had refused all the men my parents had so far proposed to me as likely husbands.

"There's not one man on earth like the one you want," my parents had often declared. These men might have position and wealth, but nowadays it is easy for them to be misled into gambling or nightclubs, and these activities are even considered to grant them a sort of prestige. When women ignored such behavior and dared marry such men, I was appalled; it was something I could not even imagine doing. I liked the fact that, so far as I could see, his character was sound and the fact that he tried to keep it that way earned my respect and admiration.

---

[1] This concept has a religious value, as monks have a better chance to succeed in missionary work or to be truly ascetic than do nuns. Buddha had forbidden women to dwell alone in a forest to meditate, as hermits often do, or to travel as missionaries, considering the fact that lone women could easily fall prey to dangerous men.

As for his mind, I thought it was wiser to consider that, rather than his looks. Every man wants to be thought manly and hates to be considered "womanish."[2] In fact, there are a great many men who do not have such high-class minds as many women and who are even cowardly. There are men who would do anything for their own benefit at a cost to others or even if it did good for no one: but this man, he was one who often went overboard in doing good for others at a cost to himself.

He was a man of conviction who stood firmly by his principles. He was a man who could decide what he wanted and walk unwavering on his path. I truly respected the fact that since he was thirteen he had decided to one day become a good editor and to that end he studied by himself, sleeping not more than three hours a day. He had this great desire to serve his country, and he could suffer a lot in being considerate of others. I believed that the qualities I admired in him might in fact be less than the reality, but certainly not more.

But then, I could not but admit that he had many faults: he felt too *ah-nar* towards others even at the risk of hurting himself. He lived in a disorganized way and cared nothing for his health. He was too humble and so good-natured that he had no care for his own possessions. He had no wish to gain fame, and indeed he would rather keep a low profile in all things. He had no wish to be known, and as such his works might be as water poured into hot sand, wasted and futile. I believed that what I feared about him might in fact be more than the reality, but certainly not less.

Apart from that, we were two very different beings: my appearance, my lifestyle were nothing like his, so would he one day resent this? I had no wish to live as he did; all my life I liked to be neat and clean, habits that I could never discard.

And, what of my parents? If they knew him well, I was convinced they would approve of him, but judging by appearances alone they would never accept him. He was so different from their other sons-in-law who worked with Europeans, who often wore Western clothes, and had the lifestyle of rising professionals. They never wore monk's slippers like him; nor did they ever carry a monk's umbrella. I worried that my parents would disapprove. For myself, I never thought his looks important. Superficial beauty sometimes hid the ugliness of reality, and so one could not be sure to find true goodness in all that was beautiful, so his looks did not matter to me. After I got home, I was so lost in thought that I did not write to him immediately. A letter came from him the day after I got home. On the top page he wrote *"I am longing for your letter, Tin Lay"* and he had pinned that to a pile of papers.

The first page read:

> ... *as the boat took away the beloved face, I felt as if it tore away my very heart. My heartbeat that was pounding in despair before we parted and you were standing in front of me, became more loud when I realized I would soon lose sight of you. I felt so empty, and I had no idea how my steps went as I came away from the jetty. The great verse that Shin Maharahtasara wrote about a beautiful and sweet face that lingered in his memory is so apt for what I feel: I cannot stop seeing your face, Tin Lay.*
>
> *The tenderness you showed towards me has now turned into this great emptiness I feel with your absence. Remember, how every time I said "I've got to*

---

[2] "Main ma lo main ma ya" is the phrase; it expresses the unfortunate and widely accepted traditional view that women have small and malicious minds.

go now," and then, unable to leave, would linger by your side? When the other night I stood by the door unable to tear myself away, you leaned on the doorframe and I watched your lovely little face in the light of the street lamp coming through the trees ... I cannot describe what I felt in my heart. I had to exercise great control!

Then the day we went to Kamayut together, all the time I dared not stare openly at your face, my little Sayama Lay[3] ... I feared my little Sayama Lay might punish me. This little Sayama Lay without saying much has taught me a lot, but I did not even dare steal a few glances at her beloved face.

You said you would think it over at home, so yes please, do think it over carefully, and I must accept whatever sentence you pass, isn't that so? You scolded me about looking after my health and told me to look in the mirror to see how haggard I have become, and I will, but really, I have no wish to see my own face. If I comb my hair I look at my hair, not my face. Nevertheless, I will obey you, Sayama, as much as possible. You too, Sayama Lay, look after your own health.

Yesterday after I got home, I opened the present you gave me. What a beautiful pair of slippers, so grand that I could not bear to wear them. I told Ko Thein Maung that I should give them away, and he scolded me that you gave them to me to wear. But please, Tin Lay, I have never worn something so grand, and can I give them away, please? I will never forget this present, I assure you. Before, I used to wear wooden clogs, and if this had been those I would have worn and treasured them. But velvet slippers are not wooden clogs, so may I give them away?

You said you might return in January, but that's a long way off. Let me count ... it's now only March. May I appeal for a reduction in sentence?

I am longing to hear your decision. Do write in tiny letters, just in case it falls into other hands. I would like to ask you to send it by registered post but did not want to trouble you ... I just want this letter to arrive safely. My heart is beating fast at the thought of your judgment; I should hear it by Thursday, I hope.

Enough for now, Tin Lay. I want to write more but I must go, Theingyi Market is burning down and so is my heart. That's all for now, my Sayama Lay.

Chit Maung
March 23

Unable to sleep I thought about him all night, seeing his face and hearing his voice. In spite of the fact that he did not seem to be a very loveable person, I knew that I could not help but adore his heart and his mind. I felt my love grow as I continued to think of him, and my tenderness for him surged to overwhelm my heart. I had felt tender towards him as soon as I had met him, and since then I knew him to be a precious gem sunk in mud.[4] Since then I had been afraid that he would destroy himself with overwork. My love rose out of my tenderness and admiration for him, and grew fresh and strong.

---

[3] *Sayama* is the feminine form for "teacher"; *Sayama Lay* means "little teacher." The masculine form is *Saya*.

[4] Burmese idiom.

I reflected on whether my love would last; and yes, I decided, it would remain steadfast forever. I had a joyful thought that loving him equated to loving my country. Not caring about whatever problems or misery I might face in my future, I decided that it was of utmost importance to make him happy, and I made up my mind that I would indeed marry this man.

CHAPTER 12

"MA TIN TIN ..."

I went out for a walk early the next morning. My mind cleared, and I felt fresh and happy. The morning air was so cool that it gladdened my heart. I walked briskly, my love for him flooding my very being, and I thought to myself that he did not know this yet!

I would write to him that very day. Daw Daw[1] Ma Yin was the first person I saw as soon as I got home. I felt such joy that I wanted to tease her.

"Daw Daw, you know what, I'm going to marry a *Bilat Pyan*[2] ICS."[3]

"Really? Who? From where?"

"Well, just someone, returned from Britain ... aren't you glad?"

"Is that so? That's good, Tin Tin, you're so Westernized, and someone who has lived in Britain must be, as well. Good, good ... "

"Would people make fun of us, do you think?"

"What for? A *Bilat Pyan* and an ICS, who would laugh at that? It would be such a great match ... who is it, Tin Tin? I'm so happy!"

"Well, Aunt, do you think it would be a good match only if I marry a trouser-wearing *Bilat Pyan*? What about a *Hpon-gyi lu-htwet*?"[4]

"What an idea ... *would* you marry one?"

"What do you think?"

"Enough of it, don't joke. Just tell me who?"

"A *Hpon-gyi lu-htwet*."

'Come on, Tin Tin, tell me, which ICS?"

"He's not an ICS, nor a *Bilat Pyan*, he really *is* a *Hpon-gyi lu-htwet*."

"All right, go ahead, make fun of me."

"Really, I mean it."

Aunt turned somewhat sulky and retorted, "But just now you said he's an ICS!"

"I was teasing you ... I've really decided to marry a *Hpon-gyi lu-htwet*."

"Who is he, Tin Tin?" she asked in a small voice.

"You want to know? It's U Chit Maung, of course."

"Really ... ?"

"So, what d'you think ... aren't we a good match?"

Aunt laughed so hard that I could not help joining in.

---

[1] "Aunty."

[2] "Returned from Britain." In wealthy circles it was considered prestigious to have a son or son-in-law who studied abroad.

[3] The Indian Civil Service (ICS) was the elite cadre of top civil servants in British India, which at that time incorporated Myanmar as the Province of Burma. Few Burmese had an opportunity to sit for the ICS entrance examination.

[4] A monk returned to secular life.

"I knew you liked each other but had no idea it would end up like this … it's going to be *so* strange! Are you *really* going to marry him? I have no objection to him, he's a good man, but Tin Tin, do you love him?"

"With all my heart and soul."

I came downstairs to write the letter, leaving her hooting with laughter.

I posted my letter after reading it over and over, and I longed for time to pass quickly so that I might have his reply. When I finally held it in my hands, I trembled with joy. When I opened it and saw it began with the formal salutation "Ma Tin Tin," I felt somewhat piqued.

> *Ma Tin Tin,*
>
> *I cannot even begin to tell you what my Tin Lay wrote … I would like to keep it all to myself. You know what she said, Ma Tin Tin, you know …?*
>
> *That she has decided to marry me! Yes! She wrote that from this day forward, being well suited as we are, we would therefore support each other and not misuse this love we share, that with firm faith and trust we would bind our love. Now, is that not wonderful?*
>
> *Not only that, but she … she asked if I were happy at last, she asked that I would make sure our love grew so that she would never have any regrets … now, isn't that sweet?*
>
> *Then, she said if I should find any fault in her to tell her so without any less loving her, and that if she refuses to change her ways, to consider her love not worthwhile … now, isn't she a good girl?*
>
> *And then, she said if I am happy in the belief that I have found one who would never go against my wishes, well, she said, I would not be at all wrong. So … is there anything more I need in my life?*
>
> *There are other sweet things she wrote that I could not tell you, Ma Tin Tin, I am keeping all the sweetness to myself.*
>
> *So let me tell you, Ma Tin Tin, that tonight I will write a long letter to her and send it by registered post. Do tell that to my Tin Lay, please, Ma Tin Tin, please ….*
>
> *Chit Maung*
> *March 26*

CHAPTER 13

A BURDEN LIFTED

I wondered how long U Chit Maung had been harboring ambitions to be a poet, but verse after verse spilled from his pen. After I accepted his proposal, almost all of his letters were poetry. We wrote to each other every day. Before, he would often quote other poets, but now they were all his own works. He wrote such beautiful love poems with indirect and polite words to hide bold meanings, and he said he had never before written love poems and never imagined he could. Sometimes he wrote poems as if they came from me until I told him tartly to write for himself and not drag me into it.

We still needed to inform the elders, and I asked him about it. He said he had no money to offer for my hand[1] and sent a long Ngo Chin[2] poem about it until I sternly asked him if he thought he was writing for a Sindaw Gyi,[3] and then he wrote back seriously.

I wrote to him that I absolutely refused to have a grand wedding. He replied that, based on the first article I had written for *Myanmar Alin*, he had guessed that I was not the type to want one and that he was in full agreement. We were both happy about it, but I was worried that my parents would not allow a quiet wedding. I told him I would do my best to get my way.

He said he wanted to marry immediately after Lent[4] but that he had no money and asked for advice. He told me to calculate how much a quiet wedding would cost and to let him know. He said his father and elder sister came from Oke Po and that they were happy about the news.

I wrote him that the wedding was still some time away and that he should visit Bogalay to meet my parents. He could put up at his friend Township Officer U Chit Tin's house, two doors away from us, and call on my parents. It was the only way to introduce him to my family. He said he would depart Yangon on Friday evening by boat, arrive Saturday morning in Bogalay, and leave the same evening. I told my family that the *Myanmar Alin* editor was coming for a visit and arranged to serve lunch at home.

That day I got up early, bathed, and dressed, and sat upstairs reading while I waited for him. Then I heard my younger sister and the doorman talking animatedly by the front door and cocked my ears. The Indian doorman of the bank downstairs, a tall and imposing figure, was always dressed in his wonderfully grand uniform. He spoke fluent if accented Burmese, and people always found it entertaining that such

---

[1] It is a tradition for the man to present his beloved with gold or diamonds upon asking her parents for her hand in marriage.

[2] Literally, "crying song," sung in classical plays.

[3] A marionette stage where classical plays are performed.

[4] The Buddhist Lent is from mid-June to mid-October.

a grand-looking Indian could speak idiomatic Burmese. Now he was complaining to my sister:

"I don't know what sort of a man this is, Missy, he stands there saying nothing with his head down. He does not seem to be collecting for charity, but he *is* so strange. Do come and look, Missy."

I knew at once it must be U Chit Maung and ran downstairs. Sure enough, I saw him standing there with a book under his arm and clutching the handle of his monk's umbrella with both hands, his head hung low. He wore his *longyi* short, and I could clearly see his horrible monk's slippers right there on his feet.

I ran up to him and brought him into the parlor. He left his slippers at the edge of the carpet and came barefooted to his seat until I took up his slippers and placed them by him. Then only with great reluctance and an air of greater embarrassment he slipped them on his feet.

I teased him about what the doorman had told me, that he had turned around as if to leave after he reached the front door. He smiled and said nothing. Father was still in Meikhtila, so I introduced him to my elder brother and sisters. All the time, he only answered questions put to him and did not look up at anyone: he sat like a dignified monk. At lunch he ate little, and he looked embarrassed that we should be giving him an elaborately prepared meal. When we were alone for a moment, I whispered to him, "Did you get my letter? Are you well? Did you sleep well last night?"

Apart from my aunt, no one knew about us and no one suspected. None of them seemed to think highly of him, and certainly his appearance did not encourage it. He did not speak as he usually did in Yangon, and I was left bewildered when he left by the evening boat. He sent a letter as soon as he arrived, however, a letter of thirty-two pages.

He wrote that as soon as he saw my house he felt so upset he wondered if he should go back. He said he only then realized that I came from a wealthy, upper-class family, and he worried whether he could ever keep me in this manner. He stressed the point that, while he was in Bogalay, he had been thinking the whole time about how poor I would be if I were married to him and that he had felt miserable.

I now realized the reason for his silence. I wrote back that I was happy he thought about my welfare but that I did not care how I lived with him, in a house or on bare ground, and that nothing mattered. Only then was he happy once again.

We planned to have everything ready by the end of Lent, in October. He wrote that he was planning to write a serial for *Myanmar Alin* and that he should get some money from it, and asked me what I wanted to read. I replied that I wanted to read anything by him and that if he should ask what kind of novel he should write, then only would I give advice. He replied that he would do his best to write whatever I thought fitting, and I told him to write one on moral issues. I knew he could easily write it and that he should write not only to please me but to please the whole readership. As best as I could, I tried to encourage him. The serial novel he wrote to earn one hundred kyat for our wedding was none other than his famous *Thu.*[5] I could safely say that this story took hold of not only my heart but the hearts of the whole country.

---

[5] *He* was U Chit Maung's masterpiece of fiction; the novel was made into a very successful movie.

He then asked if he should borrow five hundred kyat from *Myanmar Alin;* would it be enough? I smiled at this: whether we had money or not, I had arranged matters so that we would be married in October.

The whole family would be going to see Father in Meikhtila, and I had planned to tell him about us then. We took the train for Meikhtila the same day that we arrived in Yangon by boat. My whole family was with me, so when U Chit Maung came to the station with books and a letter for me, we could not say a private word.

My family was to stay about ten days in Meikhtila, and then we would go on to Mandalay. U Chit Maung and I wrote to each other every day. While I was in Meikhtila, my father and I would walk by the lake in the evenings. Often I wanted to tell him but somehow could not. U Chit Maung wrote that he wanted to know every word that passed between my father and me.

One day my father and I were left alone in the house when the others went out somewhere. I had deliberately stayed back to talk to Father. I was sweating profusely as I started to tell him.

"Father, I have met someone suitable should I wish to marry. I have decided on my own, but it would be better if you were to meet him and give your opinion. I will only marry him if you find him suitable."

"Who is it …?"

"He is U Chit Maung, editor of *Myanmar Alin.*"

"Do you know all about him, daughter?"

"I cannot say I know everything, but as far as I know he seems to have the most suitable qualities."

"Now which qualities are the ones you like?"

"He's honest and upright, Father."

"Well, that's not all that matters … how about his education?"

"He is well versed in both English and Burmese."

"Do you think you'll be happy with him?"

"Not only do I think, I believe it, Father."

"When can I see him?"

"I will arrange for you to meet him when you get to Yangon."

I wrote all this to U Chit Maung from Mandalay. When my family and I got back to Yangon, we stayed only one day and then left for Bogalay. U Chit Maung begged me to stay four or five days, but we had brought along a family from Meikhtila to work for us and with so many of us did not want to put up anywhere. I told him that Father would arrive in Yangon in May and that Mr. Rush would inform him so that he could go and see my father.

He came to the jetty to give me a letter, and he did not look happy. I opened his letter, written with a small hand on both sides of forty pages. I only finished reading it when we reached Twanté. It seemed he was unhappy because I had left so quickly, and he began his letter with a poem in Lay Cho classical form. The letter also included the full three verses of the Yatu, another type of classical poem.

When we got back to Bogalay, I sat down for one whole day and night to write to him, ninety-five pages in all. This was the longest letter I had written to him. I, too, ended with a poem. We kept on exchanging letters and poems we wrote for each other, in both Burmese and English. We discussed all things we thought necessary for a good marriage. I filed all his letters according to subject so that one day I would have the material to write a book, "My Husband."

Meanwhile, I worried how the meeting in Yangon between him and my father would go, worried that my father would not approve. When Father passed through Yangon on his way back to Bogalay, Ko Ko[6] [U Chit Maung] went to see him, using the pretext of sending some books for me. When Father got home I dared not ask how it went. He handed over the books but said nothing else so I had to wait. I sent a telegram to Ko Ko asking him to tell me what had happened.

About a week after Father got home, he called me to his side and told me that they had met each other in Yangon and that Father had had a chance to form an opinion of him.

"Are you sure you can love him your whole life?" Father asked me.

He seemed to doubt me, to judge by this query, as we two were so different in all appearances. I could not say to my father how deeply and truly I loved this man.[7] Instead, I said, "Father, is there any need to ask something like that when you know I've chosen him?"

"Well, daughter, if you are certain you'll be happy I have nothing to say against him. The young man's appearance is so different from a man of the world today and would look odd to others, but to my old-fashioned eyes, there's nothing to complain about. Tell him he can come with his senior family members to ask for your hand."

I felt this huge burden being lifted from my heart. I immediately sent word to him to choose an auspicious day to come with his family for the engagement.

---

[6] "Elder Brother," a term used by sisters as well as by wives and sweethearts who are younger than the man being addressed.

[7] For a daughter to say something like this to her father would be highly disrespectful and shameful.

CHAPTER 14

LIKE A MONK

U Chit Maung arrived in September, bringing with him editor U Sein from *Myanmar Alin*, U Lu Gyi from *Myanmar Alin*'s advertising department, and publisher U San Thein of the *Market* paper, where U Chit Maung had once worked briefly.

I had prepared a room for them on the third floor of our building and made everything ready so that they would have a chance to rest or nap as soon as they arrived in the morning. U Chit Maung wore a pale pink Mandalay silk *longyi* and a jacket of fine *pinni*; it looked strange to my eyes to see him dressed like this.

As soon as he got close enough to me, he whispered that he had borrowed the *longyi* from someone as he did not have anything good enough of his own. I smiled at that and said, "Now, Ko Ko, don't you have anything of your own?" Saying, "At present I have nothing at all but soon I'm going to own something precious," he beamed at me. Then he told me that on the boat he had given his handkerchief to U Sein to wipe his hands, and U Sein had shown the tattered thing to the others saying, now look here at our groom's hanky, and they had all laughed. I, too, laughed at that.

My family members did not approve of my desire for a quiet wedding, and my father felt sorry to give in to my wishes.

During the engagement ceremony, when U Sein introduced the groom, citing his good character, Ko Ko sat smiling slightly. Only later did I learn that at work he never got on with U Sein, who hated him, and thus to sit and listen to the unusual praises had been vastly amusing. At my insistence, U Chit Maung privately told me that U Sein held the position of editor, but that he did not even come to the office. Ko Ko was the one writing for the whole paper, in reality acting as the chief editor. I asked him bluntly why, in that case, U Sein's name appeared as the chief editor's? He said the manager of the paper wanted to change it to his name but that he had forbidden it. He said as long as U Sein lived, it should remain his position.

I was amazed when I recalled that one evening in Yangon, when I had praised U Sein's editorials to U Chit Maung, he had said nothing at all. Only when we were just about to marry did I find out he was the actual chief editor. Only from the statement at the back of the paper naming him as publisher could people have any clue that he worked at all for the paper. He had no use for fame, I thought, sad on his behalf.

After the two sides had spoken, the elders decided on October 26 as the wedding date.

No one from Bogalay knew of my engagement, and the wedding, too, was supposed to be a simple one. We firmly arranged to have only about four or five elders from each side to be witnesses for our marriage. We decided that we would not even print our invitation but write it by hand on a piece of plain paper, asking at the same time that gifts not be given.

When I told my family of this plan, my uncle, younger brother of my father, was so furious that veins stood out on his forehead. He complained to my father, "How could you give in so easily to this child? The young man has a good name and prestige, and you, too, have your own honor to think of ... and you are behaving as if there's something shameful to hide. I won't have it ... invite the whole town!" He stormed around, and when he could not get me to change my mind, marched out of the house in a fury.

I thought I would buy the bridal furniture[1] in Yangon and take it straight to our new place, instead of bringing it back to Bogalay.[2] The whole day our remarks to each other began with "After we are married ...," words that lifted our hearts with joy. He handed me five hundred kyat, saying that when he asked for a loan at the paper, U Tin, the business manager, had presented it as a gift. I gave it back to him saying that there would be expenses involved in bringing the elders here for the wedding. He asked what I would use to buy the furniture. I told him not to worry and that I would take care of it. He said he wished he had known earlier, as he had gone through such a fit of anxiety about the need for money to buy the marriage furniture. "I thought I would go down in history as someone who couldn't afford to get married," he laughed. "Phew!"

After the guests from Yangon left, I went with my aunt to Yangon to buy the furniture. U Chit Maung came along with me as we went shopping. We would be renting a small apartment on Thirty-Fourth Street and I had to buy the bare necessities. I bought a dining table with four chairs, whereupon his friends complained that we could have saved some money by buying the traditional low round table. But he told them I was not used to sitting on the floor to eat.

The small apartment was right inside the Indian quarter and felt cramped even when we went to see it briefly. On that trip, I remembered to ask how much he made at *Myanmar Alin,* and I was appalled to learn it was 120 kyat a month. In addition, he had once taken an advance of three hundred kyat for his father's use, and every month he was paying back thirty kyat, so his take-home pay was a mere ninety.

I immediately felt disgusted with a newspaper that, with a circulation of 10,000, paid so little to a person who worked day and night and who, besides, slept at his desk. I had thought it would be around 300 to 350 kyat, so I had never thought to ask before.

"Just *this*? They gave you only this much? Didn't you feel ashamed to tell people how much you get?" I asked him.

He replied calmly that if anyone should be ashamed, it was the paper. "When I started working here, the circulation was nothing like this. I never thought about the salary. I could do what I wanted here, all for my country, and for that I'm grateful and would even pay them."

"*Myanmar Alin* is surely very lucky," I retorted dryly.

Our apartment's rent was twenty-five kyat a month, which left us sixty-five kyat to spend the whole month. I had planned to get a bigger apartment but, on learning his salary, decided to stick it out here.

---

[1] Necessary new items such as bed and bedding, mosquito nets, pillows, and a few pieces of furniture.

[2] It is a tradition that after the wedding ceremony the couple be escorted to the bridal chamber that has been set out with the new furniture.

He said he was living within his means with his salary and that to earn something extra he wrote for other publications. "Do you even have the time to do that?" I asked him, and he told me that, yes, he did, he had time from three in the morning until five. I felt upset with the way *Myanmar Alin* was treating him, not because he was to be my husband, but because they were not considering the value of this person. How could a newspaper treat someone like this, I fumed. Did they think an editor could be hired as easily as a clerk?

"If I ever own a paper," I announced at the time to him, "I'd make sure to be the first in Myanmar to give good pay to editors."

When I learned to my horror that from this sixty-five kyat he had to pay back twenty-five each month for what he owed for books he had bought on credit, I resolved to get him away from *Myanmar Alin* as quickly as possible. I felt that the newspaper should at least buy the books for him, as he was working heart and soul for it. I felt very resentful and hurt about it.

I dared not think how we would survive in Yangon on forty kyat a month. He declared he would earn extra cash by writing more for other publications and told me firmly that he would get enough to keep me comfortable. He did not even think that all his hours out of the office belonged to me. He did not realize that he should eat, rest, and sleep well during those out-of-office hours to keep himself healthy; instead he kept on assuring me not to worry about money. I was filled with anxiety that I would not be able to feed him well with this meager income.

I did not want to go to my parents for the money I needed, not after I was married. It is, after all, the duty of the grown children to look after the parents. My eldest brother, although having a good job and earning well, was not careful with his money and would often ask my parents for some. Every time he did that, Father would say, "So, even after he's married we still have this responsibility," and that pained me. I had been determined for a long time that if I married a man who earned only fifteen kyat, I would live within my means and not worry my parents. So now I was not about to depend on my parents, but the thought of living on forty kyat a month terrified me. That was the first time I was unhappy about my marriage.

I had clothes aplenty and only needed two meals a day, I thought gratefully. Out of the cash wedding gift Father gave me, I bought all I needed for our new home: an iron, scissors, needle and thread, pots and pans, and even a stone mortar to pound chilies. With what was left I bought dry goods such as tins of condensed milk, sugar, coffee, rice, oil, potatoes, lentils, and even dried chilies, until all my money was gone. I stored everything away in the apartment in readiness for our return after our wedding in Bogalay.

As my boat was about to leave, U Chit Maung asked whether there was anything he could do and, on the spur of the moment, I told him to have the floors scrubbed and polished. His face fell, and I realized that although he did not speak of it, he felt bad to offer me this small and shabby place to live. During our engagement, he had told me, looking upset, that U San Thein of the *Market* newspaper had told him that keeping me there would be like caging a bird. After that I made sure I gave him no inkling of how wretched I felt about living there. He told me he would be taking a week's leave and would arrive in Bogalay with the elders on the morning of October 26. Telling me not to worry, he gave me a letter to read on the way home.

When I got home, I told Father that I had bought all the furniture and left it at our flat. Father said to me, "Now, when you are in Yangon, don't go around spending money the way you've being doing as a girl. Make sure to put aside something each month; a marriage can be stable only when you don't have financial worries. Now how much is his salary, by the way?"

I began to sweat. To ease his mind I said that, all in all, he earned about three or four hundred kyat. At the time I was paying 175 kyat each month for my life insurance, so Father asked if I could continue with it. I assured him that we could manage with the extra income from his books. I dared not tell my father that, not only would it be impossible for us to afford 175 for the insurance, but we would have only forty a month and that probably I might have to cash in my life insurance at some loss.

I realized that the easy life I had led of eating and buying whatever I wanted was about to end. My mind was busy as I mentally worked out my budget, asking myself whether I could spend one kyat a day or just seventy-five pya. While drinking coffee at breakfast, I would calculate that if I gave coffee only to Ko Ko and did without it myself, my cost would be just for the two meals, and one kyat would be sufficient. If I fed him a good curry and for myself made do with a fried egg or beans, I might manage on seventy-five pya. I would ponder while eating dinner with my family. In my parents' house, I had never washed my own clothes or cooked, and even the Thanakha paste[3] was prepared for me by my maids. But now I was determined to do all the housework myself; we could not afford a maid. Previously, one kyat was what I might give to a beggar, but now it had become a sum of grave importance to me and kept me occupied planning my budget around that small amount.

At home at all hours I smoked cigarettes and nibbled on cakes, sweets, and chocolates, and after playing a game of badminton in the evening, there would be bottled fruit juices or lime sodas: all the luxuries and pleasures that I would be going without very soon. Every time I enjoyed any of it during that period, I would say to myself, "This is the last!" and took the most pleasure from it.

Finally, October 26 came around, and he arrived. The mail brought a letter from him even on that day. This one was the last I received of the letters that had been sent every single day before we married. This one contained just one line:

Today, Tin Lay and Ko Ko are getting married.

He brought a small leather suitcase. Inside were two worn silk *pasoe*, three shirts, and two jackets: all of his personal belongings. I felt saddened about that and anxious that I would not be able to buy him anything more, as the payment of thirty kyat on his loan would take ten more months to be clear. I looked over his clothes as I unpacked his bag in my room, and he stood by me looking around with interest.

"These shoes and canvas shoes and others in this cupboard, are they yours, Tin Lay?"

"Yes, all mine ... don't you think I should wear shoes?"

"What d'you think?"

"What should I think?"

"So what if you wear shoes ... men wear them, too. There's nothing indecent about it. In time we'll see educated women wearing them all the time."

"I only wear them occasionally. U Chit Maung's wife wearing shoes would be quite a sight ... I'm going to leave them here." He examined each pair closely, smiling to himself, and I had no idea what he was thinking.

---

[3] Traditional make-up paste made from the bark of the Thanakha tree (*Limonia accidissim Linn*).

He did not look like the groom but rather like an elder who came to bear witness, and my guests kept confusing him with his friends. I took out the clothes I had bought for him to wear at the ceremony, and he complained that he would rather wear the old ones he had brought with him. I had to persuade him for some time that his old clothes were really not appropriate for a groom.

As he came down from the third floor, and we stood talking in front of my room, he stood a little way off as if he were afraid I might smell an unpleasant odor from him. He explained that his friends Tin Pe Gyi and Ohn Myint had splashed cologne on him. He looked so embarrassed about it that my heart melted. Everyone was smiling at how the groom looked shyer than the bride. During the ceremony, he sat in solemn dignity with his head down, looking for all the world like a monk rather than a man getting married.[4]

---

[4] On that day, Daw Ma Ma Lay decided to set aside as much money as she could throughout her marriage, keeping it in a bag, and to open it only on her fortieth birthday. She planned to use half for charity and the rest for their old age.

CHAPTER 15

THE FIRST SEVEN DAYS

So our wedding went off well, and we spent the seven days of his leave at my home. U Chit Maung did not look like a man on his honeymoon; rather he acted as if he were a monk who had come to spend Lent in Bogalay. How he moved and walked, how he spoke and ate, were exactly like a monk's behavior.

When his father and guests left, he stayed on not like a family member but as a visitor in my home. He did not mingle with my family but sat with his head bent in a book. Even then my family liked and accepted him into their fold and took good care of him. In this huge, three-storey building, one additional person would not make anyone uncomfortable, but he acted as if he were disturbing everyone else and looked very much embarrassed at how he sat or ate or moved, at all times trying not to make a sound.

At home, his habit was to start each morning with a pile of newspapers and to sit at a teashop. As he could not do this during the seven days with my family, he might have thought that the time dragged out to be as long as seven years. He was constantly worried about his paper, and I began to wonder if he even knew he was supposed to spend this week at leisure and enjoying himself.

The very next day after our wedding, I realized he had one unpleasant bad habit: he was too shy to be seen walking into the toilet.

After the wedding was over and he moved into my room, I had shown him the bathroom and toilet. I watched him for one day and night without seeing him use the toilet even once. The previous day he had been staying on the third floor, so I had not known of his peculiar habit. At first I was not too worried, but three or four days passed and only then did I realize it was not nature at fault but his embarrassment. I urged him not to feel shy when there was absolutely no need for it and that it would be very bad for his health. He pleaded with me to allow him to wait until nightfall, as if the whole family had to go away somewhere for him to relieve himself! I begged, I urged, I pleaded, I scolded; I had to harass him the whole time, but still he remained stubborn. I had to tell him often that no one *at all* was in the next room, that everyone was elsewhere, and to please, go *now*. Because of this, the whole seven days was a miserable time for the both of us.

My parents had given us a large room, and even in its privacy he could not relax and was overly shy to be in it unless to sleep. He always sat reading or writing quietly in the parlor. If I went near him, he would murmur, "Oh, Tin Lay, night is so long in coming." For only then, with everyone gone to bed, would he take his bath and relieve himself. His biggest problem all his life would be this embarrassment around others, and this was making everyone else uncomfortable, a consequence of which he was totally unaware. My father would whisper to me that even he was beginning to feel uneasy, and although I asked Ko Ko to please relax, it was to no avail. Within a few days I came to know all about him and thought that if he continued this way he would surely end up with very bad health.

After a week we were to leave for Yangon. I was constantly busy packing my things and storing away those I would not take. He was too shy to come into our room during the day, so I was alone and busy with my things when he did, indeed, come in, looking unhappy. I pretended not to notice and asked casually,

"Aren't you feeling well, Ko Ko?"

"What did you say to your father, Tin Lay?"

"I don't know, what did he tell you, Ko Ko?"

"I was writing when he came to sit in front of me, and he told me something about you. I felt so bad."

"Oh, what did he say? Tell me, Ko Ko."

"That you told him you're not taking the jewelry he made for you ... he said if you won't wear it, who would? He said he and your mother would be so hurt if you don't. Tin Lay, how could you have done this to him, he looked so hurt."

"Oh, that."

When my elder sister got married, she took her own jewelry with her, but when I thought it over I felt that, as a married woman, I should not do the same as I did not want to take anything away from my aging and unhealthy parents—my mother had been unwell for some time. To that end, I had informed my father I would leave my jewelry behind; at the time he had said nothing but, lying back in his easy chair, had closed his eyes tight. I had crept away softly, and when I heard how Father had gone to tell Ko Ko about it, it tore my heart to realize how much my parents loved me.

Of all his children, Father loved me best, and knowing I would be leaving him soon, I composed myself so as not to look upset in front of Ko Ko and pasted a smile on my face.

"I just said I would not take them to Yangon, Ko Ko, but actually I do feel I shouldn't take them at all."

"Your father knows you well, Tin Lay, and he would guess that you've left them for good. He feels very hurt."

"So what do you think I should do?"

"I know how you feel, but I think you should at least for a while bring them with you. Tell your father you would, to please him. I have a father but never had the sort of love yours gives to you, Tin Lay. I have never seen anyone love a child the way your father loves you. I don't think you should hurt him."

"All right, then, I'll bring them along."

I glanced at him to check if he looked relieved, but he was staring into my open cupboard.

"What is it?" I asked and looked to where his eyes were. He was looking with a surprised expression at the pile of English-language magazines on the bottom shelf. He turned to glance at me, still looking surprised.

"What a lot! Did you buy them all?" He pulled out a few and turned them over. "When did you start saving them, did you buy them every month?"

His eyes brightened at the thought that I collected reading material in English as well as in Burmese.

"I didn't buy them, they belonged to a Mr. Edwards who stayed with us once ... he worked for Steel Brothers. There were some pages I wanted to save so he gave them to me. I was about thirteen or fourteen, then."

"So what was it you wanted to save? Can't you tell me, Tin Lay?" he asked eagerly.

I made him sit on a box and opened a trunk filled with stuff I was taking to Yangon. From the bottom of the pile I took out two paper bags tied with string and gave them to him. He opened one and looked through the pictures cut from the magazines. He looked intently at every page, not even glancing at me. Time passed in silence. He took up the second paper bag and untied the strings, staring at my face all the while, not looking at his fingers prying the knots loose. I smiled at him, expecting him to say something. All the while he looked as if he were trying to make sense of my collection. Only when the string became undone did he turn back to the bag and remove another pile of cut pages from it. As before, he slowly examined each one.

I lay down on the bed, turned to look at his face. He did not look at me at all until he had carefully put back everything in place. Then he turned to stare at me. Abashed by the intensity of his look, I closed my eyes and tried to smile. In a while, my desire to know if he was still staring became so great I gave a peep. He was still staring at me, so I giggled and covered my face with my hands.

"Tin Lay … my dear Tin Lay …" he murmured softly. Only then did I dare look at him. I said nothing to him but put everything back.

In one of the paper bags were pictures from magazines I had cut out when I was thirteen: photos of the palaces and mansions of Europe—sometimes whole buildings, sometimes just the front entrances or facades or sweeping stairs. The second bag contained pages out of magazines that featured necklaces of precious stones worn by princesses, movie stars, or society women.

We were about to leave for Yangon. My family members were weepy—especially my father, who looked very much upset. I, too, felt great sorrow to be parted from my parents. I felt some financial discomfort as well, for out of the five hundred kyat that was *Myanmar Alin's* gift to us, we had spent some to bring Ko Ko's father, elders, and friends to the wedding. Ko Ko gave me 125 kyat that was left, and out of it I had secretly bought him a cotton *pasoe*, undershirt, handkerchief, and shirts that he needed during his stay with us, so I had only eighty kyat left in my hands. He would be paid only on the fifteenth, so for this trip to Yangon and until the fifteenth I only had eighty kyat and was worried my father would find out. Previously, whenever I went to Yangon I would ask Father for pocket money, usually about four or five hundred kyat, which I felt I should not do now.

The boat to Yangon would be coming from Mawlamyaing Kyun and dock in Bogalay at eight in the morning. Just as we were about to bring down our luggage, Father came upstairs to us and told me that I was to take Ngwe Zin, the daughter of the family we brought over from Meikhtila, to work as my maid. He said I must also take along a boy named Maung Thaung, a poor orphan I had felt sorry for and brought home from his village. As for the cook, he said, I was to hire an Indian chef when I got to Yangon.

As I would be living on forty kyat a month, the young people would have been better off in my parent's house. I was in despair; I had made up my mind to do my own housework and had left it at that, and now I was in a quandary. If I did not take anyone, Father would get suspicious, so I nudged Ngwe Zin and whispered instructions to her to say she wanted to stay back in Bogalay.

"My house is too small," I whispered. "I'll come back for you after we move. I dare not let Father know our place is too small, so you have to stay back."

I had to take Maung Thaung, however. When Father heard Ngwe Zin was not coming, he said I would need a female companion and declared that my aunt Daw Daw Ma Yin must go with us.

I had to take some time to smooth things over in refusing Aunt's company as well. Then, Father told my younger sister, Shwe Shwe, to take three hundred kyat out of the drawer and give it to me. I so very much wanted to grab the money, but had to pretend unconcern and said coolly enough that I still had some money so I did not need anything right now. Only when we were on the boat could I smile at the way I had put on such a convincing performance.

Father arranged everything for us and then went to bed. Before we left, we went to *kadaw*[1] him, and I had to keep my tears back when he gave us his blessings from his bed in a voice that trembled.

"Consider Maung Chit Maung's father as your own and serve him well … never forget what I have said," he said to me. In truth I could not forget his words.

My mother had suffered a nervous breakdown some years back and had not spoken since, but when we went to *kadaw* her, she gave a long blessing and ended with the words: "May this couple live together in love until old age," which Daw Daw said was a sign of great luck.

My sister and nieces cried the whole evening. I left my family and came down to the jetty, feeling heavyhearted. I knew I was not heading towards a perfect life, and yet I had to leave my family, and for that I was indeed sad.

---

[1] To pay homage by kneeling and bowing three times to the ground with hands clasped on the forehead in the same way one prays at the pagoda or when paying respects to monks. In some cases, it is an act of asking pardon.

CHAPTER 16

ONE STRANGE MAN WHO BECAME AN EDITOR

The two of us, so different from each other that no one could imagine how we could have met, settled into our home on Thirty-Fourth Street.

In the twenty-five-foot-long room, the front part became the living room and the screened back part was filled with our bed, dressing table, and dining table. The kitchen was straight through at the back without a wall or screen. In only ten or fifteen paces, a person could get from the front of the house all the way to the back. There we settled in together with Maung Thaung and Ko Ko's youngest brother, Maung San Aung, which made four occupants. This brother had disappeared from home when he was a child. Only when he was nearly grown was he found living in the Thadu Lake Village, some miles out of Yangon. Ko Ko's father had sent him to live with us so that he could go to school. Although we had to bear the extra burden, I felt sorrier for the boy than for us.

Although Ko Ko's other brother, Ko Than Tun, and his young friend Ko Ohn Myint, also as close as a brother, did not live with us, they came every day. Before we married, they had all lived together with U Shwe Kyu, Ko Ko Lay, Ko Thein Maung, and Ko Tin Pe. Ko Ohn Myint was a clean-cut, good-looking, and neat young man, still somewhat boyish, and I loved him like a younger brother as soon as I met him, and he, too, looked upon me as an elder sister. From the time he came to Bogalay for the wedding, I had liked his decent demeanor. He helped with my housework, and among Ko Ko's circle he was the closest to me.

Our neighbors on all sides were Hindus. At daybreak they would leave their homes to sell fruits such as papayas, muskmelons, and pineapples and return only in the evening. At night they would light mustard-oil fires and sit around playing drums, so it was rather smelly as well as noisy.

Ko Ko went to work the day after we arrived and that evening took me to his office. As we approached the entrance, the Indian night watchman who was dozing on his rope bed leaped to his feet and *salaamed* to us. As we walked upstairs, Ko Ko laughed and said to me that the chap had never stood up for him before nor had he ever *salaamed*. Upstairs there was a large room with the chief editor's office in one corner, screened with glass walls. The business manager's office was also set apart along the front wall. The advertising section was behind a counter. The room was ablaze with lights, and Ko Ko led our way into it, introducing me in English to each of the men working there. Then he took me into the glass-walled room and whispered to me that these men liked to tease and he had spoken in English to let them know I knew the language.

His desk was covered with scattered books and papers. Next to his desk was another where he said U Sein sometimes sat. The third desk belonged to U Tin Shein.

There was also a neat, nicely arranged Buddha shrine in the room, lit with a low-watt blue light. The blue light of the High Court watchtower's clock face coming through the windows and this little light gave a cool, peaceful mood to the room.

I saw a bookcase at the far end of the room filled with magazines in both Burmese and English. I asked if the paper bought magazines for him, and he said yes, the paper bought any book or magazine he wanted, and, remembering my anger in Bogalay when I had thought the paper did not, I felt quite embarrassed that I had misjudged *Myanmar Alin*.

There was an easy chair and one large spittoon, so I thought there must be someone who spat all the time. As soon as he settled at his desk, he said he must write the next day's part of the serial "Thu" and handed me some magazines. From the outer room, U Ba Hnin, the reporter, sang a song loud enough to tease us. One after the other, the newspapermen all made excuses to come inside to talk to Ko Ko and to look me over.

A man covered with black, greasy stuff came in saying, "Saya, copy, copy," and I wondered what it meant. Only when I saw Ko Ko hand over his handwritten papers did I understand. He said the man was the typesetter.

This man came several times to ask for "copy." I sat there looking on with interest as Ko Ko marked sheets of papers with a red pen. He was editing the news sent in by reporters; on small squares of paper, he would scribble the headlines and pin them to each sheet. I took up the papers he had edited and read them over to see how he had changed them. I did not understand why some places were marked with the words "six lines," "three lines," or "black-white," and so he explained they were instructions for the typesetter to use different-size fonts. This was the first time I learned about the process of printing, and taking up a newspaper I tried to match the new words I had learned with the font sizes I saw.

When the man came in the next time for copy, Ko Ko gave him twenty-five pya as well. The man silently took an empty bottle from the shelf and went out. He came back a few minutes later with the bottle filled with tea.

"Share it out to the chaps outside," Ko Ko told him, "and give me what's left."

I said nothing but stared at him. Ko Ko explained that the bottle was a "collective item" belonging to all.

"However good a cuppa is brewed at home, it's nothing like the tea we share this way. When everyone's broke, we'd collect a pya from here and a pya from there and buy it, then it tastes even better!"

He swiftly gulped down the strong tea[1] in the mug the man had returned to place in front of him. I said to him, "Yes, go ahead, keep on drinking so much tea, and you'll be in trouble one day."

"But, Tin Lay, the tea from this bottle clears my head and refreshes my brain, truly!"

"How many cups do you drink a day, Ko Ko?"

"Depends on how much money I have. I don't mind missing meals but I must have my tea ... however much I drink I don't feel full."

Just hearing that was beginning to make me feel uncomfortably full.

"If you're hungry, Tin Lay, let's go home. I'll come back here afterwards."

---

[1] Tea made with leaves boiled a long time with a pinch of salt and mixed with sweetened condensed milk.

Before we left, the reporters took our photo. That night after dinner he went back to the office and did not come home until two in the morning.

I had sat up to wait for him, and he scolded me for that. He took off his jacket, sat down at the dining table, and was about to begin writing when I asked if he still had to work.

"It's for tomorrow's *Market* newspaper," he replied, and continued working. I grimly said to him in my mind, "Just you wait."

The eighty kyat I had was almost gone, what with the boat fare and money for snacks and tea for his friends who came around to congratulate us. I never before had to worry about money and I felt wretched with this new problem. When he asked if we had any money left, I told him casually that "yes, we do, I brought some with me from home."

The next morning I sent Maung Thaung to the bazaar, and only after Ko Ko left around nine did I get down to cooking. Both Maung Thaung and I, unskilled and inexperienced in the kitchen, did the best we could. I had never taken an interest in cooking, and previously I had been dismissive of it, thinking it dull work that needed no brainpower. I had mistakenly thought it would be quite easy to learn how to cook.

At first I burnt myself quite often, but day by day I became more experienced. I came to learn that you really needed brains to improve and not just get it done. The first day I prepared one dish only after the first one was cooked and thus wasted a lot of fuel (as we were using charcoal). The next day I prepared every pot beforehand and, once I had the fire going, the food was cooked one pot after the other. The actual work taught me how to be frugal with oil, chilies, and onions.

As I had never imagined I would ever need to cook, the first day I had felt excited and thought it would be fun. However, in my inexperience, I had to think carefully before I did anything, so I was slow at first and in the next days tried to work faster. Thankfully, Maung Thaung did all the hard work of pounding chilies, draining the rice, and washing up, so I just had to sit and cook.

I began to suspect that a housewife could rest only if she sat the whole day doing nothing. From morning until night there was the work of sweeping, dusting, cleaning, polishing the floor, brewing coffee, offering food and fresh flowers at the household shrine, and cooking. In the afternoons, there was laundry to be done, clothes to iron, and the house to clean, and at the end of the day, the evening meal to cook. If there had been no one there to help me, I would have been busy every single minute. As for doing the laundry and polishing the floor, they were the hardest jobs and my hands began to get blisters. Often as I toiled I felt like running home to fetch my maid and the Indian cleaner. Sometimes I even wished for my family to see me like this.

At home, with a big household and each of us being fussy, my mother, in the years before her breakdown, every morning had to instruct her staff on what food to prepare for Father and each of us children, as we all liked different things. She had to arrange for many different dishes for our meals. Even at breakfast, one would demand tea, another noodles, and someone else *monhinga*,[2] *naan* flatbread, or toast. Only now by handling my own bazaar money did I come to understand how costly it must have been and felt so embarrassed that I had never given my parents credit for our bounty.

---

[2] Thin rice noodles in fish soup, a traditional breakfast dish.

Each morning I would take out one kyat and give only one half to Maung Thaung for the market, as we had basic commodities such as rice and oil already stored. I told him we would be cooking one soup and one curry. I ignored the need for side dishes such as a salad or stir fry as if they were meant never to touch our lips. One day after the next I had to keep buying this and that, things like soap or sugar, and every time I took out the small change, I reflected on how coins, too, could come in handy. If the one kyat was gone by day's end, I would worry about how I could spend less the next day. Sometimes Ko Ko would bring home guests and expect me to feed them, and then I would have to send Maung Thaung to buy more cooked rice or curry. Ko Ko would be anxious that the meal would not be ready in time and kept coming into the kitchen to check.

"You should cook a lot every day, Tin Tin; when a home is pleasant, guests will come, and if you have enough in your pots, there's no need to buy any takeaway at the last minute."

"Is that so? Then of course I'll cook more," I replied with a wry smile.

During the afternoons, locked in the stuffy apartment, I felt as if I were indeed caged. Then I would lean out the window in the front and look out over the street. Yangon might be a huge city, but there I was, in this narrow space. I wondered if in my previous life I had kept caged birds.[3] I tried to imagine how long it would take before we would live in comfort. "One day, I will," I vowed to myself.

For five or ten days I studied him and did as he wanted as much as possible. He went to bed only at about two or three. In the morning, with his tea, he read one newspaper after the other. Then he took up a book and read until eight or eight thirty. At eight thirty, without taking a bath, he would change and leave for the office. Usually he would just pick up the same *longyi* he had worn the previous day; I always had to give him a new one, which he would refuse, complaining all the time. I told him to go only around ten after he had his lunch, but he said he never ate lunch early and he always left at the same early hour.

He would return for lunch at noon or sometimes at one or half past one. During meals, he would read a book and not notice what he was eating. If a friend called on us in the afternoon he would sit chatting until two or three. All his callers liked to stay and chat with him, and as long as they were there he would not go to the toilet. If there were no callers, he would continue reading. At three, after having a cup of tea, he would leave for work. At six or seven he would return, book in hand.

I made things ready for his bath after his return in the evenings and kept urging him, but while saying, "yes, yes," he would nevertheless sit there reading until dinner time. If I spoke to him, he replied without lifting his head from his book. After dinner, book under his arm, he would take me to the office. At around ten he would ask if I wanted to go home, and only the first day did I leave early. The following days I stuck it out, and we left together around midnight. Then he would sit himself down to write articles for other papers, drinking cup after cup of tea I made for him in a pot. He might also read on after his work until around three in the morning, when I would be longing to go to bed, but I stubbornly sat on reading by his side. He used to plead with me to go to bed first, but I refused firmly, so he gave up. We never had a chance simply to talk and do nothing else; we talked while he read or wrote. At first I did not want to interrupt him, but when he, from time to time, talked

---

[3] The Buddhist belief that whatever you do to other creatures, you will suffer the same fate in the next life.

to me while he was writing, I, too, got into the habit. He could also listen to what anyone was saying to him while he read.

Late at night when someone from the office came for something, he would ask me to give tea to the man, at which I had to get the stove going. He then said it would be better to have tea ready in a flask, so I did, and if no one came to drink it, it would turn bad the next morning and had to be poured away.

He read so much that I asked where all his books were, and he told me that friends borrowed them and never returned them. He said he had his books stored somewhere else and that we would go get them some day.

One day he took me towards Scott Market but turned instead into the Royal Book Shop on the opposite side of the road. He browsed a long time, and at first the Indian shopkeepers seemed to think I was another customer. My legs began to ache, so I sat down on a stool. When Ko Ko looked over at me, I would gesture with my eyes that we should leave; he would nod his head, but keep on looking at books. He took down a magazine and read the whole thing. The shopkeepers seemed to know him well and left him alone. Only after he had picked out some books did he go to the counter and sign for them, and then I realized to whom he owed money for his books. He announced to the Indian owner that he was now married and that he would be taking back his books. The shopkeepers beamed at me and hurriedly called a horse carriage, which they loaded until it was full. Only then did I understand that he bought his books here but kept them stored at the back of the shop, to be carefully looked after by his shopkeeper friends, instead of taking them with him. We came home in a rickshaw with the horse carriage following us. The next day, he fetched a book in English that was being rebound from a small stall in Thirty-Second Street.

"This is the book I treasure above all others," Ko Ko told me. "I would not exchange it for a whole cupboard full of books. The language is so difficult no one else wanted to read it. Just by this book one can learn how to be a successful editor. I saw this in a secondhand shop, and I've read it perhaps fifty times. I saw so many things in there that are exactly like my life. I've never seen a book that touches me as deeply as this."

Because of what he said, I did not put this book in the bookcase but stored it away carefully in our cupboard. The book was titled *Queed*,[4] about one strange man who became an editor.

---

[4] Written by Henry Sydor Harrison (1880–1930), published in 1911.

CHAPTER 17

"SHOULD I LEAVE YOU ... ?"

Within ten or fifteen days, I knew everything about Ko Ko; I watched him like a hawk as well as talked to his close friends and family. Through the many facts I gathered, I came to learn much about him. There were some qualities that made me admire him even more, some that made me wretched, some that were funny, and some that made me fear for my marriage. There were things I liked and could accept, there were things I liked but could not accept, there were things I did not like but must accept, and there were things too difficult for me to like or accept.

They were all part of his character. Out of the reluctance to offend, he could never show his disapproval of anyone else by word or expression. He easily felt sorry for others, so it was easy for others to cheat him. He never got angry, so some people dared treat him without respect. These things I learned in our early days influenced all that happened later in our marriage, and so I never forgot them.

One day we went out and, as we did not have the time to go home for lunch, he took me to an Indian food shop in front of Thuriya Press. The shop was not clean, and I declined to eat; when the waiter came up, Ko Ko ordered for one. The waiter turned away without asking what Ko Ko wanted, and while I was looking around for another waiter, the first came back with a plate of rice and a dish of chicken curry.

"We haven't even ordered yet!" I said sharply.

"Mem'saab, Saab's been eating here for nearly a year, and he always eats the same thing."

With that the waiter turned away.

"He knows me well by now, Tin Lay," Ko Ko said to me. "Night or day, since I've ordered the same thing for five months, they no longer ask. Saves a lot of time."

"You could eat the same thing for so long?"

"If I like anything I can eat it forever. When I used to pay U San Thein to have a Tiffin carrier brought to me every day,[1] once there was *ponyay gyi*[2] in it, and he asked if I liked it. I did very much, and said I could it eat it every day. It did appear every day, and I ate just that and I didn't complain, but others eating together[3] with me got tired of it so I had to tell U San Thein to stop. I could eat just that my whole life."

A dedicated and committed mindset, indeed.

One evening we were walking back from Yaygyaw, the eastern part of Yangon, and as it looked about to rain, we stood waiting under the portico of the *Rangoon*

---

[1] Housewives make extra money by supplying home-cooked meals in a Tiffin carrier (a steel container, usually a cylinder, comprising several stackable sections).

[2] A dark brown bean paste made only in Bagan. Otherwise described as a tender pork stew with bean paste and a savory, nutty flavor.

[3] In schools or in the workplace people share their lunch boxes' contents.

Gazette offices to get a rickshaw. There he recounted a story from his past that to this day remains in my memory.

He had formerly lived in Hnin Pan Street, near where we stood, and he told me that once in heavy rain like this he was walking home when a man came under his umbrella, so Ko Ko had held his umbrella to cover this man as well. The rain got too heavy, so they both stood right here, in front of *Rangoon Gazette*. Ko Ko said he noticed the man slowly pulling Ko Ko's wallet out of his pocket, but so as not to embarrass the man, he had pretended not to notice it and even looked elsewhere and thus lost his wallet with one kyat and five pices.

"People will step all over him," I thought, feeling more annoyed by than admiring of his need not to offend others.

Ko Ko's close friend, an artist, U Ohn Lwin, once told me something about him.

"We were all living at Hnin Pan Street then, a group of men of all sorts; some were employed, some jobless, and most were living off U Chit Maung. He'd come back around two or three at night and the front door was kept unlocked so that he could come in without disturbing anyone. Once, you know what he did? I felt like hitting him! He tiptoed in as usual, with some Montlay Pway crispy pancakes, and he disappeared to the back where the bathroom was. I was awake, and I went after him because I wanted to see what he was doing and to relieve myself at the same time. He was sitting in the back room eating the pancakes. I asked him why he couldn't eat them in the front room, and he said the noise of pancakes in his mouth might wake up others. How *loud* could it be, that he needed to be so considerate of others?"

One day I sat down to think what I must change about him and what to accept in silence, and I drew up a grand marital plan in my mind. When he came home that night, he stared in consternation at my packed bags and neatly tied-up bedroll, all set out in the front room.

"Tin Lay, where are you going?" he asked in alarm.

"I'm ready to go back to Bogalay, Ko Ko, as soon as you tell me to leave."

"What? I don't understand … why am I going to tell you to leave?"

"Let me say something, Ko Ko. We've been married nearly a month, and you know best why you married me. You have such a good heart, more than I could ever have guessed. You would give away the clothes on your back if anyone asked you in the street. There's give and take in life, and I know how pleasant it is to give, give, and give. But in our marriage, if U Chit Maung's wife were as generous as U Chit Maung, we wouldn't have a reed mat to our name. Only when people begin to notice that U Chit Maung's life has turned around for the better after his marriage would our union mean anything. For that to happen, U Chit Maung's wife surely cannot be as generous as he is, and so it seemed I might have to accept earning a bad reputation to stay in this marriage. I could bear having a bad reputation, but what do you make of that, can *you* accept it? This idea of total generosity from both of us could not be part of our married life. So, what do you think, Ko Ko?"

He sat down heavily in a chair and hung his head and looked lost in thought.

"Ko Ko, there are a number of things I do not like about you. Some of them must be changed, and as your wife I have a duty to do that. If you can't accept that, what's the use of me being here?"

"What things, Tin Lay?"

"The way you insisted on having food ready not even knowing if any caller would turn up; the tea I had to make nightly for reporters who often did not come, and I had to throw out the next morning; these are things one should not do even if one had plenty of money. In the Jataka story of Widura, there's advice on frugality, to save a fistful of rice from the daily pot so that after some days there would be extra rice left over. So now, what should I obey, that lesson or you, Ko Ko?"

He smiled at that.

"Before I married you, I thought I could change some of your bad habits. But if you resist change, my efforts are meaningless. I've been talking to you about taking care of your health since long before we were married, and are you doing that now? You go to bed late, the whole day you sit at a desk, you don't bathe regularly, you don't eat regularly, and these are the things I must change. If you don't agree to it, there's no point in being married, is there?"

"But Tin Lay dear, my work hours cannot be limited ... I have to work twenty-four hours a day, you should understand that."

"I didn't say you mustn't work, and it's not true that you can't limit your time. What if I arrange it so that it won't hurt your work? Just tell me if you agree to it or not."

He kept smiling but said nothing.

"I *will* change the way you eat and sleep and live, Ko Ko, and I'll stay with you only if I can do that. If you think there is no need for change, just tell me to go, and I will. Should I leave you?"

"Please don't go, my Sayama Lay," he laughed.

CHAPTER 18

WORST DAY

The next morning as Ko Ko drank his tea, I put out the clothes for him to wear to the office. Just then the Indian barber arrived. He had the barber shave him rather than do it himself because he said it was a closer shave. I told him to get a haircut at the same time, but Ko Ko demurred, saying if he had a haircut he would have to bathe, but I begged so much he agreed to it. Afterwards he said there was no time and that he would just wash his face and go, and I again begged him to bathe. I swept up the hair clippings from the floor and suddenly a thought struck me, and I swept them up into a paper bag, sealed it, and marked it 24 November 1938, and put it away in the dressing table drawer. After he had his bath, when he saw that I had put out the silk *longyi* he wore at our wedding, he protested.

"It's too new, Tin Lay, give me another one."

We argued back and forth.

"You have to look polished, Ko Ko, or else people will look down on you. You always wear shabby clothes."

"Does it depend on the clothes if people respect you or not? I don't like that idea."

"I don't mean that, Ko Ko, but you do need to wear good clothes. Even Buddha decreed that the monks in his Order have to wear their robes neatly, by wrapping the robe up to enfold the whole length of the arm. Then the people would look upon them with respect. I can't bear to see you wearing frayed things every day. It is said that even a basket needs a tidy rim, and you have to wear clothes to suit the place."

He sighed loudly and complained how hot it would be, but wore the *longyi* after all. I pretended not to hear his grumblings and went on doing things in the kitchen. He called from the front door, "I'm off now, Tin Lay," and I smiled to see him looking so good with a fresh haircut and new clothes.

"Don't keep your eyes downcast, Ko Ko," I called out to him, "or else the children might go to hell for stepping on your shadow."[1]

At *Myanmar Alin* there was a group of messenger boys ranging in age from ten to fifteen. They wore white shirts, pink *longyi*, and pink scarves around their heads and looked so sweet. Ko Ko laughed and ran downstairs, knowing I meant these boys when I said "children." I wrote down briefly in a big leather-bound book what took place that morning.

I went every evening to *Myanmar Alin*, but that night I excused myself from his room and went downstairs to look at the presses. I peered at the typesetters doing their work. I knew that at night there were few people supervising them, but they were a capable and responsible lot. I felt admiration for the business manager for having things so well under control. I was very interested in looking over the whole

---

[1] Buddhists believe that anyone stepping on a monk's shadow has committed a sin.

business of publishing a paper. The men explained to me what I wanted to know, and I spent about two hours in their domain. As I climbed the stairs back to Ko Ko's office, with each step I was building in my dreams my own newspaper business, brick by virtual brick.

That night when we came back, I pleaded for him to go to bed and not work.

He agreed, but as we settled down he said that he needed to write a novel or something ...

"I need to earn more, with my salary we can't survive."

"Yes we can," I assured him, "we don't have a big family yet. You can do it later."

The next day at lunch, I pulled away his book as we sat down to eat and demanded whether he was reading or having his meal. After lunch, I urged him to have a nap, but for two or three days he resisted, either sitting up to talk with callers or lying in bed reading. I finally forced the issue by checking the visitors through the peephole, and if they were the sort to come merely to chat, I would tell them he had gone out. I also had to hide his book, and then, complaining and arguing, he would finally fall asleep. I gave him tea only in the afternoon, and mornings and nights he had to make do with coffee. When he complained that all this sleep was keeping him from work and from earning some extra cash, I had great trouble getting him away from the table. Only because the *Market* newspaper was run by a friend did I allow him to write for it, but for nothing else. Every day I racked my brains about how to deal with the constant battle of getting him to rest.

I firmly believed that in six months his cheeks would fill out and he would be far healthier, so I grimly kept to a timetable and battled on a daily basis for him to keep to it. If he felt miserable with all this nagging, only I could know how miserable I felt doing it. Meanwhile, his youngest brother, Maung San Aung, said he did not like Yangon and went to live with their father in Oke Po.

Nearing the end of the month, I was desperate to have my money last until payday and as desperate for my family not to find out about my life. The situation was such that I had stopped drinking coffee, as I needed to serve it to callers. Maung Thaung noticed all this and sometimes would sit crying silently in the kitchen. The two of us ate little and made sure Ko Ko did not notice. We always waited lunch and dinner for him,[2] and as he usually came home late, we would be very hungry by the time he arrived. I could bear it, but felt so sorry for Maung Thaung that I sent him home to Bogalay, warning him repeatedly to tell my parents I had a cook working for me.

After Maung Thaung left, when Ko Ko saw me cooking he looked unhappy and tried to help, but I drove him out of the kitchen. He kept urging me to write home to request a maid. I thought how badly he would feel to know that the absence of a helper was better than the absence of money and made sure he would not know how broke we were.

December 29[3] was the worst day of my life. I did not believe any other was as filled with such burning anxiety. I had bought half a small chicken from the vendor that morning, planning to cook chicken curry and lentil soup. I only had twenty-five pya left in my hand and reminded Ko Ko before he left in the morning to be sure to

---

[2] It is a cultural tradition that other family members not eat before the husband or head of the household is home.

[3] Probably in 1938, the year of U Chit Maung's and Daw Ma Ma Lay's marriage.

send Ko Ohn Myint to me if he should come to the paper. There was enough rice only for lunch, and I wanted to send Ko Ohn Myint to pawn something.

As I cooked, my mind was busy elsewhere, wondering which piece of my jewelry I should pawn. I did not want to pawn what my parents had given me without their knowledge or permission, but there was no help for it. I finally decided to pawn a diamond brooch, as I could reclaim it as soon as he got his salary, and I waited impatiently for Ko Ohn Myint.

At about half past one o'clock, Ko Ko came back, but not alone: he brought his friend U Shwe Kyu, publisher U Sein, and Ko Bo Gyi of the CID.[4] As soon as I saw them, my limbs turned numb and my heart almost stopped; I knew for certain I would have to give them lunch, I was duty-bound. The curry was just enough for two people at two meals, so it was not much, and I felt ashamed of it. I felt desperate. There was no one to send out to buy something, and I had no money.

When he said the guests would be staying for lunch, I tried with great care to keep my smile intact. But I felt hot and cold all over and knew that if I stayed on in his presence he would notice something was wrong, so I turned back into the kitchen. I set out all the food I had and prayed desperately that he would not ask for refills, meanwhile serving them without sitting down to eat. I felt like running to hide in the bathroom. Maybe he did suspect that the rice would not be enough, for he ate little but talked a lot. I could not begin to tell anyone how miserable I was. After eating with relish, they all went to sit in the living room. Ko Ko stayed behind to tell me Ko Ohn Myint had not come and that a telegram came from my father saying he, my father, would be arriving tomorrow morning.

I wanted to drop dead then and there. Father would be miserable to stay in a small place like this, and surely he would notice we had no money and certainly no cook working for us. I wanted to cry, but knowing that I could not even allow tears to well up in my eyes, I desperately controlled myself and, taking the telegram from him, pretended to be overjoyed to be seeing Father again.

I did not want to eat any lunch, and besides there was nothing left to eat.

Ko Ko and his guests sat talking in the front room, and they went back to the paper together. I repeatedly asked Ko Ko please to find Ko Ohn Myint and send him to me. Ko Ko, too, seemed worried about Father's visit.

After they left, I had no will to do anything, so I sat by the window looking out for Ko Ohn Myint. Every time someone turned into our street, I would hope it was him and fall back in despair when it was not. I had no idea where he lived, so I could not go after him myself. I comforted myself that Ko Ko would surely get hold of Ko Ohn Myint, but the thought of Father arriving the next day would enter my mind to keep me agitated with worry.

By evening, I was leaning out the window hoping to see Ko Ohn Myint. I was thinking that if Ko Ko sent a messenger home for something, I would write a note reminding him to find Ko Ohn Myint. But no Ko Ohn Myint arrived nor any messenger. I felt so weak that I went to curl up on the bed. Lying there unhappily, I thought of what Ko Ko had told me once.

"Before I got the job at the *Nawrahta* paper, I was flat broke. I slept at my friend's house in Insein, Ko Bo Gyi of CID. Then I heard that the Insein jail superintendent wanted to learn Burmese, and I went to see him. For daily two-hour lessons he offered me twenty kyat a month. Then he said, 'The best instructor could be hired for

---

[4] Criminal Investigation Department.

fifteen but I offer you twenty.' I knew the fair amount is forty or fifty kyat, and I knew he could afford that. And I said to him, 'Well, Superintendent, you might wait till doomsday to get a good teacher at twenty a month; I, for one, will hire my vast knowledge in Burmese to those worthy pupils who offer more than double what you now pay. Goodbye.'

"At that time, Tin Lay, I was really broke and starving, but that gave me the impetus to hope all the more and to try harder. You do gain something through desperate situations."

Starving now gave me the impetus to hope all the more and to try harder; I pondered on his words and took heart. I turned my unhappy thoughts to hopeful ones of how I would help this man achieve the success and fame he so richly deserved, and in this way I eased my worries somewhat. I waited to hear his footsteps and wondered how I could manage his dinner with twenty-five pya. Around seven in the evening, he came back, and when I opened the door for him he said he had sent someone twice to look for Ko Ohn Myint but could not find him. Seeing my face, he asked in alarm, "Are you all right?"

Grasping at this straw, I said, "I don't think I feel too well, Ko Ko. I didn't even want to cook. Do you like rice salad?"[5]

"Yes, I do, I often eat at that old lady's stall in Thirty-Ninth Street."

"Is that so? I'd like some, let's go there."

We went out, and I was so relieved that I had thought of the cheap rice salad. I had never eaten at a roadside stall before, but I made sure he thought I would, this time. When we got there, I told the woman to prepare one plate of twenty-five pya's worth of salad for him.

"What will you have, Tin Lay?" he asked.

"I wanted to before but now I feel a bit nauseous. If I eat anything I'll really be sick, Ko Ko. You go ahead."

He looked unhappy at the thought of me feeling ill and, not knowing we had no money left, he kept urging me to eat something else, such as Faludah. I did not have the heart to say anything to him, so I just grimaced as if nauseated and shook my head at him. He ate his rice halfheartedly, feeling sorry for me. If he knew the truth, he would not have eaten a bite. I thought to myself, this man eating at a roadside stall … this is not right, and lost in my own thoughts I stared at him.

When he finished, I asked as I would normally do, "Do you want another helping?" and the reader might imagine my voice came out with a tremble. But actually I said it brightly as if I had the money in my pocket, and I wrote down truthfully in my diary that night that only because I knew for certain he would not ask for another plate did I dare to utter these words so confidently. I also wrote that in my twenty-one years of life with regular meals every single day, this was the first time I had missed both lunch and dinner.

---

[5] Rice salad is a mix of rice, shredded cabbage, roasted chickpea powder, bean sprouts, fish sauce, and onion oil; it is inexpensive street food.

CHAPTER 19

MY LONE JOURNEY

We would walk to the jetty early the next morning to meet my father ... just for the exercise, I said. Before we could leave, Father arrived with his Indian butler in tow and, as soon as he came in, told me to prepare his bed in the front room.

"I'm not feeling too well," Father said, and lay down. I knew at once that at the first sight of our place he had been surprised and upset. Ko Ko also seemed to realize it and went off to work looking unhappy.

I took ten kyat out of Father's jacket and gave it to the butler to go to the bazaar.

I prayed that when Ko Ko returned he would have his salary in his pocket. I knew what Father was going through, so I dared not go near him and dared not walk around since he might call me. At about ten in the morning Father got up from bed and took a bath. He said nothing as he changed in the front room, but going to the back to bathe, he had glanced around at our room and the kitchen, and how everything was set out. I was terrified of what he might say, but, merely telling me he was going out for a while, he left the apartment. I felt very relieved.

Just before Ko Ko came home, Father returned and, sending his butler downstairs, told him to "bring up everything in the car" and sat down in the living room with his feet up on the coffee table and his eyes closed, as if in exhaustion.

As soon as I saw the first load the butler carried in, I felt like sobbing my heart out on Father's breast. He knew I loved Cadbury's Chocolate Biscuits, so there were tins of it, as well as other biscuits; there were tins of butter and canned fruits; Nestlé's cream; sweets and chocolates, all from Barnard's Store, as well as coffee, condensed milk, sugar, and seasonal fruits such as mangosteens and rambutans. Just by looking around he had guessed that I had been deprived of the things I liked and had hurried out to get them.

Ko Ko arrived just after Father and, seeing the stuff piled on the table, stood still in shock. Glancing over at Father sitting as if exhausted in the living room, Ko Ko, too, dropped into bed and lay there unmoving. Seeing my father and husband suffering like this, I felt like curling up in a corner but instead calmly went about setting out lunch. Ko Ko came out and kept whispering urgently, "Did your father ask anything? What did he say?" and scolded me for not giving Father lunch earlier. "Eat the food that he has brought in his presence, where he can see you, so he'll be pleased," Ko Ko urged.

I just smiled or nodded or shook my head to what he was saying, as I did not feel like uttering a word. We called Father and sat down to our meal, but none of us could eat. Only when I was clearing the table did Father speak to Ko Ko for the first time.

"Maung Chit Maung, you eat lunch too late, it's not good for you," he said and went back to the living room.

Ko Ko went to sit quietly by Father and stayed there the whole time before he left again for the paper; he sat with his head down, listening respectfully to whatever Father said. When he left, Father called me over and demanded to know why we were living in this place.

I said we were trying to find a bigger place and that this was temporary. Father pointed out all the things he disliked about the place.

"Your bed and dining table are practically side by side, why couldn't there be a separate bedroom and dining room?" he fumed. He tackled me about not having a maid, and I said I could not get one easily just now, and he demanded why I had not let him know. He asked point-blank if we could manage on Ko Ko's salary, and I replied coolly that yes, we could, easily, and for him not to worry.

As soon as Ko Ko came back that night, Father demanded that we move to a bigger place in a better neighborhood.

"I want you to do that before I leave," he insisted. I persuaded him that it was never easy to find a good place in Yangon, and that to avoid moving often, I would find the most suitable place as soon as I could.

That evening, Ko Ko came back with his salary plus a twenty-five-kyat bonus. Now the rent's taken care of, I thought with relief. The next day Father came back with a horse carriage loaded with rice, oil, and other dry goods. During the four or five days my father stayed in Yangon, he took me wherever he went: to the Shwedagon Pagoda, to the shops, and to the cinema, and he took both of us to have meals at the Continental Hotel,[1] and the Bombay and Savoy Restaurants.

Callers who came when Father was with us were amazed to see him combing out my hair himself; they had never before seen such a love displayed by a father for a daughter. Ko Ko recounted to the callers with relish how my family was very close and how well Father looked after us. His closest friends now felt sympathy for me, unlike before. Father left for home after repeatedly urging us to move as soon as possible. Ko Ko promised him he was going to write novels to supplement our income. I had begged him not to work so hard, but as Ko Ko had already promised Father, he kept insisting he would write these novels, and for my part I was trying hard to dissuade him. As it was, we had no means to move to a better place.

Father kept sending letters demanding to know if we had found a new place, and when I replied we were looking around but so far had found nothing yet, he would write back to say that we were not trying hard enough. I greatly feared that Father would turn up again, and I wrote to him that we would surely move soon and kept giving all sorts of excuses.

After paying the rent and repaying the loan to the paper, as well as the debt to the bookstore, Ko Ko used the remainder of his salary, about one-third of it, to buy new books and magazines, so it was not easy to manage with the rest. Having to be so careful every day, I even came to feel stingy about feeding myself. I had no wish to drink coffee or eat anything apart from meals. I was sure Ko Ko guessed we were short of money, but he did not know exactly how bad off we were, as I made sure he would not know. When we went to bookshops, he always asked me if he should buy any of the books he liked, and if I saw him put down one I knew he wanted, I would buy it, come what may, even though I knew my own situation. I felt somewhat horrified at myself. I wrote down all our expenses, and his monthly expenditure on books was often higher than the household expenses. I doubted if the paper could

---

[1] Where Trader's Hotel is now.

afford to buy all the books he wanted. For his personal needs, he never spent one pya beyond buying books or tea, and still his expenses exceeded mine.

He also had his family to look after, and it was embarrassing for me that we could not support them as much as they needed. Looking at me, no one would believe we had no money; in fact, people thought we did not give to charity because we did not want to. I did not want anyone looking down on my husband, and I never let on to anyone, even his closest friends, that we were barely surviving. To all, I pretended we were well off enough to be good hosts when they came calling. Father, however, sent Daw Daw Ma Yin to live with me, and with her I could not hide anything, so my poor aunt also went without while feeling deeply sympathetic for me. I often opened my heart to Aunt about how I had to keep Ko Ko from knowing about our lack of money month after month. I wanted to prevent anyone, especially my husband, from knowing all this and even wished I could somehow manage to hide this miserable reality from myself!

For four or five months, I managed to keep him from doing extra work and tried my best to look after him. Nevertheless, it was only I who thought about taking care of his health, while he as usual disregarded it, so my efforts were not as successful as they could be.

I had to remind him every day to bathe, and if that did not work, I would nag him, and if that did not move him, I would beg almost on my knees. The worst thing about our marriage became the daily task of getting him into the bathroom every evening after he came home from work. He thought it a waste of time, as he would rather read. When he was immersed in a good book, it made him unhappy to leave it, and it made me unhappy to try and get him away from it. Only when he noticed tears welling in my eyes would he go into the bathroom. Even then, I could be assured he was really bathing only when I heard the sound of splashing water.

Once I thought I could tease him into it and wrote a verse on how fresh a person would feel after a bath and how it removed the unhealthy "heat" from the body and eased all aches and pains. I hoped that if I showed it to him as soon as he came home, he would immediately march into the bathroom. That he did after reading my poem, but he came straight out at once after washing his face, saying it was too cold to bathe, so my poetic effort came to nothing, like water poured into hot sand. I huffily wrote in my diary that my poem must have been very weak or else his reluctance to bathe too strong.

One would think that since we loved each other so much our time would be full of tender moments; not at all. The love poems he wrote before our marriage seemed as if they had never been his works; he now seemed to have nothing to do with love poems, and he seemed nothing like other men as well.

One day, soon after we were settled in Yangon, we returned from the bookshop by horse carriage and sat facing each other. He told me to spread out my palm, and he drew on it with his forefinger, and thinking he was reading my palm, I opened my fingers wider.

"What do you see, Ko Ko? Tell me ..."

"I'm not looking at the lines," he said, looking up in surprise.

"What? What are you looking at then?"

"Well, my friend Shwe Pane Thaung, the bachelor, said if you want to hold a girl's hand, you pretend to read her palm," he spoke shortly, without the slightest hint of a smile—and looking shy and embarrassed, he then bent his head to a book. I stared at him, and then closed my eyes tight.

I cannot write what a rush of tenderness I felt towards this man at that moment, more than at any other time. He was a man living outside of man's social boundaries, I thought, and it was no wonder people called him a monk. If I called him Ko Ko in front of others, he would look deadly embarrassed, and he, too, never called me Tin Lay in public, things I had to understand and forgive.

There was no time for tender exchanges between us as all his time was spent with a book instead of me. In my diary, I wrote that marriage was like a lone journey in a desert, a dry, painful life, but the diary was the only place where I confided such a thing. To maintain appearances, I made sure that not a hint of it escaped me by word or expression. If he were busy with his books, I would simply take out his love letters and read them over and over again. After six months, I became used to this arid life with a writer, but with love and understanding towards him, I happily and contentedly accepted my fate. I had total trust in him that he would be completely faithful and love me deeply all his life. Although he never whispered sweet love words, it did nothing to lessen our love.

He studied English literature more than Burmese, and although he was a strong nationalist who never used any Western-made products, his manner of treating a woman was very Westernized. He gave way to me in climbing up or down the stairs or by helping me in and out of cabs or opening doors. He treated me gently and with consideration and was always exceedingly kind. If he had to point out whatever wrong I was doing, he did it gently and by explaining at length. For all this, I loved him not only as a husband but also as I would a father or a teacher. Every night when I would *kadaw* him before going to sleep,[2] he would give his blessing, wishing for me to have all my desires fulfilled, and I always felt that because he had said so, they would be, indeed.

---

[2] Traditional act of respect for parents and husband.

CHAPTER 20

IS THE WORLD COMING TO AN END?

Constantly having to worry about money made me realize that, with Ko Ko's salary, I could never hope to give him the sort of life he deserved. I believed that we could make more money if we published a newspaper or journal on our own, and I asked him what he felt about it. He resisted the idea at once, declaring so vehemently that he could not leave *Myanmar Alin* because a replacement for him would be difficult to find, that I dropped the matter and tried to think up other ways.

One day, while waiting for Ko Ko to return for lunch, I sat idly looking through his files of the *Market* paper. Suddenly I had an idea and felt impatient to see him. When he came back, I asked him what he thought of publishing the series he had written for *Market* in a collection under the title "Is the World Coming to an End?" and asked whether we could make money out of it.

"No one would buy it if it comes out now," he said. "I'll write a new one."

"Now, Ko Ko, don't start about writing a new book, not now ... let's wait until you are really healthy. But why do you think this book won't sell?"

"It's not the right time, Tin Lay ... this book would be too early. The articles were written in 1935, and as there's no war, who would want to read it?"

"If you advertise, I'm sure people will be interested."

"But why do you want to publish this particular one, Tin Lay?"

"So that it won't give you more strain, I had to find something already written. It does seem like war is coming, so I'm sure it would sell."

"It can't be published as it is, Tin Lay, politics keep changing all the time. I need more facts. Moreover, we'd need money to publish ... the costs of paper, printing, binding. If I write something new, someone else will invest in it, so please let me do it."

"Just tell me what you need to know and how to find it; I'll help you with the research. As for capital, I have a life insurance policy at Sunlight, and I can cash it in, and there we have it. If we publish ourselves our profits are bigger."

"At Sunlight? Then cash it in quickly, Tin Lay, war's coming for sure."

"So we'll publish this book, right?"

"As you wish, then, Tin Lay, but I doubt that it'll sell."

He did not sound very enthusiastic, but I was determined to publish this book. The next day I went to Sunlight to cash in my policy, and I received eight hundred kyat. I worked day and night over this book. Every evening I was at *Myanmar Alin*, and thinking that if I had my own printing press it would be much easier to publish his books, I took a deeper interest in the workings of the press and tried to learn more about it. He was busy with his own work, so I took care of finding the material he wanted. If he wanted to know about a particular statement made by the British minister of defense, I had to look through the English newspapers. If he asked me to find a paragraph he had marked in blue pencil in the Japanese newspapers, I did. I looked through all the Japanese papers and set aside all war news marked in blue. As he instructed, I would look through reports filed by news agencies to get particular details.

When he mentioned he needed a book titled *Should Japan Declare War on Britain?*, I went to City Book Club bookshop on Pansodan Street and bought a copy. There I saw a book by two Japanese, Otana and Ihotan, titled *When Japan Goes to War*, and bought it as well. Ko Ko borrowed a book from Thakin Than Tun[1] titled *The Decline and the Fall of Imperialism*, and I copied out the passages he marked.

He told me there were marked passages in other books, and sure enough, there they were, marked in blue, and I now realized how useful it was for him to have that blue pencil always in his pocket. I marveled at how he remembered the many passages he had marked in so many books. There was a lot of new material to collect, but the passages were already marked by him, so it was easy enough for me to find. We had the book printed at his friend's press, and as each chapter was done, my happiness grew at the thought of the complete book coming out soon.

While he expanded his manuscript, I made sure he could do it in peace, and I sat by him, reading the pages he finished. To encourage him, I told him that I already knew he had a brilliant mind, but had not realized how talented he was: "I never knew what a talent you had, Ko Ko. We'll soon be out of living like this, I swear."

In the preface, he wrote that "this manuscript was completed in 1935 and is now published as a book in 1938, and it was necessary to add the facts that have emerged in the meantime. I could not spare the time from my job as an editor, and it fell upon my wife to fulfill this need."

I was pleased at the thought that he would gain some fame for this book. He said he would print 1,500 copies to sell at half a kyat each. I told him to sell it for one kyat, but he said in that case people would not be able to afford it, but I was confident it would sell. I was so confident that I would be able to move to a better place that I told my friends to keep their eyes out for one. However, when the book came out, it took about ten days to sell around two hundred copies, and I knew I had been too optimistic. Ko Ko kept saying worriedly, "I told you it won't sell, Tin Lay," so I coolly told him that it would sell gradually, but I felt frustrated whenever I saw that stack of books.

We did move, however, to an apartment on Thirty-Eighth Street. My hopes had been so high that I had planned to move to a bigger one with the rent of seventy-five kyat, but had to settle for one at forty, on the same street.

---

[1] Thakin Than Tun was minister of agriculture in the wartime government of Dr. Ba Maw and a leader of the Communist Party of Burma (BCP). The BCP revolted against the government in 1948, two months after independence. The party collapsed in 1989. Thakin Than Tun, who was the brother-in-law of Bogyoke Aung San, died in 1968 during an internal BCP purge; a member of his own party shot and killed him, then fled and surrendered to the government.

CHAPTER 21

RULING BY THE PEN

Ko Ko's salary was raised to one hundred sixty-five kyat after we moved to Thirty-Eighth Street, and after taking out rent and loan repayments, we had about sixty kyat left. Besides, without me having to say a word, Father would send, often enough if not monthly, two or three hundred kyat, so I could buy my husband all the books he wanted. We never missed good English-language movies either, and I always fed him well, including nutritious drinks like Horlicks and Ovaltine. He began to look much better, filling out where before he had been gaunt, and even began to put on weight. I had him wear new *longyi* of silk in various weaves and colors, and he no longer looked shabby.

"U Sein[1] was teasing me for wearing a Bangauk[2] *longyi*," he said to me. "They'll think I've changed."

"For sure you'll even change some more," I said.

"Please, Missy, I think this is bad enough … I feel so uncomfortable with new clothes!"

He refused to wear pastel colors, so I had to buy him clothes in dark and somber tones.

"Get something for yourself, too, Tin Lay, don't keep buying things just for me," he would often say.

Now, when I went with him to the paper during the evening, I began to help with his work and became very interested. When he was writing breaking news, I could not wait until he was done but would stand over his shoulder to read every word.

When, after completing a page, he crushed it into a ball and threw it away to begin all over again, I would pick it out of the wastebasket and file it away at home. I learned that in newspaper work one has to be prepared for future news. Once when Gandhi fell ill, and Ko Ko prepared an obituary, I was very surprised and protested, "He's not dead yet!"

Ko Ko had to make very quick decisions about what to include and which piece of news would be timely. I would watch him expectantly, hoping he would not be wrong, and he would look up at me and say, "That's why it's fun to work at a paper!"

When I saw that the news turned out to be correct the next day, I would be relieved, but as I was already beginning to worry for the next issue, I was constantly on tenterhooks. Working at a newspaper looked like a risky business, like teetering on the edge of a precipice.

---

[1] A reporter at *Myanmar Alin*.

[2] Silk of a plain but distinct weave, named after "Bangkok."

"You know, Tin Lay, when we heard the news of King Edward's abdication, it could be taken either way: that he *would* abdicate or he *has* abdicated. I found a photo of Mrs. Simpson, and with that, I wrote 'has abdicated' and put it on the front page.

"The next day, none of the English papers had any news of it, and among the Burmese papers, only mine did, so people were calling up each other about it, and they didn't know what to believe … even if the English papers did not have it, they couldn't disbelieve it, either. The governor was so mad, his chief secretary, Mr. H. Craw, called me to the secretariat. *Thagyi Gazette* publisher U Khin Maung took me there, and that day I was wearing a cotton *longyi* and wooden clogs, and I went clumping into his office. He didn't ask me to sit down, but I pulled up a chair and did so. He glared at me and asked, 'Who are you?' and I replied shortly, 'Chit Maung, executive editor of *Myanmar Alin*.'

"He asked me to name my source for the news of the abdication, and I told him I didn't come here to be interrogated. He got really angry then, veins about to pop on his forehead, and demanded whether I had thought beforehand what could happen to me if the news turned out to be incorrect. I asked him if he realized I was the executive editor. Then he pounded his fist on the desk and said, 'This news is not yet confirmed, we've had no word from London. I demand you put in a correction in tomorrow's paper, or else we will sue you.'

"'Chief Secretary, I am not responsible for your government, as I am only responsible for *Myanmar Alin*, and I am indeed deeply sorry that your government did not get your news in time. As it is correct, I have no need to place a correction in the next day's paper. Very soon, I'm sure, you'll receive word from London, and then your government will be wiser.' He was so furious! We left, and as soon as we got out of there, U Khin Maung told everyone what I had said to the chief secretary. MP Gangha Singh, that big chap, was so pleased he gave me a bear hug and swung me around. You need to be thoughtful and be prepared to take risks in this business, Tin Lay."

I wrote it all down in English in my diary, as he had told me.

Every day *Myanmar Alin* commented on the economy, religion, politics, or society. The paper had no hesitation in pointing out the weaknesses of government and did so sharply. *Myanmar Alin* became a very powerful voice, strong enough to face the government. Whenever news of government departments' misdeeds came up in the paper, no one dared ignore it, and the personnel concerned made sure these things were corrected, and because of that I saw the truth of his saying that a newspaper governs a country by the pen.

All the while that he was doing his work, he was also studying every aspect of governance and the financial situations of other countries. I was bewildered and asked why he was interested in finance, did he want to be a finance minister? He explained that an editor had to comment on all aspects of politics and governance and therefore needed to know as much as the governing body.

We kept buying bookcase after bookcase. I tore out all the pages he had marked in magazines and filed them separately according to subject. He bought books on politics, economy, education, science, and history; and biographies of great personages, as well as novels and poetry. He read them all. He studied each subject in depth, and after he had looked into law books, I noticed him walking the thin edge of danger—as a Burmese saying goes—at *Myanmar Alin*: his criticism of government departments became stronger, backed by his new knowledge of law concerning how to avoid pitfalls.

He kept all references he had used while writing the editorials, and these after so many years grew into a big pile. I took back from Ko Ohn Myint the old articles in English he had written for various publications and got some more from his friends that I compiled and kept safe at home with other files. I also kept a file of hate mail according to the subject under discussion, whether it was political or whether they were from readers who could not believe that he would be so cruel as to part the sweethearts in his fiction. Also, there were letters from readers who disagreed with his editorials or other news.

While putting away those letters, I remembered what he had written to me before our marriage about an editor's role, and I copied it and filed it with the hate mail. It said, in English,

> *It has long been a trite observation that no reader of any newspaper is so humble as not to be outspokenly confident that he could run that paper a great deal better than those who actually are running it. Every upstanding man who pays a cent for a daily journal considers that he buys the right to abuse it, nay, incurs the manly duty of abusing it. Every editor knows that the highest praise he can expect is silence. If his readers are pleased with his remarks, they nobly refrain from comment. But if they disagree with one jot of his high-speed dissertations, he must be prepared to have quarts of ink squirted at him forthwith.*

He looked at all the papers I was filing away daily and told me they should be of use one day.

CHAPTER 22

BEHIND THE IRON SCREEN

One day U Chit Maung came home for lunch looking disturbed.

"Things are going to change at Do Bama Asi-ayon," he told me. "You'll see some interesting things tonight, Tin Lay."

He explained, "The association will split in two. Thakin Ba Sein and others went to Dr. Ba Maw to request the release of Thakin Tun Oke. Dr. Ba Maw will use this opportunity to polish his political image by publishing the release order. We must stop Dr. Ba Maw from issuing this statement, as it will be a political disaster ... the Do Bama Asi-ayon will lose a lot of strength if the statement comes out. Right now there's nothing to lead us but the association. When I criticized some Thakin in the paper, people resented it, and I had to do it only because I did not want the association to fall ... they *must* be united. But if it splits, I must do something to help it remain as strong as it was. I feel so wretched, Tin Lay."

That night at the paper, the chairman of the association, Thakin Thein Maung, and Ko Ko sat talking gravely. I sat by them, noting down every word. After Thakin Thein Maung left, Ko Ko began to write the news, and I noticed that he was thinking deeply over the matter. He looked suddenly much older, and I thought to myself, no wonder his hair has turned grey in his twenties. I sat there looking at him, forgetting to blink. Before the copyboy came in, I hurriedly pulled the pages from him and read them over.

He asked, "What d'you think?" and I replied briefly "Good," but felt a deep sadness because of this situation. The politicians such as Thakin Ba Sein, Thakin Aung Than, Bo Sekkya, Thakin Tun Oke, Thakin Nyi, Thakin Lay Maung, and Thakin Thein Maung had all been my friends since my activist days in Bogalay, and they had encouraged me to make speeches when they came to hold political meetings. I had looked upon them with admiration and respect since those days. Thakin Nyi especially had been pleased that a Westernized, fashionable young woman like me was active in politics, and he encouraged me a lot, and I earned his respect and affection. When all the men I knew were breaking away from each other, I felt deeply unhappy, and Ko Ko, knowing that, tried to comfort me. "It's nothing new for political parties to split, Tin Lay," he said, "let's hope it's for the best."

The next day Thakin Kodaw Hmaing[1] sent a note by messenger asking Ko Ko to publish his statement of resignation from the association in the next day's paper. Ko Ko got up in alarm and said, "I've got to go to him, I've got to get there in time and ask Saya Gyi[2] not to resign, or else all my plans will fall apart!"

"What plans, Ko Ko?"

---

[1] Thakin Kodaw Hmaing was a highly respected elderly writer and great nationalist, and an honored member of the Do Bama Asi-ayon. He passed away in 1964 at the age of eighty-nine.

[2] "Saya Gyi" means "great teacher."

"If the Thakin association splits, there won't be anyone left with Thakin Thein Maung. Remember how I told you once that students should become members? Now is the chance; I believe that only when the students become active can we make any headway in our fight. It's time students enter politics. Remember, students were at the forefront when people in Britain protested against Chamberlain's appeasement of Hitler? And students took the lead in India when Gandhi's Civil Disobedience started, and they were jailed by the thousands. If we could get student leaders into politics, and if they became active, we'd gain our independence all the sooner. I must talk with Thakin Than Tun about it, we *must* get the students involved."

Late that night, we took a cab to Kyeemyindine, where Saya Gyi Thakin Kodaw Hmaing lived, to beg him to change his mind about resigning. I was deeply worried to see Ko Ko so torn between his paper and politics. He was seldom at home, going either to the Naga Ni Book Club[3] or the Do Bama Asi-ayon.

One night, he said he had made an appointment to meet Thakin Than Tun and Ko Nu. "Ko Nu said he does not want to put 'Thakin' in front of his name if he joins the association," Ko Ko told me. "I must also get Ko Aung San[4] to join the movement; I *must* do my utmost to persuade them. If they join the face of politics will change; just you wait and see, Tin Lay."

He went off to meet Thakin Than Tun and Ko Nu at the Botahtaung Bridge, and I sat down to write in my diary all the details of the Thakin movement. I was longing to know what they were talking about at the bridge. When he came back, I greeted him with the question about how it went, and he smiled and nodded. That night I saw clearly his parallel lives—as a newspaperman and a politician. I realized that he did not become an editor because of his great interest in literature, but to use his position as a vehicle to change the future of our country. I finally saw the truth, that he became an editor only through his great commitment to politics. He knew that someone like him was necessary in the newspaper business to support the course of politics, and thus far he would not leave this job to enter politics. While he was immersed in the role of an editor on the sidelines, I did not want him to leave all that to enter politics, but one day, I vowed, I would urge him to do so.

At the end of the detailed notes I wrote on the Botahtaung Bridge meeting involving Thakin Than Tun, Thakin Nu, Thakin Thein Maung, and U Chit Maung, I added a line that one day I would make him enter politics.

---

[3] The "Red Dragon" Book Club, very much a leftist club, was a meeting place for politicians and literati. It also published a lot of leftist material, mostly translated.

[4] Ko Aung San was to become Thakin Aung San and, later, he led the Myanmar Independence Army as General Aung San. He is the hero of Myanmar Independence. He was assassinated on July, 19, 1947. A rival politician, U Saw, was convicted of organizing the assassination.

CHAPTER 23

A TIME OF CHAOS

On June 26, 1938, I gave birth to my eldest son. That very day Ko Ko went to the Do Bama Asi-ayon and entered the membership for his newborn son in the name Thakin Aung Khin. The same way that the father in the movie *The Good Earth*, based on Pearl S. Buck's novel, cried "My son!," Ko Ko, too, holding the baby up to his face, kept on saying "My son! My son!" After my son's birth, I could no longer go with my husband to the paper every evening as I used to.

I had given birth prematurely at seven months, and as soon as I telegraphed my father, he rushed down to Yangon in alarm. Father took upon himself the work of looking after a new mother in all the traditional Burmese ways, and so Ko Ko did not need to take leave from his work. Father, however, could only get a week's leave, so before he went back he urged me repeatedly to move to a bigger place.

After he returned home, he sent my aunt and nieces to look after me, as I had not completely recovered, so we were a bit crowded at home. One morning at about nine, Ko Ko was at the office and I was at home with the others. I was lying in bed when I heard noises from the street, and I got up to peep out of the window. A large crowd of Indians ran screaming into our street. I could see people fleeing in terror on the main road, and I wondered if a fight had broken out between the Indians and the Burmese.

Suddenly, some of the Indians spotted me at the window, and crying "Barama! Barama!"[1] came up to my building. My heart jumped to my throat, and I closed the window and ran inside. I told the others that a fight had apparently broken out between the Burmese and the Indians, and I felt very frightened without Ko Ko at home. The noise of fighting, the sound of violence, and cries of pain resounded from the street below. As I was a new mother, my aunt and Ma Chit, a niece living with us as a companion, warned me to keep very calm.[2] If the Indians should come up and break down our door, we would most likely be killed. I peeped out the window at the houses where other Burmese lived, and diagonally across from us, at the third floor window of their apartment, I saw Ko Par, son of U Ba Thein, officer of the telegraph, and I called out to him.

As soon as our street became clear of fighting, Ko Par came over to us and said we should all move with them to the telegraph office building, as here we were unsafe with so many Indians living around us. Just as I was wondering whether I should move, another crowd of Indians ran into our street, and the beating and fighting began all over again. Ko Par said he and his family would be leaving at once and urged us to come along. I could not decide; on the one hand, I was terrified that

---

[1] "Barama" is a mispronunciation by the Indian population of the word "Bama," meaning "Burmese."

[2] It is believed that too much excitement could cause new mothers to have a fatal fit.

Ko Ko might be beaten to death if he came running home, but I also feared that he would not know where to find us if we left. My aunt and nieces all begged that we should leave, saying we could send a message to him once we were safe. Their faces were pale and looked terrified, and so I swept up my diary and his copy of *Queed*, as well as my jewelry and baby things, and went with Ko Par and his family to stay in the telegraph office. I locked the apartment, but I was not at all sure it would remain untouched.

The room we were given to ourselves in the telegraph office was used for the wireless and had glass windows along all the walls. We could be easily spotted from the street, and when Indians passed by, my aunt and others were so afraid they would hide under the table and gestured to me to hide as well. I hugged my baby to my bosom and felt desperate just looking at them. On our way here, we had seen bloodied people, and although I was not easily frightened, I felt my nerves almost giving way. Without Ko Ko, I felt utterly desolated. Ko Par called Ko Ko at the paper, and he said there was a crowd blocking the road near *Myanmar Alin*, so he could not come home, and that he felt relieved we were safely inside the telegraph office. He said he would come at night in U Ba Hnin's car. I was much relieved when Ko Par relayed the message.

Just at sunset, the terrifying calls to arms and the noise of fighting on Dalhousie Street pierced my ears like nothing I had ever heard before. Ko Ko came with U Ba Hnin around seven in the evening, and as soon as I saw his face, all my terrors fled as if by magic, and in an instant I became unbelievably strong.

"I was so worried about you, Ko Ko, I can only breathe now. You can't imagine how frightened Aunt was. On our way here we saw people bloodied and injured, and without you I felt so desolate and my heart was thumping so hard. How are things at the paper?"

"Not so good. The Indian crowd wanted to come in and destroy the paper, but I gathered a group of men and I was going out to fight them, but the business manager called us back and shot his pistol in the air so no one dared to come in."

"You were worried about us, weren't you?"

"You can't imagine how much. I was planning to leave as soon as the crowd dispersed when I got Ko Par's call. Did you lock the flat?"

"Yes, but whatever happens, Ko Ko, it's our fate. I am so grateful to Ko Par. Since morning, Aunt has had nothing to eat, and there's nothing here. Ko Par brought us some coffee. Do we have to stay here?"

"Ko Par and his family are here, and it's safe, so it won't do to go elsewhere. You have to stay here until things cool down, Tin Lay. If there's anything you need from home, give me the key. I'll go in Ko Ba Hnin's car."

"I think we need bedding, Ko Ko, we can't sleep on the cement floor. For you, too."

"Not for me, I can't sleep here."

"What did you say, Ko Ko? Where will you sleep?"

"At the paper; now it's most urgent that I am there to make sure the paper comes out. I can't stay here at any cost, Tin Lay, you'll just make the best of it here on your own."

I felt bitterness well up inside me. I could not bear to think of the prospect of staying in this building, scared out of our wits, without his protection. I felt hurt that he could leave an ill new mother during this time of terror. I knew well enough that getting a daily newspaper out under any circumstances was most important, but we were not at home but living in an open hall. I felt that even if we were not afraid to stay the night, it was not proper for women to be in such a situation. I felt he should know that a new mother especially needs to be careful or else many ailments, one after the other, might sicken her and the child. I wanted him to acknowledge that I was as important to him as his paper.

He brought over the bedding, and saying, "I'm off now, Tin Lay, I'll come tomorrow if I have time," he left. I felt so desolate I could only nod my head. As soon as he was gone, the hurt inside me welled up, and thinking what my father would have felt to see me thus abandoned, I tried to hold back tears that were threatening to spill over. My aunt and nieces were frightened, and unhappy for me, since I had watched my husband depart, but dared not say a single word to me. They huddled in a corner watching me out of the corners of their eyes. Ko Par came up often to tell us not to worry, and I felt better, but after he left we sat up staring at each other, not daring to sleep.

We sat up until dawn. Every time the baby cried, I thought of his father leaving us and wanted to cry too. I was bitterly hurt that the paper was more important to him than I was, but I gritted my teeth and bore the pain.

With morning, we had to decide how to prepare our meals; someone would have to go home to cook. There were no food shops near us, and the streets were deserted. Ko Par said to come home with him if we wanted to cook, and my niece Ma Chit, trying hard to be brave, said she would. I could not be sure Ma Chit would be safe, and if possible I would have done it myself, but as I was in no condition for it, it was useless for me even to volunteer, as none of them would agree to it. Poor Ma Chit left with Ko Par, walking from the corner of Pansodan all the way to Thirty-Eighth Street. Watching them from the upper storey of the office, I thought that if something happened to Ma Chit, it would be Ko Ko's, as well as my, responsibility. He should be finding food for us, I thought, not letting Ma Chit venture out into danger.

If I had argued with him, maybe he might not have left us, but I consoled myself that if the news got into the paper, people who were planning to come to Yangon could be warned. He came back around two in the afternoon, and we asked each other simultaneously, he to me, "Are you well?" and I to him "Did you go to the toilet?"

He said yes, and I did not bother to answer his question.

The *Myanmar Alin* covered the racial violence in the day's paper, and we learned more fully about it. He was happy to get a chance to write against the government and satisfied to have managed to put out the paper at a time like this.

"Don't worry about me," he said. "Everything's arranged for my food and all."

I gave him lunch from what Ma Chit had cooked and brought over, but he ate only a little.

"I'll come again tonight," he said, but I told him not to take any risks and not to worry about me. He did not even remember to ask where we got the food he had just eaten, and I thought how uncaring he could be.

The violence got worse; even the military police could not control the situation. Every neighborhood of Yangon erupted with racial hatred and fights. We became used to living at the telegraph office and did not feel as frightened as before.

The worst thing was to see poor Ma Chit go out every day to cook at our apartment and to bring back the food. I felt so sorry for her I could hardly bear to eat it. I also worried for Ko Ko, working his heart out at the paper, and I prayed with *metta*[3] for him to be safe. I kept muttering to myself anxiously about whether my husband remembered to go to the toilet, and Aunt in the middle of all this kept teasing me, "Well, why don't you walk over to the paper and make sure?"

The next day, when Ma Chit and Ko Par were late coming back after cooking, I leaned out of the window, watching out for them, sick with worry. Late in the morning, I saw them hurrying back, and while I helped take down the pots stacked on her head, I saw Ma Chit's tear-stained face and my amazement turned to fear.

"Ma Chit, Ma Chit, what happened?" I asked in fright.

"Only because I care for you so much, Tin Tin, that I dared go out every morning. This morning when I came down the stairs, an Indian chased me so I had to go up again and lock myself in. I was so frightened, and only when Ko Par came for me did I dare come out. My hands and feet feel like ice ... if I have to go again every day ..."

She sat down on the floor and sobbed, her face on her knees. I felt a piercing pain in my heart and, staggering to the window, leaned on the sill. I knew that Ko Par came in and left after telling Ma Chit to give me lunch, but I did not greet him, and I had no idea when he left. I stayed at the window until Ko Ko came back in the afternoon.

"Were you waiting for me? Haven't you had lunch? Aren't you feeling well?" Ko Ko asked tenderly. I could not even raise my head, and he became worried.

"Tin Lay, tell me, what happened?"

Finally, I lifted my face. "Ko Ko, please take us to the jetty tonight, please let us go back to Bogalay."

"I can't do that, Tin Lay, there's fighting at the wharfs, too. I got all of Father's telegrams in a bunch today, six in all. I think he was sending one a day."

"What did he say?"

"A lot of things ... asking if we were safe, to come back if we could, and to leave the paper at once ... all sorts."

"That's right, Ko Ko, please, in any way you can, take us to the boat for Bogalay tonight."

"Did something happen?"

"I feel so upset ..."

"Well, Tin Lay, we have to go through it like everybody, it's just for a while ... things will cool down. Just have a little more patience, all right?"

"It's not because of me, it's because of the others that I want to go back."

"Did they say they didn't want to stay?"

"It's not a question of just staying here, Ko Ko. Ma Chit has the worst of it. I feel so unhappy to tell you, have you any idea where we got our food?"

"You're eating with Ko Par's family, right?"

"Not at all, Ko Ko. Ko Par's family had to go home every day to cook, and Ma Chit also went every morning. Today she came back crying, she was so afraid ... can you imagine how I felt?"

"Oh dear, Tin Lay, I had no idea ... " His face fell, and he looked far unhappier than I had been. His head hung down, and for minutes he stood silently as if turned to stone.

I realized that he was uncaring of me only because he cared so much for his country, and my hurt disappeared forever.

---

[3] *Metta* means "loving kindness."

"If we can't go, is there an empty flat near the paper?"

"Not yet, but if there were, how could we move? And it's impossible to return to Bogalay."

We could not think of anything more to say.

Aunt said to us, "Is there space at your office for us to stay one or two days? When things quiet down a bit, we can return to Bogalay, and then afterwards get a new place near the paper. Your work, Maung Chit Maung, has no regular hours, and when something like this happens, what's to do? It's time for you to get a place near your work, but right now, perhaps, it can be arranged to have our meals with the staff of the paper? It's impossible to stay on here."

"Yes, Aunt, I'll come and fetch you all tonight, and I'll inform the manager."

It was better to have us stay at his workplace rather than to have him come where we were because this was less disruptive to his work, so, feeling embarrassed towards his colleagues, we moved into his room, which he cleared out for us. I had been keeping tight control over myself so as not to collapse, but once we were at the *Myanmar Alin* offices I could not help myself and fainted dead away and became very ill, almost dying.

We stayed about four or five days at the paper and returned to Bogalay. I knew my father would refuse to let me return to Yangon until we had found a place near Ko Ko's work, so before I even left for Bogalay we found a spacious apartment on the upper floor of the building two doors down from *Myanmar Alin*, over the Maha Swe Company. The rent was ninety kyat, and Ko Ko worried we couldn't afford it, but I said firmly that even if it were a hundred, we had to take this place so long as he was working at the paper.

"I'll just have to ask Father for the rent, there's no help for it," I said, but he protested that I should not, he would ask the paper for a raise.

"I have never asked for a raise before," he said, "so I do feel embarrassed about it."

"Do whatever you think best, Ko Ko, but do make sure to pay the advance for the place, and take care of your health," I reminded him before we left.

While we were living at the newspaper office, it was forced to close down by order of the government for one day, and there was an editors' meeting. Because it was closed down, I have never seen such a strong anti-government editorial as the one that appeared in the next issue. In my diary, I wrote down all I knew of the racial violence and of what was said at the meeting, and I saved the editorial from that day's issue in my files.

When we got back to Bogalay, I found my father ill in bed. He had been too worried about the violence in Yangon, and I learned he was even vomiting blood. I did not dare say a word about our stay at the telegraph office and told him we had been safe at *Myanmar Alin* all the time. I told him we had found a bigger place right over the Maha Swe Company, and he was very relieved.

"The rent is too high," I said, but even while still collapsed in his bed, Father comforted me, saying, "So what, I'll pay it!"

I came back to Yangon as soon as I received a letter from Ko Ko saying he had moved our things to the new apartment and that it was peaceful again in Yangon.

I would have liked to stay by Father's side when he was so ill, but he urged me to go back, saying, "Maung Chit Maung's all alone … go back … go back," and so I left. And as the flat had no partitions, he gave me some money to have wooden ones made.

CHAPTER 24

CIVIL DISOBEDIENCE

So now that we were installed near the Sule Pagoda on the top floor of the Maha Swe Company, we arranged for carpenters to partition off rooms, as the apartment was just one big hall. We were now very close to Ko Ko's work, and I complacently thought he would come back early for lunch or drop in more often, but that was not the case at all. He went to work at eight every morning, came for lunch at one, and went back at three, and came back for dinner at eight, and then from nine to one or two in the morning he would be back at work, in the exact same way as when we were living on Thirty-Fourth and Thirty-Eighth streets.

Looking at him working so hard, I knew how successful he could be if we had our own paper, but every time I suggested it he would say he could not leave *Myanmar Alin*. I had no success at all in this matter, which made me very frustrated. However, he did get a raise to 195 kyat, and after paying the rent, we had 105 left, but as usual other expenses, such as repaying loans and buying books, kept our budget tight, and if my father had not insisted on sending us something each month we would have lived very frugally indeed.

My husband's commitment, body and soul, to the paper was so strong that he harmed his health through work, although he did not ask for even one privilege in return, but even remained humble. One day he was so ill he could not go to work and wrote a leave-of-absence letter to send over to the paper. I read it after he finished writing it, and then I tore it up and sat down in a chair, staring at him.

"Tin Lay, what have you done? Why did you tear up the letter?" he asked in alarm from the bed. I had no wish to answer him and turned to look out of the window. He kept asking, and I kept silent, furious with him.

If he had written, "I would like a day's leave as I am ill," it would be normal, or to say "Please give me a day's leave" was perfectly acceptable. But to write as he had done, "I appeal to you to give me a day's leave," made me so angry when I thought of him working all hours of the day, apart from meal times and sleep, and then *appealing* for one single day's sick leave. When I could find my voice, I finally questioned him, "Tell me, Ko Ko, are you a clerk? Are you an office boy that you must *appeal* to them?"

"How short-tempered you are, Tin Lay. It doesn't matter whether it's an editor or clerk or office boy, if you want a day off, you appeal."

"So is there a rule in your office that appeals must be written if anyone wants sick leave?"

"Of course not, Tin Lay, I wrote it of my own choice, and what's so bad about it?"

"Think of it, Ko Ko, as an executive editor you have no need to be so humble. I know it is noble to be humble, but there's a time and place for everything. If you are constantly humble, everyone around you, those higher or lower, will come to expect it as a matter of course, and when a time comes when you cannot be humble, people will resent it more. This humbleness of yours means disregarding your own honor, your own value, and if they resent you when you can no longer be humble, it's not their fault, it's yours. I don't care how you behaved before, but now that you are my husband, please don't lower yourself so much, I beg you."

He took up another piece of paper.

"I'll do it for you, Ko Ko, I'll write that, as my husband is ill, I would like to inform the paper that he will not be coming to work today."

Quickly saying, "No, no, don't do that, Tin Lay, I'll do it," he wrote a note that said, "I request a day's leave as I am ill."

"Now do you like it?" Ko Ko asked. I replied that to request was at least better than to appeal. At times I felt very frustrated, wondering if he knew anything of his own worth.

Although he was humble and gentle towards his colleagues and friends, when he met the British and administrators from the government he could be cold and sharp. Once, U Kyaw Min of ICS[1] phoned him, telling him to attend a press conference at the Secretariat. Ko Ko demanded sharply, "Who is this calling?" and as soon as the other replied, "Kyaw Min, ICS, Secretary," Ko Ko said, "Please send a written invitation, otherwise we will not be attending," and dropped the receiver. I smiled at him and said, "Now aren't you the arrogant one?" and he muttered "I don't know what they think editors are." I found out then that his tongue could be rather sharp. If he were talking to an Englishman, he could be so sharp as to make even me feel awkward. My British friend, who worked for Steel Brothers, remarked to me privately, "If your husband were in the government of independent Myanmar, he would kick us all out."

Apart from his attitude towards government personnel and British society at large, he was unfailingly polite and gentle, even humble, to everyone he met. People knew him only in connection with *Myanmar Alin*, and because of his demeanor, it would have been hard for others to discover his true talents. Although Burmese society was unaware of him, the British administrators knew how sharp his pen was; one high official even tried to persuade him to take a good position in government if only to lure him away from his work.

Yangon might have regained peace and quiet, but it was not so at home: Ko Ko would often be deep in discussion and argument with the likes of U Saw[2] and Thakin Nu and other editors concerning plans to put out a paper calling for civil disobedience. At the time, the carpenters had not started work on our apartment, so I could hear all they said while I was putting my baby to sleep.

I noticed that U Saw seemed very eager to be arrested and jailed once civil disobedience began. Many others were also willing to be jailed, but not because they had an agenda to gain political points. I knew that if they went ahead as planned, Ko Ko would surely go to prison. I could see how strongly he felt for both his work and for politics. He told me to go back to Bogalay if he were jailed, and since I did not want to worry Father, I said I preferred to stay in Yangon. Ko Ko would not agree to

---

[1] Indian Civil Service, the elite cadre of top civil servants in British India.

[2] U Saw was a prominent and ambitious politician who was accused of conspiring to assassinate General Aung San and six of his cabinet ministers; the successful attack took place on July 19, 1947. He was found guilty and executed after Myanmar achieved independence in January 1948.

it and kept urging me to go home to my parents, and I could do nothing but write home about it. My younger sister urgently wrote back saying that Father, as soon as he heard the news, had become ill and had been vomiting blood more then ever before, and to please have consideration for our father's state.

I did not know what to do, caught between anxiety for Father, on one hand, and my unwillingness to ask my husband to give up his plan, on the other. After Father's stay at the Yangon General Hospital, Father's doctor, Colonel Morris, had told us that Father would not last in his present condition, but that two things might prolong his life by perhaps two or three years: if we provided him with good, tender care and kept him happy. I was alarmed to imagine that if I went home because my husband had been jailed, it might worsen Father's ill health and send him to his death. I kept remembering how he had whispered to me from his bed, when so weak and ill, telling me about how worried he had been during the racial violence. He loved me so much that it was he, and not my husband, who had tenderly smeared turmeric paste on my face after I gave birth.[3] Ko Ko had often said he had never seen a parent love a child this much before.

I asked Ko Ko, "What if you didn't sign the civil disobedience paper?" and he replied, "Can you even begin to imagine what would happen?"

"Is it really necessary?" I insisted, and he replied, "Of course it is. I've got to do it, there's nothing more to be said," and I felt disheartened.

I sat down to think as soon as he left for work. His going to jail was certainly going to affect Father's health, and it would be my fault, in a way, so for Father's sake I decided Ko Ko must not go to jail. If it were only for myself I would not mind, and if Father were no longer alive, or were quite healthy, I would have easily let Ko Ko do what he wanted. I was very anxious for Father's health, but at the same time I thought that if Ko Ko withdrew from this plan to carry out civil disobedience, he would be seen as someone who did not stand by his convictions, and that people would lose respect for him. This thought burned in my heart. I felt caught in this fire between my father and my husband, and my thoughts whirled in my head. I had never before talked privately to the paper's manager, U Tin, but after Ko Ko left for work, I went to see him. U Tin was surprised to see me. I told him in detail that although I hated to ask my husband to give up his involvement in the civil disobedience plan, I must consider my father, who was gravely ill, and asked him to lend a voice to my pleas. He looked sorry for me and said he would do what he could.

"I'll talk to him," he said.

When Ko Ko came back in the afternoon, I gave him my sister's letter and told him how I went to see U Tin. He did not say a word, but went to lie down on the bed.

I knew exactly what was going on in his mind, and my heart was aching as much as I knew his was, too. I felt disgusted with myself for having done something that conflicted with my desire to support my husband. I thought of the honor I owed my parents, and that I was fulfilling my part, but even that did not ease my pain. My husband neither spoke to me nor looked at me before he left for work, looking deeply upset. I felt worse than before and felt like running after him to tell him to do

---

[3] Applying turmeric paste is a traditional health remedy to keep a woman's complexion clear after birth. Burmese fathers as a rule do not perform such personal things for children, especially daughters.

whatever he wanted, even if Father should die, and caught in the confusion of my mind, I fell into bed and sobbed and sobbed.

He came back around nine, and as I was preparing dinner for him, I heard him call, "Tin Lay!" from the bedroom. I went in, and he said, "Just look in the mirror to see how thin you have become ... don't worry, Tin Lay, this plan may not even arise. Just because of U Saw, we might have to reconsider whether we should do it at all. I feel very sorry for Father, and rest assured I will make sure he lives longer. If I withdraw my name, people will talk, but I cannot care about whatever they might say."

Tears rolled down my cheeks. I was really happy for Father's sake, but the words "whatever people might say" pierced me to the core. Of all the things that I owed my husband, I thought that this debt was something I must repay at any cost. I prayed that during my lifetime I would be able to repay the debt incurred by my husband's effort to shield my father's life, and wrote it down in my diary.

Afterwards, whenever Ko Ko remarked even casually, "I think Ko Nu is upset with me," I wanted to tell everyone that it was me who should be blamed. Now, with this book, I finally have the chance to make it public, that if any censure were to fall, it should be on my head. Ko Ko had always been committed heart and soul to serve his country's needs, and I want to make it clear that he was never one to put his own interests first.

By then rooms had been partitioned off in our apartment, and we had bookcase after bookcase made. He read so much that his eyesight was already bad; although he ate, slept well, and was putting on weight, his eyesight deteriorated further, and his hair turned greyer. Every time he had his hair cut, I kept all the trimmings in paper bags, now packed into my dresser drawer.

In the evenings, I accompanied him to the office as I did before, to help choose the out-of-town news, and, at home, I would make notes on whatever he wanted. I would read the novels slated to be serialized in the paper to see if they were good enough. Some writers were unknowns, but they wrote well, and on my recommendation, one novel titled *Fisherman* by a newcomer was serialized.

By that time, I had became friends with writers and had become acquainted with politicians. Out of all the writers we knew, Ko Ko most liked and admired Saya Gyi P. Monin. When Saya Gyi was planning to go back to his hometown because living expenses in Yangon were so high, Ko Ko was very upset and went to talk to the manager of *Myanmar Alin* and also begged Saya Gyi P. Monin not to leave. Soon P. Monin began writing the "Lay Pway"[4] column at the paper and stayed on in Yangon.

During the time the coalition government[5] was in power, *Myanmar Alin* was able to feature more detailed accounts of parliamentary news than any other paper. My husband also asked me to make sure to file all statements issued by parliament, and I kept all books and notes pertaining to the parliament in a separate bookcase. All the pages of the contents of this bookcase were slashed with his bright red ink strokes, and we began to call this the Bright Red Cupboard.

Ko Ko had an exceptional analytical mind for politics, and he could foresee political moves a few steps ahead. He would often find and suggest leads for political reporter U Sein, and sometimes he would go with him, and I would often go along as well. One night, we accompanied U Sein when he went to interview Prime

---

[4] *Lay pway* means "whirlwind."

[5] *Nyunt-baung asoya,* a government made up of various political parties.

Minister U Pu at his residence. U Sein went in, but we sat in the car in the driveway and laughed with each other about how the prime minister had no idea that the editor who would make short shrift of his pronouncements in the next day's paper was sitting right there in front of his house with his wife. U Pu's household staff probably thought we were friends of U Sein along for a ride.

Not only was news of parliament fully featured in the paper as a result of my husband's diligence, but he also dug out all the behind-the-scenes stories, and thus he had little time to rest or eat well. His health began to suffer, but still he persisted in working hard to be a responsible editor. He was as quick to scent political news as if he were a hunter in a forest that he knew like the back of his hand. The politicians in government who wanted to win him over were usually fooled by his apparent willingness to let them do so, and afterwards he was able to analyze and calculate their steps and write his views, which hit the bull's-eye every time. I filed all such news items under my own heading: "a rare editor."

CHAPTER 25

THE 1938 REBELLION

The 1938 rebellion was a landmark event in our country's history. The moment we heard that one thousand oil field workers from Yenanchaung,[1] led by Thakin Po Hla Gyi, would be marching to Yangon soon, Ko Ko became busier than ever, attending more and more meetings with politicians. When we received the news that in Magwé,[2] Thakin Po Hla Gyi and other leaders, such as Thakin Ba Din, Thakin Ba Maung, Thakin Khin, and three monks, had been arrested, Ko Ko barely came home for his meals. I filed all his published comments and analyses on the strike, including his severe condemnations of the coalition government. I was determined to write a book one day titled "My Husband," and for that I had been collecting all published materials, as well as my own notes on his verbal comments concerning the various situations. As he became more busy, I, too, was fully occupied with filing material for future reference.

The Do Bama Asi-ayon, led by Thakin Than Tun, Thakin Soe,[3] and Thakin Hla Maung, declared that people were needed to lead the strike force, and many young men became interested. It was a time when Ko Ko was writing articles in the paper to inflame this interest. Various organizations and political groups held a meeting in a rest house at the foot of the Shwedagon Pagoda to discuss how they would welcome the strike force into Yangon, and I went along with Ko Ko, who was busy discussing matters with the politicians.

The organizers in Magwé had elected new leaders to march with the strike force to Yangon, and the University Students' Union president, Ko Ba Hein, who was in Magwé at the time, held a rally and gave a speech to the strikers. The police had arrived with a warrant to arrest him, and on that day Ko Ko was so busy responding to this news he drank more tea than ever before.

"This government is digging its own grave!" he muttered in glee, quaffing down mug after mug of tea the whole day and writing furiously at his desk. I could not make out why he was behaving like this. In Magwé, the government had sent out mounted police with batons to sweep in among the nonviolent and unarmed

---

[1] Yenanchaung is a town in central Myanmar where crude oil seeped out of the ground, triggering the start of the colonial-era Myanmar oil industry, which was largely destroyed at the start of the Second World War. Prior to colonialization, the wells had been leased by the Burmese king's government to indigenous, hereditary operators known as *Twinsa*. "Yenanchaung" can be literally translated as "smelly water creek."

[2] A town in central Myanmar.

[3] Another communist who later led a faction separate from that of Thakin Than Tun. Thakin Soe was the major author of pre-war socialist and communist literature in Myanmar; he translated a number of Marxist-Leninist terms into Burmese using many Buddhist philosophical concepts. Unlike Thakin Than Tun and General Aung San, he refused to work with the Japanese prior to and during the Second World War, arguing that Japanese fascism was worse that British colonialism.

demonstrators, beating them up and arresting hundreds. He featured the full news, and he wrote such strong comments that the public could clearly see the divide between the rulers and the ruled.

The Do Bama Asi-ayon issued statements, but it was *Myanmar Alin*'s news that reached the readership in all towns, and with his pen Ko Ko managed to call to arms people from all over the country to support this national association. The Yangon police kept a close watch on all politicians, like a paddy bird waiting for fish, and as Ko Ko was deeply involved, I was worried that he, too, might be arrested.

When student leaders were arrested, Ko Ko wrote so cleverly to inflame the resentment of the student body at large that I could not help rereading what he had written and, as usual, kept all his writings on file. I would always remember the pleased expression on his face when he looked over at me from his desk and, raising his pen to make a point, said, "Wait and see, it won't be long before the students rise up."

On the night of December 13, when Vice President Ko Hla Shwe of the University Students' Union was elected president, the union headquarters[4] was packed inside and out, and the air resounded with thunderous applause and cries of support. I can say it was the night that students wholeheartedly and en masse stood up to join the political movement.

When the next day's issue of *Myanmar Alin* featured the speeches made at the Students' Union, and headlines of the news of the event were featured in very large fonts, I can still recall how it shook the country. I asked Ko Ko anxiously if it was just the students out there or was anyone supporting them, and he smiled and nodded, yes, there were supporters. The next day a conference of all Yangon students was held.

The coalition government continued to issue new orders to restrict the students, and while Ko Ko himself was not on the stage with the politicians who were loudly denouncing the government, he was writing strong condemnations and chipping away at the stability of the rulers with every word from his pen. The coalition government had come into power by promising to give each peasant five acres of land, and with these attacks on the students everyone lost faith in their promises and felt only disgust. Ko Ko used to say that governments rule not over but under newspapers and that a powerful paper could bring down a government; how true were his words, I thought.

It was the night of December 20. We walked back to the paper around eight in the evening. On the way, I asked him about what the students would do, as rumors had been circulating that they would be doing something definitive soon. "They'll have to do something," he replied, but said nothing more.

Around ten that night, "Tet Hpon Gyi" U Thein Pe[5] came to talk to Ko Ko. To give them some privacy I went to stand by the window. They whispered for a time, and then U Thein Pe left hurriedly. Ko Ko went on editing, the copyboys kept running up to ask for copies, and we did not have a chance to talk. Only when almost all the copies had been sent down to the press did he turn to me and ask

---

[4] This landmark building was destroyed by dynamite by the military on July 7, 1962, during student demonstrations protesting the plans of General Ne Win to halt student political activity. General Ne Win had announced this plan following his coup d'état of March 2, 1962, which abolished the multiparty democratic government.

[5] U Chit Maung's friend, who had written a novel on the "modern monk," *Tet Hpon Gyi*, and thus was afterwards known by this name. Later he took the pen name Thein Pe Myint.

softly, "Do you really want to know what the students are up to?" I nodded my head several times and leaned close to him.

"I told Ko Thein Pe that the students should surround the Secretariat," he said. "They'll do that early tomorrow morning."

"But what if the government finds out before morning?" I asked in alarm.

"I told them to be very careful about keeping it secret," he said. "They will bring all the students out as if to march in a demonstration only, and once they're gathered in town, they will surround the Secretariat."

"But the government won't stand for it … remember how in Magwé they sent out mounted police to beat them up."

"I did warn them about that, but there are many students willing to risk their lives. This is the only way to shake the country, shake the world. If they surround the Secretariat, no one in government would be able to go to work, and the outside world would be cut off from here, as no news would get out. There's no action stronger than this. It's been decided that the political situation needed a new impetus, and this is the only way to do it."

While we whispered together, Shwe Pein Thaung, a writer friend, dropped in, and we could not say anything more. What a plan Ko Ko had hatched! I was longing for the next morning to see the results. That night we came back home late from the paper and talked about politics deep into the night. I could not sleep, worrying that the plans might be discovered, but Ko Ko slept peacefully. We both got up early the next morning.

While he was reading the papers, I changed, determined to go out and witness the events.

"It's still early," he called out to me, "the students won't be here yet."

"I think it's better to go wait for them," I said.

"Are you going alone?" he asked, so I said I would take someone with me.

As soon as he left, I went next door to Dr. U Kyee Myint's apartment, and, with his wife, I took a horse cab towards the Secretariat. Near the *Thuriya* newspaper building, we came upon a large group of students marching towards us, so we told the cabby to stop a while at the corner of Sparks Street.[6] Led by one among them, the students sat down in front of the gates of the Secretariat. We had the cab drive all around the Secretariat, which covered one whole block, and I saw with my own eyes how disciplined and calm the demonstrators were. I was happy that my anxiety of the previous night came to nothing, happy to see the students successful in their effort. We looked on for a while and came home. When Ko Ko came back for lunch, I told him what I had seen, and even as we were speaking someone came with the news that the students were being beaten up.

"I have to go," Ko Ko said, "do you want to go too, Tin Lay?"

"Of course," I replied immediately. Ko Ko left, and I went with Ko Ohn Myint, and as we arrived in front of *Thuriya* paper again, there was such a crowd that we had to push our way to the front. The police were dragging away the students and hitting them with batons. The crowds looking on screamed abuse at the police, their voices so filled with anger and hatred that it chilled my blood. As I saw the students falling under the blows, the relief I had felt earlier this morning was replaced by such despair I could not even voice it. I even wanted to bash up a few policemen myself. When the mounted police charged towards the crowds and pushed us back, Ko Ohn

---

[6] Sparks Street has since been renamed Bo Aung Kyaw Street.

Myint and I were carried along with the crowd. We could not push our way through the people, so we returned home in dejection.

I was highly agitated and could not sit still the whole afternoon. I wanted so much to go over to the paper and longed for evening to arrive. I tried to read, but I had no interest in the printed words. Dr. Kyee Myint's wife came over to ask me about the beatings, and I gave her a full report.

Near dusk, I heard my husband's steps, which I knew well, on the stairs. Tonight they were leaden steps, slower than usual. As soon as I opened the front door, I saw the look of pained anxiety on his face and, pretending not to notice, asked him nothing so as to offer him some peace. He sat making a list of the wounded, and then handed to me the photos taken at the scene that he had carried home between the pages of an English magazine. I asked him if these photos were going to be published, and he said, yes, of course, but to keep them hidden for the time being, and he told me all that had happened. Then someone came with an urgent message from the paper, and after he left I went to put the photos on the bed.

I watched him from the veranda walking towards his office, and I knew how upset he must be at the carnage. By eight at night he had not returned, and I knew that he would be very busy at the paper. I kept going out to the veranda, hoping to see him, and suddenly I saw many cars pulling up to his building. I realized at once why he had brought home the photos. I ran to wrap them up in a piece of clothing, and then I hurried over to Dr. Kyee Myint's apartment and asked him to hide them. Then Dr. Kyee Myint accompanied me downstairs to use the phone at the Dagon Store, from where I called *Myanmar Alin*'s manager, U Tin, at his house to tell him the police were at the newspaper office. I went back upstairs and watched from my apartment with a fast-beating heart until the police left. After a while, I saw Ko Ko hurrying home. I ran downstairs to meet him, and he told me, as I suspected, that they had come to seize the photos. I told him they were safe at Dr. Kyee Myint's place, and his eyes lit up as he said, "Good for you!"

I returned with him to the office, and we came home only at dawn after the fourth printing of the paper, bringing one copy back with us.

The breaking news of the death of the student Ko Aung Kyaw shook the country. We felt so miserable about it, more than if a blood relation had died. Ko Ko tried to comfort me, saying that there was nothing anyone could do. "The strike succeeded much more than expected, and we'll honor Ko Aung Kyaw and share our merits with him.[7] He died a noble death and our country owes a lot to him. We can only hope our deaths will be as honorable."

At home, I offered a *Soon Kyway* ceremony[8] on Ko Aung Kyaw's behalf, and Ko Ko was pleased with that. I went to the funeral, but the crowd was so big I could not go near the tomb and came back very disappointed. People thought the students were following U Saw's advice in surrounding the Secretariat, and I felt so miserable about it all that I told no one but close friends about Ko Ko's role.

When the students decided to go on a hunger strike, Ko Ko remarked that it was a wrong move, so I noted down in my diary that he had not agreed with it. Just the day before the coalition government fell, I was at the market and heard a shopkeeper call out, "Get a pair of Dr. Ba Maw slippers!" Startled, I turned around to see the

---

[7] Sharing merits even with the dead is part of Buddhist belief.

[8] Offering food to monks before noon and arranging to have them recite sutras and prayers.

seller holding out a pair of leather slippers with white straps. I told Ko Ko what I had seen, saying,

"I wonder if Dr. Ba Maw will ever rise again in politics, because the students pray for him to die, the people pray for him to die, and now even slippers are being named after him."[9] Ko Ko said that in politics things never run just one course.

"Right now, Dr. Ba Maw may be under people's feet, but in time he might be over their heads again. At one time in England, chancellors rose and fell like hot air balloons: now Gladstone's up and then Peel's up and once again Gladstone and then Disraeli and once again Peel. In politics, it's not always ascent or descent. In Britain, even if the populace comes around throwing stones at your house, you may well be voted in again. If you are prepared to survive the fall, you never lose in politics."

After U Saw's government came to power, one day we were out in a horse cab shopping, talking politics the whole way. As we approached the Iron Market,[10] I asked my husband teasingly, "Now when shall I see you as a political leader, Ko Ko?"

"Don't ever wish to see me in that role," he replied.

"Why?"

"There are far too many in this country who want to be political leaders and too few who want to be editors. It's easy to be a political leader, Tin Lay, but to be a successful editor is not as easy. In a country you need good, responsible leaders, and it's as important to have good, responsible editors. If you want a good government, you need to have good editors."

"So you are an editor because of politics and not because of interest in literature, wouldn't you say, Ko Ko?"

"I must focus on politics as long as we are not independent. My politics is not about power or position. I prefer to be a social reformer rather than to aim for political power."

"But you have studied so much about administration and government, if you don't use this knowledge in governance, where then?"

"Well, I will make use of it, and I *am* making use of it. There are two ways to use knowledge, Tin Lay … to do it yourself or to work behind the scenes."

"So which do you prefer?"

"I prefer to work behind the scenes so that there will be benefits, but no one will know who is responsible. Day by day, I realize this is the most urgently needed way of doing things. Behind the politicians there should be someone who is a responsible person, who has a good mind and can reason out things carefully and calmly. The public need not know he exists; the public need not applaud him. The public need not know what he is doing, and the government need not know what he is doing. He should be giving advice and guidance to good political leaders from the sidelines so that the leaders can remain straightforward and do the right thing. His main responsibility is to keep the politicians from making mistakes. In other countries, the politicians are out there raising their fists and talking loudly, but behind them there are brilliant minds that no one realizes exist, working out everything so work gets done smoothly and faster. Here, no one even considers being such a person; as soon as individuals enter politics, they all want to get up on the stage, and the moment

---

[9] To have one's name associated with footwear (or animals, especially dogs) is a great insult.

[10] "Iron Market," the literal translation of *Than Zay*, is located on Lanmadaw Street. It sold drygoods and was replaced by a new building on the same site in the 1990s.

they step on stage they think they have achieved fame and that their work is done. Tin Lay, you'll never, ever, see me go up on a stage."

"But if the advice is not taken and nothing good happens, what can anyone do?"

"Well, you have to try to make it happen."

"But if the advice is not followed at all?"

"We still have to try."

"But if they refuse to follow the advice at all, not at all?"

"We have to show them the way ..."

"So then, how many years is that going to take? Don't you think you'd get things done faster if you did it yourself? Just watch, one day you'll be up there in the forefront."

"How can you say such a thing? I keep telling you I won't be at there out front."

"You say so now, but one day you'll be pushed there."

"Pushed? Who will push me?"

"The politics you have studied so hard all your life, Ko Ko, that'll push you."

"Now, I must disagree with you here, Tin Lay."

"Wait and see, Ko Ko. This Iron Market will be witness to what I say: that one day you will be at the forefront as a great political leader, respected by all."

"So, I am to get up on the stage?" he laughed in reply. He shook his head at me as if in denial.

I said what I did not because I wanted it to be so but because I knew it would happen and because it should. Every single day I had watched him study education, administration, health, economics, finance, religious affairs, internal affairs, and trade, and I knew for sure that one day these studies would be of use to him in a certain suitable position.

CHAPTER 26

UPCOUNTRY

Winter turned to summer, and then the monsoon came again. Our baby son, who was not yet a year old, suddenly took sick and passed away. This was the first tragedy we faced in our marriage; we could neither get over it nor find comfort, and it remained a constant pain in our hearts.

We held a *Soon Kyway* ceremony at our house on behalf of our son, and although Father was too ill to come up to Yangon, he wrote a long letter of consolation and suggested that Ko Ko take leave from work and that we both should travel. He said that if we wanted to, we should come see him as quickly as possible. Saturday was a day off from work, so we left for Bogalay by Friday night's ship. We told Father we would like to travel upcountry, and he gave us enough money to see us through.

The day before we left Yangon, Ko Ko came home from the paper with two tickets on an Irrawaddy Flotilla Company[1] steamer for our return trip, each ticket for two persons. I was wondering why it should be two tickets, but Ko Ko explained that the manager had given him tickets for two in upper class and two in second class so that we could choose whichever we wanted.

"Then, Ko Ko, give back the second-class tickets. We won't need them."

"How do you know, Tin Lay? Maybe we might need them later?"

"Do you think so? Then leave it, Ko Ko."

We were going up by train, and Ko Ko wrote ahead to make sure he would be meeting *Myanmar Alin* reporters at every stop. I told him that I had heard of the Governor having a separate carriage reserved for his library when he traveled by train and said I wished we could have one too, for him, and Ko Ko thought I was teasing him. But in fact, as he and books could never be apart, I really did want to bring enough books to fill a carriage.

Along the way, he met with the reporters who came to the station during stops, and Ko Ko asked them in detail about the political parties in town, the nature of the townspeople, the economy, society, and crime rates in order to gather as many facts as possible during each stop. At one station, he asked the reporter how many businesses there were owned by immigrants such as Indians and Chinese, and when the man did not know, told him to find out and send the data to him at the paper.

As the train neared Mandalay,[2] he remarked on how much the country owed the Crown Prince Kanaung.[3] Ko Ko said that G. E. Harvey, who wrote our country's

---

[1] The Irrawaddy Flotilla Company (IFC), based in Glasgow, Scotland, began services in 1865 on the Irrawaddy River (now spelled "Ayeyarwaddy") with four steamers and three barges.

[2] Mandalay was the last capital of the last Myanmar monarchy, the Konbaung dynasty.

[3] Crown Prince Kanaung was the son and designated heir of the second-to-last king Mindon (r. 1853–1878). Prince Kanaung had tried to modernize Myanmar, but he was assassinated in 1866 by jealous and resentful nephews, who fled for sanctuary to the British and the French.

history, was deliberately misleading students and future generations when he wrote that the British took over "Burma" not to destroy it but to save it.

"But the English public did not like it that the British government representatives were using all sorts of excuses to colonize countries," he continued. "They held protests, and they condemned the way wars were fought. Fitch wrote that the East India Company was greedy to claim whatever they could lay their hands on. Then, their leaders gave the excuse that the Third Anglo-Burman War[4] of 1885 happened because the Burmese were 'unfair.' Even the English people and their historians knew that was a lie. Randolph Churchill admitted as much, and the writer of the book *Friends of Burma* said so quite openly. Their idea of teaching such rubbish in our schools is really a plan to mislead us."

"So what exactly did Randolph Churchill say?"

"That the British government, fearing the influences of the French on the Burmese court, annexed the country despite the will of their own parliament."

"And what about Harvey?" I asked.

"He said the British annexed our country 'not to destroy what was there but to fulfill what is not there.' We have to consider whether, during the past fifty-four years of British rule, they really did as he said. They *did* fulfill needs, but we have to remember it was more for their own sakes than with any goodwill for us."

"You often said, Ko Ko, that the British have destroyed many things since they arrived here … what exactly were they?"

"Yes, we have to address this, too. Most of the students and clerks serving under the British seem to think that there was no progress of any kind during our king's time. Actually, the people under the monarchy had a more complete life. They had the traditional skills that are now lost, such as knowing the scriptures well and being well-versed in classical poetry and literature, astrology, herbal medicine, and astronomy, having skill in traditional weapons such as bow and lances, and skills in carpentry, carving, architecture, and blacksmithing, skills in horse riding, elephant training, et cetera … all the arts as listed as the eighteen manly arts. Apart from that, they knew about the use of organic dyes from barks, roots, flowers, and plants, and how to spin and weave by hand, and how to make pots, whether glazed or terracotta. Also, the arts of working in gold, bronze, and iron, cutting and polishing gems, carving figurines or floral motifs in wood or ivory or marble, and making fine basketry and lacquer wares. In the old days, they worked in these professions all over the country, but now such skills are dying out. These were good productive skills that should be upgraded, but they are almost gone by now, so the government can't even keep them alive. Most people nowadays wish only to learn English to serve as clerks and have forgotten that we had traditional professions. Under Prince Kanaung's direction, we had the telegraph, and factories producing glassware, bombs, and weaponry. We produced carpets, silks, and velvet, we had our own mint, and as for foreign languages, people learned to speak English, French, Italian, Chinese, and Hindi. Now where are the fifty or so factories we used to have? What

---

[4] In November 1885, the Myanmar king was exiled to India, and the British annexed the entire country to India following this Third Anglo-Burman "War," in which British gun ships traveled up the river, apparently bringing exiled Prince Nyaung Yan to take Thibaw's place, and thus arrived in Mandalay almost unchallenged. In fact, the "prince" they carried on board and prominently displayed, posed in the bow of the leading ship, was a clerk dressed in royal costume. Unknown to the subjects of the Konbaung dynasty, Nyaung Yan had died a few months earlier in British India.

would the British answer to that? They know we are fiercely nationalistic, and that is what they fear. Think what a bitter pill it is to swallow that they say they came to save us. I feel so sad for the young students having to learn the British lies about our history. I want to write a book."

"Good, Ko Ko, make sure to write it when you have the time. What will the title be?"

"Title ... ?" He sat thinking, a blue pencil in one hand and a copy of *A Burmese Arcady* in the other, one finger marking the pages. He gazed at the passing landscape of paddy fields and turning to the back of the book wrote on an empty page,

1. What annexation has brought
2. As things are and shall be
3. Is this Liberty?
4. What then is Liberty?
5. Will democracy bring Liberty?
6. Democracy or Revolution?
7. How to make a Revolution?

He showed me the above outline and said, "This is what the book will be. I only need a title."

Later he decided to call it "Fight for Liberty," but he could not finish it, and so no student ever read his views.

When we arrived in Mandalay, we were met by my husband's good friend U Ko Ko Latt, reporter and agent for *Myanmar Alin*, writer Mya Myo Lwin,[5] and U Kywe. They wanted us to stay with them, but we went to stay at our friend U Hla's house. All through our stay in Mandalay, these good friends made certain we saw every sight and were so hospitable that we felt both joy and embarrassment.

We climbed Mandalay Hill to pray at the pagoda on the top, and we toured the old palace. As we walked around the palace pavilions, Ko Ko told me details of royal life, and seeing the fifty destroyed factories around the old city that Ko Ko had mentioned, I felt desolate, especially when I saw the glass pillars in the palace that had been produced by one factory. Before I was married, I had visited Mandalay twice, but only now, with Ko Ko explaining things to me, did I feel I was seeing it for the first time.

Ko Ko was deeply interested in history and had a deep respect for old traditions and culture. He would often say that the value of a people could be gauged from their history. What he said inside the palace made me realize that he was not only admiring the skills of the artisans who built the palace, but he was also expounding on the lifestyle of the past, the people's attitudes, and the nationalistic spirit. "So that is why he feels so strongly about conserving old cultures," I thought to myself.

We went to see U Bein Bridge[6] in Amarapura,[7] where our friends took photos of us, and we traveled to Sagaing, and Ko Ko compared for us the Sagaing Bridge,[8] made of iron, and the U Bein Bridge, made of discarded palace timbers, and pointed

---

[5] Mya Myo Lwin was a well-known Burmese writer of fiction.

[6] A mile-long wooden bridge that spans a man-made lake, Taungthaman.

[7] An old royal capital, as are Sagaing, Inwa, and Shwebo.

[8] Also know as the Ava (Inwa) Bridge, until recently it was the only road and rail bridge crossing the Ayarwaddy (Irrawaddy) River, located south of Mandalay.

out that they were equally durable. We visited the pagodas of Sagaing and the Old People's Home in Mingun founded by a nun, and then we traveled on to Shwebo. There we went first to honor King Alaungpaya's[9] memory at his tomb.

I thought I would write a detailed account of all that my husband said on this trip and took notes to copy in full in my diary at home. We took an Irrawaddy Flotilla steamer to Inwa,[10] bringing with us Mya Myo Lwin and U Kywe, and so the spare tickets came in handy. We visited the Lawka Tharahpu Pagoda, and when we were looking up at the place where British soldiers had climbed the spire of the pagoda to signal with lights, I saw Ko Ko grit his teeth in fury, and knew how deeply he felt this insult to religion.

I gazed across to Mandalay and thought, "When will we be free?"

We saw the ancient monastery in Inwa where Dhammazedi and Dhamma Pala[11] studied. We took a horse carriage to go around Inwa, and I shall never forget the driver, Maung Khway, who was quite knowledgeable about history and who accurately and rapidly gave us detailed information on each site. We saw everything: the moat, the old walls, the old city, and if we passed by slabs of stone inscriptions, Ko Ko would stand there unmoving, reading every word. We wanted to go on to Bhamo, but not wanting to be away from Father too long, we returned home by steamship. Our friends saw us off, and we told them repeatedly how grateful we were for their kindness.

In the upper-class accommodations, there were only the two of us and two English gentlemen from the Burmah Oil Company. I complained that seven days on the ship would be so boring. As soon as the ship sailed, I flopped face down on my bunk and began to write in my notebook. I kept putting questions to my husband about things I could not recall, and he would answer as he read a book. "What are you going to do with all this, Tin Lay?" he asked, so I just told him to wait and see. He had no idea I wanted to write about him: I would read whatever he wrote, but he never read anything of mine unless I asked him to.

I got up to take a bath at sunset and, as usual, as I had to do in Mandalay, urged him to have his. He would not leave his book, so I told him that we would be dining with foreigners tonight, and he got up reluctantly. Afterwards, he insisted on wearing comfortable old clothes and looked in horror at the *pinni* jacket and silk *pasoe* I had put out for him. I was in despair and declared that he could go alone to dine, as I would not be joining him.

"Why not, Tin Lay? Of course you have to eat."

"We'll be dining as guests of the captain, so you can't wear these old things, and you must wear a jacket to look respectable."

He grumbled that he was losing all his liberties and remained stubborn, so without a word more to him I began to put on make-up and to dress in my best from head to toe. Then I turned to him and said, "Now we'll certainly look good together won't we? Why bother wearing a shirt at all? You should take it off and go in your undershirt."

---

[9] King Alaungpaya founded the Third Myanmar Empire and the Konbaung Dynasty.

[10] The old capital, known as Ava by the British.

[11] Dhammazedi and Dhamma Pala were two monks of the Mon race of the south who lived in upper Myanmar in the fifteenth century and served as religious mentors to a Mon queen who later escaped Inwa and ruled in Bago (Pegu) as the great Queen Shin Saw Pu.

Looking at me, he smiled and said, "Well, you look grander than at our wedding, as if you're off to a party. Out of consideration for you, Madam, I will change," and he changed into the clothes I had put out for him. I smiled to myself.

The captain sat at the head of the table, and he introduced us to the two English men. They, too, were dressed for dinner. Ko Ko sat with great dignity, and silently ate his dinner. I wondered if the others would think he knew not a word of English, as he sat there eating whatever the steward put in front of him and I alone carried the conversation. The gentleman sitting directly opposite asked me if I were Burmese, and I said yes, pure Burmese. He said that Western dress suited women only if the person were well-formed but that Burmese dress complements anyone, plump or slender, and that the style and designs were elegant and beautiful. I glanced sideways at Ko Ko and smiled at him discreetly.

"The dresses worn in court were different from what we wear nowadays," I told them. "The royal costumes were more beautiful and intricate." One of the English gentlemen described to his companion the court dress he had once seen and marveled at the gold and silver embroidery.

They asked me where we were returning from, and I told them that my husband had some leave and that we were traveling upcountry. Bit by bit, I managed to bring Ko Ko into the conversation, and as soon as he got on the subject of British rule, Ko Ko talked at length. The English listened with interest to his views. The captain excused himself, as he had to look after the ship, but the two gentlemen sat on asking my husband questions until late into the night. They asked him where he had stayed longest in Europe during his student days, and he replied that he had never traveled north beyond Mandalay, let alone outside of Myanmar.

During the whole trip, he read book after book lying in his bunk and often remarked to me that it was most pleasant to read on a ship. He only went out for meals. When we reached Thayet, we asked permission from the captain and went ashore for an hour, sightseeing all over the town.

At teatime Ko Ko complained privately to me that he could not get as much tea as he wanted and that he longed to sit at a proper teashop again. At Minbu, the ship sailed away before he returned from meeting a reporter on shore, and I hurriedly sent a steward to tell the captain, worried that we would leave Ko Ko behind. As the ship turned back slowly and again docked at the jetty, I saw no sign of my husband and was wondering if I should go after him when the captain called me over. He pointed to my husband sitting immersed in a newspaper at a teashop near the jetty and, laughing hard, hurried ashore himself to get Ko Ko back on board. I had to explain to the English passengers about his habit of sitting at teashops.

I had never been to Pyay[12] before, so when we docked there I suggested we disembark to spend some time there and then take the train to Yangon. This we did, and Dagon Shwe Hmyar,[13] who was in Pyay, took us all around. We came back by train, and when we arrived in Yangon, Ko Ko wrote in *Myanmar Alin* under his pen name, "Shwe Lin Yone," an article titled "Ruined Cities" about the ancient capitals we had visited in Upper Myanmar. Mya Myo Lwin also wrote about our upcountry trip.

---

[12] Pyay is a central Myanmar town and site of the ancient capital of the Pyu race (second through ninth centuries). It is known as Prome by the British.

[13] Dagon Shwe Hmyar was a famous writer.

I told Ko Ko I would like to thank the *Myanmar Alin* manager, U Tin, for the trip, and he agreed, and we hosted a dinner for U Tin and his wife at the Continental Hotel. I had only once talked briefly to U Tin before, but at the dinner I found him to be a very pleasant and honorable person, which was apparent as soon as one saw him. U Tin's wife was a gracious and gentle lady with a good heart. She spoke softly and was very charming. We felt we were friends, and afterwards they invited us to call on them.

CHAPTER 27

BIRTH OF *JOURNAL KYAW*

Ko Ko continued working from eight in the morning to one in the afternoon, then from three to eight at night and again after dinner from nine to one or two in the morning. One day, he said something strange. It was strange as well as being most welcome, for it was something I had been longing to hear since we first got married.

"Tin Lay, U Tin told me that because *Myanmar Alin* is now a public company, some shareholding directors do not like me. He advised me to begin doing something on my own. I think he said this because he was worried about me."

"Long may U Tin live and high may he rise," I blurted out, happy at the thought of being free at last.

Ko Ko continued, "I wonder if U Saw is behind this: he is really afraid of what I may write. As he's now prime minister, he would not want *Myanmar Alin* to get at him. I can't be sure he did not pull a few strings."

Ko Ko kept on thinking aloud about his suspicions, but I was so happy I was not at all interested. In my mind I was already seeing "our" printing presses working at a great speed inside "our" publishing house. I told him to resign immediately so he could begin working on our own newspaper, but he kept on insisting stubbornly that he could not leave before they fired him, so my dreams of a daily faded into one of a weekly journal.

We thought hard about what to call it. Ko Ko calculated the letters according to astrology, while I could not be bothered with all that but decided that our journal would be better than everyone else's—in fact the best—and chose the name *Journal Kyaw*.[1] My husband did more calculations and said this name would last long but asked me if it did not sound too vain?

With the blue and red pencil he always had in his pocket, I sketched out on a piece of paper the words "Journal Kyaw U Chit Maung." He took the paper from me and said, "But I'm still working for *Myanmar Alin*. I don't think I should have my name as editor here. We'll have to use another name."

I asked him again to resign, somewhat resentful at this stubbornness, but he still shook his head. He was so adamant about it that for the time being we decided I would be named the editor. I took away the piece of paper with the name "Journal Kyaw U Chit Maung" written in red and blue and pasted it on the cover of my diary. Inside, I wrote a dated entry describing how *Journal Kyaw* came into being.

To inform Father and to borrow the capital necessary, we left for Bogalay on the night before one of my husband's days off. I was exhilarated by the thought that something I had been longing for and planning for was about to bear fruit. I was

---

[1] *Kyaw* means "fame" or "better." The English name for the paper was "The Weekly Thunderer," although the paper was published in Burmese, "just to remind the British that there was something thundering at them," according to U Ohn Myint, close friend of the couple, who spoke with the translator.

convinced that, although not many people might have heard of Myanmar Alin U Chit Maung, many more were going to know Journal Kyaw U Chit Maung. With each thought, I felt untold gratitude towards U Tin for bringing it about.

As soon as Father heard we were going to set up our own business, he declared, "It will definitely be successful, my daughter, as much as you wished."[2] He was very happy and said that I would surely succeed because I did not have the gentleness of most women and that my strength of character would see me through anything I set my mind to do.

When we returned from Bogalay, we put out an advertisement in the paper announcing the debut of *Journal Kyaw,* and the immediate response totaled orders for 3,000 copies. When we informed newsagents outside of Yangon about it, the letters asking for copies far exceeded what we expected.

When Ko Ko was at work, I sat at a desk at home writing receipts for the money and replies to the newsagents. We had no building yet where we could set up the presses, so for the time being we thought we would pay the *Myanmar Alin* to print the journal for us.

Ko Ko was working at three jobs at once, his pen never out of his hand: writing news for the *Myanmar Alin* newspaper and articles for the *Myanmar Alin Magazine* and for our journal. He wrote the editorials for *Journal Kyaw,* as well as the fiction, the political news and analyses, and he even translated articles. The whole paper was entirely his handiwork. If he did not have his pen in hand, his head would be deep in a book as usual.

As for me, I was the business manager, I was the clerk, and I was the office boy, and I was, of course, the one to wrap and post the journals. I was doing the job of five people. Ko Ohn Myint wanted to help, but as he was already working as editor for the *Toh Tet Yay*[3] paper, he could not get permission to take on another job, so I battled on alone. As the workload increased, we hired a clerk, and together with him I continued working at home. It was only because of my past trips every evening to *Myanmar Alin* and all I had learned there that I could do my work successfully, and for that, I am forever in *Myanmar Alin*'s debt.

The journal came out sometimes with my name listed as editor, sometimes with Ko Ohn Myint's, but U Chit Maung's name had not yet appeared in it. How Journal Kyaw U Chit Maung finally got this name was as follows: one night, my husband came home at about eight o'clock and, soon after, editor Ko Saw Oo followed. Ko Saw Oo told him that the government was insisting that the news of a bomb exploding near the steamer *Adamson* was incorrect and that government officials were asking for their own denial to be published the next day in *Myanmar Alin*. Ko Ko said that the news came from a reliable source, that he had full confidence in it, and that for a paper to print anything bordering on a retraction would damage the image of the paper.

"I have no confidence in any explanations from the government," Ko Ko said. He told Ko Saw Oo there was no need to publish the government's denial.

Instantly, there was uproar; apart from U Tin, there was another managing director of *Myanmar Alin* who insisted that the denial be printed. Ko Ko said that the paper might belong to the investors but that, for the sake of the readers, he would neither deny the truth nor hide any news, and he refused to print a retraction. He

---

[2] The author's father has by now recovered slightly from his illness.

[3] In English, "Progress."

went back to the paper that night without having his dinner, and when he did not return well after midnight I began to wonder what was happening. There was no other big news at the time; only this explosion. I wondered whether he was late because of his disagreement with the management of the paper. He came back very late.

"Was there something important going on?" I asked him at the door.

"I suppose so, Tin Lay," he said tiredly.

Only then did we have our dinner, and during the meal he merely asked about the progress with our journal and about letters from out-of-town agents. I asked him why he was late, and he said, "I'll tell you later."

After dinner, we went into the living room and sat down.

"I had words with the publishers," he said.

"Was it because of the ship?"

"Of course. The director insisted I publish the government's statement, and I refused. Thuriya U Pu Galay was there, too. I said that as long as I am executive editor, something like this is not going to appear in my paper. They may think I'm being difficult, but actually it's for the sake of the paper, you know."

"So, what happened, Ko Ko?"

"Well, there we were, one side saying yes, the other no, and the typesetters not knowing what to do."

"And then?"

"They said that the editor must follow the orders of the directors. When I said no, they said in that case I should resign."

"Well, then, Ko Ko, you resigned then and there, didn't you?"

"No I didn't, I told them to fire me. I'll leave only when they fire me."

"My goodness, Ko Ko, how faithful you are, how loyal! So why didn't they fire you?"

Just then someone knocked on the front door, and it was the night watchman of the paper, bringing a letter signed by the director, stating that "Chit Maung"[4] had been fired this very night. As the tone of the letter was very rude, I would have been furious if my husband had received it under any other circumstances, but now, I felt like honoring the director with a threefold *kadaw*. As long as Ko Ko was working at *Myanmar Alin*, he could not assume the title of editor at *Journal Kyaw*, and now finally he could let the country know he was the chief editor of our publication. I did not care about the manner in which Ko Ko was allowed to leave *Myanmar Alin*, I was just happy that my wish had been fulfilled. Since that day, I have considered this director a true benefactor: because of him, Ko Ko would be known as Journal Kyaw U Chit Maung.

Ko Ko meanwhile was feeling sorry for U Tin, saying he would be upset at the news. We learned later that U Tin had tried his best to persuade the others not to let Ko Ko go.

The next day, not only *Myanmar Alin* but all other papers, both Burmese and English, featured the announcement of the *Myanmar Alin* directors that "Chit Maung" had been fired, and Ko Ko sat reading everything with interest. I saw with fury in the proof pages of *Journal Kyaw* that in the masthead he had written "Editor: Chit Maung," and I asked him why it could not be "U Chit Maung." He replied calmly it was good enough as it was.

---

[4] Not to use the prefix "U" is very rude.

"Now, Ko Ko, my name as business manager appears as Daw Tin Hlaing, and you, yours appears as Chit Maung. Do that, yes, keep on doing things like that, go on being humble, and so that's why they dared insult you by putting the announcements in all the papers. Well, editor, can't you be nice to *this* business manager, too?"

He laughed heartily at that and said, "Yes, Madam Manager, please do as you wish," so I changed it to "U Chit Maung."

I insisted that he write an editorial stating that he had left *Myanmar Alin* and would henceforth be in charge of *Journal Kyaw*, but he wrote it in a way that would not cast any slur on *Myanmar Alin*'s image. If I had not been there, he would not have written it at all, and people all over the country, guided by the announcements of the *Myanmar Alin* directors, would have thought that Ko Ko was at fault. I found him amazingly free of vindictiveness or resentment.

The next day, he went to *Myanmar Alin* to hand over his duties to another editor. In the same way that Ko Ko felt a great attachment to *Myanmar Alin*, so did U Tin feel strong attachments for us. He helped in any way he could to make our business run smoothly and always had the time to answer my questions with patience.

Soon after Ko Ko left *Myanmar Alin*, Ko Saw Oo also left and came to work for us. The two editors, two clerks, and one business manager, me, worked in our apartment. While we were all of us busy with *Journal Kyaw* affairs, suddenly the government closed down *Myanmar Alin* for publishing an article titled "The ICS." [Indian Civil Service] Ko Ko trembled with rage at this and immediately wrote the following strongly worded editorial in the *Journal Kyaw* about it.

Why Was the Myanmar Alin Closed Down?

We must put some hard questions to the government, which we expect to be answered clearly.

According to the order by the government, the Myanmar Alin *is no longer allowed to be published, and it was closed down suddenly on November 28, 1940. The reason given by the secretary of the Internal Affairs and Defense Department was that the November 26 issue of* Myanmar Alin *contained an article titled "The ICSs," which violated the Defense Code Sections 34 (6) (F) and (Q). Given the contents of this article, the government said, this news was to be considered inflammatory, and the government contended also that the article would create misunderstanding among the subjects of His Majesty and that it harms the security of the people. In addition, this paper, they said, had once been censored and the publishers have been warned thirteen times not to publish certain articles, and for the security of the country, the* Myanmar Alin *has been ordered to close down according to section 51 (1) B of the Defense Code. Also, if this order were to be defied, the publishers could face charges according to Section 3.*

We have many questions to ask concerning the sudden closure of the paper. If we were to accept it as true that the article on the ICSs that appeared on November 26 was inflammatory and would create misunderstanding among the subjects of His Majesty and harm the security of the people, then, if an ICS or any ICS officer oversteps his official boundaries, are we to keep the news out of our papers? Are we not to discuss it, are we not allowed to say we disapprove of it, and are we not to warn higher authorities so that necessary action can be taken? We would like to be enlightened on this matter.

In our view, if an official commits a misdemeanor, we would need to inform the government so that necessary action could be taken, but one publication was summarily closed down for an unforeseeable length of time because it performed this task. Would it not be better, would it not be more reasonable, if the government would command the said official to clear up his own problems to the satisfaction of all parties concerned? If he could not do that, would it not be wise to transfer him to another place, or do whatever necessary to keep the peace?

We clearly see here the speed with which the authorities closed down the paper and the slow pace of their inquiry into the problem, for which we are truly amazed and much saddened. Only after many hours had passed following the closing of the paper did the government come out with a statement explaining that they were indeed looking into the matter. The fact that the government went so far as to close down the paper that reported this problem showed plainly enough that their move was not the result of any fear that the news would spread, but was punishment against the newspaper for publishing the news.

The statement explained how the government was taking action against reports published in the Burmese papers that described one government ICS commissioner stepping into the grounds of a pagoda in Mingaru Village of Maubin Township without removing his shoes. "As soon as the news appeared," the statement continued, "the government asked for an inquiry into the matter but as the first report was lacking in detail, a fuller report was ordered. After receiving this fuller report, the government would not hesitate to take action. The government has announced itself to be the supporter of Buddhism, as the citizens know full well." In this case we must now ask the government if there remains any reason to close down Myanmar Alin, and we demand an answer from the government.

If the government were to study the works on political science and economy such as Liberty in the Modern State, The Press and World Affairs, and The Press, they would realize that their summary closure of the paper was not fair and that the act was overly harsh.

We would like to remind the government that anyone in service does not only serve the state, but that he himself is one among the ruled. Thus he should not, according to the government's own words, as "a subject of His Majesty," create enmity between other "subjects of His Majesty." If he had done so, he too deserves to be summarily punished, as Myanmar Alin was summarily closed down.

If one government official has created a problem that could have far-reaching negative effects, he does not deserve the privilege of being investigated at leisure. If what was reported in the paper was considered inflammatory, what of the person who committed the act? What of the speed with which the paper was closed down and the leisurely pace of investigating the matter? How would the government answer these questions, and would these questions, too, be answered with punishment? We would like to point out to the government the error of its ways in taking summary action, and to advise it to recant on their decision of closing down Myanmar Alin.

The day after the above article appeared, U Kyaw from the Secretariat called to ask Ko Ko not to write so strongly. Mr. Prescott, chief of police, phoned to tell Ko Ko that an order had been issued to arrest Ko Ko and that he had strongly advised against it.

"Please don't write anything like that again," he asked.

Ko Ko ignored everyone and called an urgent conference with publishers, editors, and journalists of Yangon at the *Journal Kyaw* office, which meant our home, in order to find ways of having the ban lifted from *Myanmar Alin*. He told me to entertain all of them well, so I had tea and cakes provided by New Light Bakery and made sure they were served well. Ko Ko fought for the rights of *Myanmar Alin* with all his heart and soul; he was a man who found strength in fair fights.

CHAPTER 28

JOURNAL KYAW MA MA LAY

My father, not yet completely recovered from his illness, came to Yangon as soon as he could get up from his bed. He immediately complained that having the newspaper's workplace set up in our home was not a good idea. He told us to leave the office where it was but to find a good house and garden to move to. So we moved again to a house in Alone Township owned by the Irrawaddy company and bought typesetting equipment for the office. Father then insisted on buying us a car to commute to work from Alone and back, and I had to beg him, saying if he was so determined to buy us a car, please buy us a printing press instead, as we needed it more. We then rented a friend's car for our use. Previously we had been printing at Naga Ni Press, but now we rented a room in the Yegyaw neighborhood, on Montgomery Street,[1] and put our printing press there, together with our typesetting equipment. In the mornings, Ko Ko would go straight to the press and I to the office, and so we took separate routes.

We each took 500 kyat from the paper as our salaries. After all the expenses of the paper had been paid, with the remainder we opened a separate account for Ko Ko's library and bought as many books as he wanted. *Journal Kyaw*'s circulation was over six thousand a week and now we could afford to buy any book Ko Ko wanted. When we were young, Father had insisted on all of his children learning accounting by working at the bank, saying that you could never be sure who would go into private business.

When my turn came to study accounting, although both my parents and the directors of the bank urged me to do so, I had refused, saying I would not like to work under the British. My younger sister became highly skilled at accounting, so much so the bank directors were very proud of her and arranged tea parties in Pyapon[2] for their senior accountants to meet her. After she married, her knowledge of accounting was only useful for her in making the grocery and laundry lists, while it turned out that, after all, I was the one who needed it most.

Although I had refused to learn accounting, I had grown up with people around me talking about it and working on it every day, so I was able to keep my accounts in strict order, and as a result, as big as our business grew, there was no waste whatsoever. I firmly believe that at work, at home, or in matters of state, discipline is the most important factor. I am convinced that it is due to discipline that wars are won, countries prosper, and wealth accumulates. Our office regulations were rigidly followed by everyone, including myself. I impressed on out-of-town reporters and

---

[1] Montgomery Street, now named Bo Gyoke Aung San Street, was the eastern portion of the road that bisects Sule Pagoda Road, while Commissioner Street was the part that ran to the west.

[2] A town bigger than Bogalay and a regional center.

agents the need for discipline, insisting that for any endeavor to survive for long, discipline was the key.

The project that I had dreamed of every evening while sitting by Ko Ko's desk at *Myanmar Alin* had now materialized. I learned a lesson in the process, namely, that to have a goal and the will to work for it meant you would achieve success at the end. Taking this lesson to heart, I set myself higher goals and resolved to reach them. As I always like to make sure that everything runs smoothly, I suffered more stress than did my husband. He worked as if he were in my employ. Unless the business side urgently needed his attention, he usually ignored it and left it to me, so that I would remark to him, how could he allow me to be so burdened? He was entirely without greed, and he lived his life as peacefully as he could. So when I realized that he really needed to be free of worry over such mundane matters in order to concentrate on his writing, I willingly took over the management. We did not have a place big enough for both the journal offices and the press, so I kept a lookout for a suitably large place.

Journal Kyaw did, indeed, become widely read all over the country. Ko Ko said to me that a journal had to offer knowledge as well as news, and in order to do that he needed to read more, and this he did, getting as much information as he could on various subjects to pass on to his readers.

As for his health, since I now had him under my eyes all the time, it had improved tremendously. As there were telephones at both the press where he worked and the office where I did, I could check on him at any time. I had achieved my desire to keep him in comfort. I kept my house well cared for and nicely furnished so that he always came back to a pleasant home.

In June 1939 my daughter, Khin Lay Myint, was born. With a nanny to look after her, I could continue with my work. I had three or four maids to look after the housework, each capably taking care of her own duties and each faithfully following my regime of discipline. My father came to Yangon to undergo treatment with Dr. Kondu, so I had day and night nurses looking after him. Overseeing the family affairs, the household matters, and the journal management kept me very busy.

My father's condition did not improve, so his doctor suggested we should send him to Kalaw, a hill station in the Shan State.[3] A month later Ko Ko and I followed, but Father's condition had not improved so we brought him home. On our return from Kalaw by train, we were in the first-class compartment, which had four bunks. Father and I were in lower bunks and my uncle, who had stayed with Father in Kalaw, slept on the one above mine. Ko Ko, however, did not sleep a wink but sat by Father the whole night. About midnight I woke up from a fitful sleep and saw my father holding Ko Ko's hands and saying quietly to him, "Bless you, my son, my son," and I felt happiness rise and choke my throat.

After we arrived back in Yangon, the doctors said there was nothing more they could do. When Father took a turn for the worse, I sat near him and recited the Buddhist sutras softly to him so that his mind would be on pure thoughts as his spirit left his body. Ko Ko, too, without telling me, had run to fetch our family monk, who resided in Kyeemyindine, so both of us had the same idea as to how best to say farewell to Father. Just as the monk arrived, Father passed away peacefully, listening

---

[3] The weather is very mild and cool in Kalaw, and the air is fresh, surrounded as it is by pine forests.

to the sutras I was reciting in a whisper. I felt as if a mountain had crumbled to dust; Father had always been there to look after me, and he was no more.

I had no wish to continue living in a house with such a tragic memory, so we moved to Fiftieth Street. I tried harder to find a place where our business and our home could be together. One day we heard of a newspaper office closing down in Yegyaw where our press was and we planned to rent it from U Tin Maung, its publisher.

Before we could finalize matters, I told Ko Ko how every time I went to our press in Yegyaw, on Montgomery Street, I had noticed the spacious New Burma Clinic's building next door to it and thought how wonderful it would be if we could rent that building so that the press, office, and home could be in one place.

"The owner lives there himself," Ko Ko said when I told him. "He's surely not going to rent it."

So I said nothing, but one day as we walked back from U Tin Maung's place after some discussions, I could not help remarking that I still wanted the New Burma Clinic space instead. Just as we arrived at the building where our press was, I looked up and there, right next door on the upper-storey veranda of the clinic, was a sign, "To Let."

I smiled meaningfully at Ko Ko and pointed to it. He turned to me with wonder and said, "You know, Tin Lay, your father always said you would get what you want and he was right!"

I immediately ran up to the owner's apartment and then and there signed a lease for 250 kyat a month for the whole building. By the time we moved into this building, the clouds of World War II were gathering over Yangon, and at night no one dared to turn on the lights too brightly. Even the shops had their lights dimmed so that everywhere there was darkness, as if a storm would break out at any moment.

Since my wish to have work and home in one place was fulfilled, I settled down quickly and worked harder than before as we waited for the war to break out over our heads. Our living quarters were upstairs. The front part of the ground floor was set up as the journal's management and commercial office, the middle section had the editors' desks, and at the back were our printing presses. We had to buy another press as our weekly circulation reached almost nine thousand.

Ko Ko would go down to his office at first light, and then visitors would begin to arrive. Over cups upon cups of tea they would discuss all sorts of matters, and by the time I came downstairs at nine I would see him surrounded by many of his friends.

We would take a lunch break from one in the afternoon until two, and still the visitors kept coming all through the late afternoon.

It was up to me to make sure that the journal came out on time. Every extra hour cost us more, and when Ko Ko did not finish his columns on time everyone else had to wait, and the overtime wages began to add up. Ko Ko, as usual, was too embarrassed to tell his visitors to leave, and so the typesetters had to wheedle and urge him all through the day to produce enough copy for them to work on. If they could not get enough copy out of him, they would come to my desk to complain and give me their overtime slips.

No matter what I might say to Ko Ko, he only wrote at night, busy as he was the whole day with an endless stream of visitors who came to talk about politics and the war. But come night time I doubt whether there was anyone on earth busier than my husband. He would write late into the night and then would sit and read international newspapers or books until dawn. I sat up with him, and I had to beg him to go to bed. I worked at my desk the whole day, and then at night I had to supervise the typesetting and printing of his columns, work that should have been done during the day. It was always well past midnight before I could finally go up to my bed, and sometimes it would be near dawn. I shuddered to think what it would be like to publish a daily newspaper if a weekly was relentlessly using up my time and energy like this.

My work was to deal not only with Yangon distributors but with agents from all over the country, as well as to manage the office operations. Moreover, when there was not enough copy to fill the pages I had to drop everything else and write something.

Once the submitted short stories were not good enough, and Ko Ko did not have the time and Ko Saw Oo had no idea what to write. As something had to be done quickly, I gritted my teeth and wrote a short story titled "If Only He Knew." I used the name Ma Ma Lay, a name I used when writing nonfiction for our weekly. I had no experience whatsoever in writing fiction.

When my story came out in print, U Ohn Khin phoned Ko Ko to tell him how much Dagon Khin Khin Lay, a well-known writer, loved it. Ko Ko had not even read the story yet, and only Ko Saw Oo had done so and had accepted it for publication. I later found Ko Ko's comments on this matter in his diary, in which he wrote every day. When I published his diary, I had left it out because at the time I did not want anyone to know that I was "Ma Ma Lay."

Excerpt from U Chit Maung's diary:

> When I wrote about Dagon Khin Khin Lay, I also thought of the unknown writer, my wife. I must say that I married her because of the articles she sent to Myanmar Alin, and since that time I knew her to be a talented and thoughtful writer. Before we had even met and I had no idea what she looked like or what type of a person she was, just by reading her articles that were far superior to others' I had thought to myself, "How wonderful it would be to have such a wife!" and indeed my wish has come true.

> So, it is apparent that my wife even before she met me was a good and thoughtful writer. After we married and she began writing for Journal Kyaw as Ma Ma Lay, a few of my friends knew it was she, but even they thought that I had written them in part or whole. That is not at all the case. She wrote whatever she wanted to and it was up to me as an editor to write a heading or subheadings, and I had no need to do more than this, the normal duties of an editor.

> On one occasion we urgently needed a short story. We had a pile of submitted manuscripts, but neither Ko Saw Oo, a writer himself, nor I could find anything that was up to the standard of Journal Kyaw. At the time, Ko Saw Oo was too busy to write one and as for me, I could barely finish the articles I had to write, let alone a short story. But the matter became pressing, and it seemed as if either Ko Saw Oo or I would have to write one by the next day, so my wife, the business manager of the paper, announced that if there was no one else, she would write one. Ko Saw Oo read it before it went to press, but I did not, and only when I saw it in Journal Kyaw did I realize it was indeed well written. Some people even thought I had written it.

    A few days ago she wrote an article titled "The First Responsibility of Women" under the name Ma Tin Hlaing, Journal Kyaw, *and it was printed in the* Myanmar Alin *daily. My friend the cartoonist Ko Hein Soon told me that many people were saying it was I who wrote it.*

    I myself would rather read than write, and I only write when it is truly necessary for me to do so. I have never urged my wife to write, nor have I told her not to, and I have kept quiet on the matter. But when she continues to produce good writing people assume I have a hand in it, but whatever people might say, it is clear that her writing is hers alone and not mine, and there is simply no need for us to give an explanation.

CHAPTER 29

PERSONAL AFFAIRS

As the saying about married couples goes, "One rows at the bow, the other at the stern," so it was that we traveled together in life, and one might think our path of marriage ran smoothly, without any bumps or thorns. Actually, there were indeed annoyances that came out of our differences. It was fortunate that before my marriage I knew all about U Chit Maung and had made up my mind to take the good with the bad. In some marriages there are problems when the husband has a bad attitude, but then problems can also arise when he is far too nice.

At the office, people hated me and thought him nice. I did not want to take on the role of supervising everything and so I tried to push him into that position, but he did not want it and worked as if he were under *my* supervision, as if he were an ordinary employee.

If I called in a debt, he would beg me not to do so and to wait until that person decided to pay me. If, on the other hand, our paper owed somebody, he would keep pestering me until I paid up. If he were the business manager as well as the editor, we would have gone bankrupt; he was always extremely reluctant to ask for payment. If he wanted me to do something concerning our work that was not according to procedure, I would resist him, but in personal affairs I usually let him have his way just for peace, even if I knew it was wrong.

On a daily basis I had to be aggressive with him about eating well and to make sure of his good health. On top of the strain of it all, when he was unreasonably too nice to others who took advantage of him, I would feel really wretched. I wryly thought that this daily misery might well be as bad as that suffered by the wife of a man who comes home drunk every day!

At home we had a young boy working in the kitchen, and when I spoke to him I addressed him as someone younger than myself, but Ko Ko would talk to him as if they were the same age. I begged Ko Ko not to do that in case the young boy lost respect for him, which is very likely to happen in such a case, but to no avail. I told Ko Ko that since I treated the boy according to his age (which was not even twenty) while Ko Ko did not, it would seem as if I were the head of the household and not him. I did not want anyone to think that. In spite of my pleadings, Ko Ko could not bring himself to speak any less than in this extremely polite manner.[1]

Ko Ko also would neither address the maids directly nor look at them, so that no one would think him familiar with unrelated women. He only spoke to the kitchen boy and that with such respect that I knew it was just a matter of time before the boy became too full of himself. In our house, besides the maids and the boy, I had a distant cousin, Ma Kyi, living with us who supervised all of them.

[1] The use of different first- and second-person pronouns, as well as the tone of voice, marks the manner of speech and is an important aspect of Myanmar's culture.

One night we had gone to bed very late. On our floor there were eight rooms, including a shrine room, our bedroom, another room for my daughter and her nanny, one for the maids, and another for Ma Kyi and a young maid. Around three in the morning I heard Ma Kyi call out "Elder Brother! Elder Sister! ... Elder Brother!" from her room, and we both got out of bed in a hurry and ran to the room. The door was locked and when we called her name and pushed at the door, Ma Kyi opened it and said, "That boy—that boy—he tried to get into our room through the window. When I screamed he went behind that door," and she pointed to the door that led to the veranda.

When I went to look, there was the kitchen boy, cowering behind the door. Another man in Ko Ko's place would have given the boy a good thrashing. I waited for Ko Ko to do something and stood there with my arms folded, and Ma Kyi stood close behind me. Instead of being angry as we expected, Ko Ko talked to the boy mildly, in the manner of a father to a son or a teacher to a student.

"How could you do something like this, to insult young women by entering their room? It's obvious you wanted to attack them at this time of night. This is not something a good man should do."

The boy squatted on the floor and listened with bowed head. I was furious at what the boy had done and angry with Ko Ko at the way he was handling it, but I kept my temper in check so as not to disgrace him in front of the others. Suddenly Ma Kyi ran into our room and came out holding the long sword we kept there for security, and in one movement she brought it down on the boy's head. If I had not grabbed Ma Kyi from behind, he would have been decapitated. The blade slashed into his shoulder, and blood flowed everywhere. I pulled Ma Kyi into our room and left her there to calm down, and without even looking at the boy I went out to stand on the veranda. I thought to myself, "if Ko Ko had not been so weak with the boy, he would never have dared do something like this, and even now he is not showing any anger. All this happened because Ko Ko was being too nice." I felt bitterly unhappy.

Ko Ko was busy all through what was left of that night, reporting the matter to the police and taking the boy to the hospital. I stood on the veranda throughout the entire time, for two solid hours. When everything had been taken care of, Ko Ko came out to where I was standing to tell me that the boy was in the hospital and that the wound was severe. I exploded at that and turned to him, saying, "If you had at least slapped the boy a few times on his head, all this wouldn't have happened. I told you not to talk to him as an equal. Next time it will be *us*, your family, that scum like him will dare to insult."

Only then he apologized, saying it was his fault and that it would not happen again. In all his life, he had not even kicked at a dog, let alone injured a human; and this was just one example of how I suffered through his goodness.

CHAPTER 30

WAR

In my diary I wrote down everything that happened to our family and at the paper, and about how when we were in tight spots U Tin would come to our help or give advice.

We continued publishing our paper, and all was going well; we had money and could spend as we liked, but I never forgot the past and would compare what we had now with what we did not have then. The words Ko Ko once said to me, "You do gain something through desperate situations," never left my mind. The book titled *Is the World Coming to an End?* that we had published[1] with what little money we had at the time finally sold out briskly as war came nearer. I had once had to console myself that one day it would sell out, and now I was delighted that my wish had come true.

Ko Ko said he wanted to write another book titled "The Looming War," and I persuaded him to write a serial for the journal first, rather than a complete book, suggesting that later we'd compile the articles in book form. The series was illustrated with the drawing of a Golden Eagle, which was the translation of Ko Ko's pen name, "Shwe Lin Yon." The articles were so popular that circulation jumped even higher. There was a restriction on paper so we could print only ten thousand copies, but according to the orders that came pouring in we could have printed a lot more.

As war seemed more and more likely, people became very anxious, and bomb shelters were being built everywhere. Most men sent off their wives and children to remote villages, thinking it would be safer out of the city. I, too, sent off crates of clothing and dry goods to be stored in Thingangyun,[2] at Myanmar Alin U Tin's house, where he had moved recently. We could not get a house in Thingangyun, so if war came to Yangon and we had to flee, we planned to stay at our friend Shwe Pane Thaung's small house, also situated in Thingangyun.

At the start of the war in 1941, we also began publishing an evening paper, *Nay Sin Kyay Hmon.*[3] At that time, I was heavily pregnant and still continued to work for both papers. On the morning of December 23, 1941, when the Japanese bombed Yangon for the first time, we were all working at our desks as the planes approached the city. As soon as the sirens wailed, the staff became jumpy with fear, but I gritted my teeth and went on with my work. When the bombs began to fall, Ko Ko dragged me behind the stacked piles of paper. The household staff from upstairs, including my baby daughter and her nanny, came down and huddled near us. Only when

---

[1] The book was published in 1938.

[2] Thingangyun is a far suburb of Yangon.

[3] Translated as "The Daily Mirror."

Khin Lay Myint was brought downstairs did some workers discover we had a daughter.

I felt wretched listening to the explosion of the bombs, thinking that this momentous work I had strived so hard to set up would surely be destroyed. But thinking of the English sayings, "Destiny destroys what man creates" and "Half is better than nothing," so much like our Burmese saying "Fate decrees life," I reflected that however straight we carve our paths, if Fate wanted to destroy a path, there was nothing much anyone could do. I consoled myself that it was already a great accomplishment to be where we were at present, even if we were only halfway up the road to success. When the bombers finally flew away, the city was left utterly devastated. Within the same day, the population left their homes and fled to the outskirts or to the countryside. We, too, moved out to Thingangyun as planned and thought that we would work out later how to continue with our business.

We told all our workers that they could come and live with us in Thingangyun and that we would feed them as well, but if they wanted to leave Yangon, we would give them the money to do so. Some decided to come with us, and some left. We moved to Shwe Pane Thaung's house that very day without taking any of our personal or professional property. When we arrived at the small house where he lived alone, we found out it was big enough for this bachelor but not for the ten of us. We hardly had room to move around.

Every morning Ko Ko would leave with his workers to write and print the papers while I stayed home. I arranged to have all communications transferred to Shwe Pane Thaung's house so that I could work from there. I knew by then that there was no longer any hope that we would be able to carry on as usual, but as Ko Ko wanted to continue working, I thought I would support him in any way, regardless of whether we made any money or not.

Things got worse day by day. From morning until night and from night until morning, the planes came in one wave after the other, and bombs fell ceaselessly, and so people hardly came out of the shelters. Ko Ko and his men would walk home to Thingangyun from town, and they would have a short rest while I set the table for them. In spite of all, I would make sure to serve a good dinner. One evening while we were at the table Ko Ko told me that it was different for those left in town. "They hardly have any food because there are no food stalls. There are very few people left, and cats and dogs are starving to death all over town." I felt choked, unable to go on eating, when I heard this.

My elder brother kept sending telegrams from Bogalay, worried sick that in my last stages of pregnancy I was still living in Yangon. Whenever I remarked to Ko Ko that we should leave everything and just go live in Bogalay, Ko Ko would say, "You should leave, Tin Lay, but as long as we have this stock of paper I'll continue publishing as long as I can." I knew that if I left he would hardly get anything to eat, so I swallowed my fear, thinking, "Well, we'll die together if we must," and stopped thinking of leaving Yangon. Myanmar Alin U Tin came over to say he and his family would be moving to Thonze, a small town farther north, and urged me to leave Yangon, especially in my condition. Everyone else, including our workers, kept urging me to go.

One night when everyone else was asleep, Ko Ko pleaded with me to move to Bogalay. When I said he, too, should come, he said that until the population of Yangon was ordered to leave he would stay on to publish *Journal Kyaw* "even if he could publish one page."

I knew I should leave; if I gave birth now, there was no doctor, no medicine, and I would not even be able to move to avoid the bombs. I knew all that, but whenever I thought of it, my fear was fleeting. However, the fear of leaving him without anyone to care for him and the thought that if he should die in an explosion I would not even see his body—this fear was so strong that I stubbornly refused to go.

He was unhappy about this situation even as he went to work every day. I wrote down in my diary all that he told me during that time, including which of his friends had fled Yangon and who had moved where. One day when the bombing during the day was more intense than usual, he came home rather late. As soon as he got home, he urged me strongly to leave the next morning. He said if the boats stopped running it would be extremely difficult to leave at all. Saying I must leave, he went to borrow U Ba Tu's car to take me to the jetty early the next day. I felt wretched that we would be parted.

Ko Ko was refusing to leave Yangon not because he had a salary to earn nor because he was making money, but because he felt he should continue to give news to the country, despite any risk to his own life. I did not want to accept this at all. I was unable to sleep the whole night, racked with worry. I had to leave to ease his mind, but I still worried about how he would eat or live, and I felt very unhappy when I thought of it. I was to leave both my husband and my work, which day by day I had come to enjoy.

The whole night I repeatedly urged Ko Ko not to forget to bathe and to use the toilet regularly and not to stay overnight in town. I pleaded with him in tears, begging that he would somehow join us in Bogalay if the boats stopped running. Near dawn he said he felt worried about my safety and that he would accompany me to Bogalay and then return the next morning. I felt so relieved and thankful that I could hardly say a word in reply.

In the morning I asked all our workers please to look after him and told them to buy more groceries for the kitchen. As we drove though the devastated city on our way to the jetty, I reflected on the fact that however hard we might try we were helpless against Fate.

The boat docked at Bogalay at about five in the evening. As we walked home from the jetty, all the neighbors came to their front doors to scold us for staying in Yangon this long. Out of their anxiety for us, they were so vehement that I felt very embarrassed. When we got to my house, there was already a large crowd of our relatives, including fearsome Gyi Daw[4] Nyunt, who had all gathered here as war refugees. Immediately, there was a tremendous uproar from all of them, berating us for not coming to Bogalay sooner.

My elder brother was so mad he was almost at the point of beating me. Instead, boiling with compassionate anger,[5] he sat me down at once and scolded me until midnight. Then I, too, went to bed, as everyone else was already asleep, but I could not close my eyes. The words Ko Ko had said to me, that "there are very few people left, and cats and dogs are starving to death all over town," rang in my ears, and I was worried sick about him. I watched him with tears running down my face as he slept, and I prayed that some day people would know and appreciate how much he had been willing to risk for his country.

---

[4] Gyi Daw means "Elder Aunt."

[5] *Karuna dawsa*, or an anger that arises out of affection and worry.

I had married him out of love and untold admiration for his will to serve his country with every moment of his life, uncaring of his health and comfort. I knew better than anybody that while even politicians have both personal and political lives, he alone stood out as someone who had completely erased his personal life. I felt a deep gratitude for that as well as for all that he had done for me. All that night I thought over how much he meant to me and I finally decided I could show my love and respect in only one way.

At four in the morning I shook him awake because the boat would leave at five. He got up hurriedly and went downstairs to wash his face. I ran on tiptoe into the room where my Gyi Daw Nyunt was sleeping and woke her up softly so no one else would know. When she opened her eyes I bent down close to her ears and begged her in a whisper, "Gyi Daw, please come with me to Yangon. I don't dare cut the umbilical cord myself when I give birth and please, you've got to come with me."

"How can I do that!" she yelled, startled nearly out of her wits and I hurriedly clamped my hand over her mouth and kept on crying and pleading with her, keeping my voice low. I knew that fierce Gyi Daw Nyunt was the only person I could ask, as she was not afraid of anything. If I were not with child I could just sneak away, but as my time was drawing very near I had no idea what to do by myself at the time of birth and, besides, I was terrified of giving birth alone. To make her feel some pity I knelt down and repeatedly *kadaw* several times. Finally, wiping away her own tears, Gyi Daw said, "All right, if you want it so badly, I'll come with you," and much relieved, I ran to pack.

I woke up one maid after the other and whispered to them to get our stuff ready without making a noise or waking anybody else. When Ko Ko came back upstairs after his wash and saw me getting my things ready, he stood there stunned. He kept on urging me not to come back with him and said he would not allow it, but I ignored every word and directed the maids to carry the stuff downstairs. He ran down after me and kept on pleading with me to stay.

"Think of it, Tin Lay, you are heavily pregnant and with all the bombs falling, aren't you afraid?

"Yesterday you agreed to leave Yangon and now you want to go back, what will your brother say?

"Please, Tin Lay, don't come with me, I beg you, I'll come to you as soon as I can.

"I'll wake up everybody and tell them you're leaving."

He pleaded and threatened and tried to make me stay.

I carefully drew the iron gates apart, trying not to make a sound. Leaving the keys with the Indian watchman and telling him to lock up after us, I hurried out of the house. Ko Ko and Gyi Daw followed in silence as we walked to the jetty. On the boat there were no other passengers apart from us returning to Yangon. I could well imagine the uproar in the Bogalay house come morning.

All along the trip Ko Ko kept scolding me but I stubbornly sat still and did not say a single word in reply, letting him vent his anxiety. Perhaps he wanted to taunt me into breaking my silence, for just as we were about to dock in Yangon he said to me, "Then why d'you keep saying it's all Fate, material things are not permanent? And that you can build up everything later?"

Only then I spoke for the first time since we left and told him that it was neither for money nor my work but only out of my love for him that I was back in Yangon;

and, please, not to disregard my *cedana*[6] this way. Only then did he stop his scolding; he clucked his tongue loudly in exasperation and muttered that he should write a book on it.

Our workers who were waiting at the jetty for Ko Ko's arrival were astounded to see me. The whole of Yangon was deserted and when we got back to Thingangyun I stopped working and concentrated only on cooking and serving all of them as well as I could manage. When more bombs fell directly on Yangon, I worried about him working there while I was in Thingangyun. If our neighborhood were bombed there was nowhere to hide and, in my condition, not far that I could run. At these times I felt afraid and tears would well up in my eyes, but as before I kept up my spirits by telling myself, "We'll die together if we must."

---

[6] *Cedana* means goodwill, good intentions.

CHAPTER 31

A TIME OF DEVASTATION

The bombing grew very fierce, and only when there were almost no people left, even in Thingangyun, did Ko Ko decide that it was no longer possible for him to continue working in Yangon. Even if he had wanted to, his workers were not willing to stay on, and so, finally, he agreed to move to Bogalay and to continue publishing from there. We arrived in Bogalay as usual, around five in the evening, and the very next morning at nine o'clock I successfully gave birth to our son, Maung Chit Shein.[1] We got to Bogalay just before the boats stopped running, and thus we barely escaped the worst devastation in Yangon.

Ko Ko's staff hired boats to bring to Bogalay things from the Yangon office, such as our stock of paper, desks, tables, and the press, and furniture from our household, as well as Ko Ko's collection of books. We rented a house in Bogalay and kept our publishing business there. A few days after I gave birth, we moved to a rented house on Post Office Road, as my brother's house was getting cramped with so many people. We set up the printing press and began to publish, but as all lines of communication with other towns had broken down, we simply gave away the printed journal to the Bogalay townspeople.

Then Ko Ko had nothing to do but read to his heart's content, and so I could not understand what he was doing when he spent all his time drawing a detailed map of Bogalay on a large sheet of paper. He went out to check all routes into town and would come back to mark them in colored pencil on his map. I asked him what he was doing, but he merely replied, "Just in case it's needed," so I thought to myself that there would be a good reason for it even if I did not yet know its purpose.

Then he wanted to be introduced to the young people of town who were without any political party affiliation, and so he became acquainted with Ko Thu Daw and Ko Ohn Kywe, sons of our neighbor U Maung Gyi. Then my brother introduced him to Judge U Tun Myint, and Ko Ko asked the judge if it would be possible to form a home guard for the town.

"Sir, the authorities will agree to something like this if you propose it to the Session Judge," Ko Ko told U Tun Myint, and I noted that he wanted the judge to take credit for the idea and for him, Ko Ko, to remain in the background. I was already used to him working this way just to get things accomplished without bothering about who would get the credit.

Led by Ko Thu Daw, the young men of the town were eager to form a home guard that had been "suggested" by U Tun Myint, and as they would need to be armed, Ko Ko discreetly hinted that it would be wise to choose the members well, and I wrote down exactly what he said in my diary. When U Tun Myint returned

---

[1] Maung Chit Shein later changed his name to Maung Thein Dan.

from Pyapon with the permission, the home guard was formed at once with the young men selected by Ko Thu Daw and Ko Ohn Kywe.

Ko Ko remarked to the town's chief of police, who often visited his friend, my brother, that if only he were to personally take charge of training them in firearms, the young men would surely learn faster. The police chief was happy to do so when it was put to him this way, and soon he was busy with training the young men how to shoot straight.

Ko Ko often visited my brother to talk to the government officials who liked to gather there to persuade them not to leave the town when and if orders came for them to do so. The political party in Bogalay was Thakin Ba Sein's party, and Ko Ko had nothing much to do with them.[2]

When orders indeed came for the government authorities to flee Bogalay, Ko Ko gave a signal to Ko Thu Daw and the others to implement a plan they had worked out. So that the home guard could keep the arms and ammunition that were stored at the police station, the young men simply walked in and walked out, calmly carrying away the guns. As soon as it became known that the authorities had fled, men from outlying villages and from across the river gathered like flies and came into town wielding knives and swords, bent on robbing the rich townspeople. It was a terrifying sight.

Then Ko Ko spread his map in front of the well-armed home-guard members and told them who should stand guard where and who should block which routes. When the "invaders" saw the armed men blocking every point of entry into Bogalay, they could do nothing but strut around and wave their swords in bravado. All the elders gathered at my brother's house to discuss the safety of the town while Ko Ko sat reading quietly at home, as if he had had nothing to do with the matter.

Even the judge of the criminal court, U Mu, at first had no idea of Ko Ko's involvement and said to me while working with the home guard, wiping away the sweat from his brow, "Well, well, everything's falling apart, and your husband's just fine, isn't he, sitting there reading his books." I nodded my head several times, not in agreement but in satisfaction that my husband would do important things behind the scenes without anyone being the wiser. He would often say that he liked to help others anonymously, and I felt deep satisfaction and joy at what was happening.

Then the politicians went all over town announcing that they had taken control. As they had almost no weapons, they demanded that the home guard hand over its arms to them. The politicians did not want the arms to be in the hands of townsfolk, as the British were still in the country, in Mandalay at the time. The Thakin faction also feared the guns might be turned against them. As the political party in Bogalay was not the one led by Thakin Ko Daw Hmaing, with whom Ko Ko had a good relationship, he found it impossible to go to the Bogalay Thakins and tell them to trust the home guard, as it was he who had taken the first steps in forming and arming them. The Thakins did not trust anyone who was not in their faction, and although Ko Ko tried hard to negotiate between these groups, he was unsuccessful.

With all the tension caused by the unrest around us, plus the mistrust between the young men and the politicians, everyone was in a state of terror. Besides, men with unsavory reputations got themselves involved with the politicians, and thus the

---

[2] As noted earlier, the Do Bama Asi-ayon had split into two factions, with some members willing to work with Dr. Ba Maw in the Freedom Block and the other faction willing to go against anything or anyone who had been previously allied with the British.

demands for the home guard to surrender their arms grew more aggressive. The home-guard members protecting us against bandits were sons from good families, and everyone agreed that it would be highly dangerous to give up the arms to the politicians who were now working with men of dubious character, but no one dared say anything. The home guard continued to be diligent in their work.

One day the political party announced that Bo[3] Yan Naing[4] would be arriving in town that night and that by order of Bo Yan Naing, the home guard must surrender their arms to the party immediately. Ko Thu Daw and his comrades came to ask Ko Ko what they should do, and Ko Ko told them it would be best to follow this order. By ten o'clock that night, Ko Ko was already in bed. We heard the sound of machine gun fire announcing Bo Yan Naing's arrival. The home guard went with their weapons to U Thin's house where Bo Yan Naing would be staying and gave up their arms. At about ten-thirty there was a knock at our front door, and when we opened it, there was a car and message sent by Bo Yan Naing. The message said he "would like to meet U Chit Maung as he just heard he was living here" and would Ko Ko come to see him now?

As he dressed, Ko Ko talked to me.

"We need some sort of administration set up for the town. The Thakin are not going to allow the officials of the previous government to take any posts, they will want to form it amongst themselves. If they form an administration with people of little or no ability, the town will suffer. The administration must be entrusted to these government officials, but with the Thakins holding the strings, and that's the only way to have a stable and strong administration. If these men of experience are left out altogether all over the country, they will have no place to go, if they have not left with the British. Or they may well side with the Japanese. Then the country will continue to suffer without able men in places where they are needed. What a great shame that nothing was prepared for a situation like this!"

He returned around one in the morning. He said he told Bo Yan Naing that he had planned for the home guard to retain their arms when the British left because he knew the arms would be seized and that there was an urgent need to protect the town, and that he was not friendly enough with the politicians in town to work with them on all this. Bo Yan Naing asked him to administer the town, but Ko Ko had refused, saying he must get back to Yangon. He told me that he had advised Bo Yan Naing to return the arms to the home guard and to use ex-government officials in the new administration.

When the Thakin party hoisted the Japanese flag, Ko Ko went to the Thakins and urged them to fly the Burmese peacock flag alongside it and to "let the Japanese see this."

The politicians in town, who were from Thakin Ba Sein's faction, knew that Bo Yan Naing was more closely affiliated with Thakin Ko Daw Hmaing's party. So to strengthen themselves, these politicians went to fetch Bo Myint Swe's troops, who supported them. When Bo Myint Swe arrived, he wanted to appropriate the home guard's weapons, but since Ko Ko was still in town and had the support of Bo Yan Naing, Bo Myint Swe did nothing but settle his troops in town.

---

[3] A military rank.

[4] Yan Naing was a member of Thirty Comrades, a group of thirty young men who went to Japan for military training, led by Thakin Aung San.

Ko Ko worked as much as he could for the affairs of town, and at the same time sat at his desk for entire days to prepare a plan of administration, titled "When Myanmar Gains Independence," with a pot of green tea by his side. He even made up a list of people most suitable to be sent as ambassadors to various countries. I asked him what was the very first thing to do after independence, and he said a new currency must be issued. I wrote that down as well as other comments he made on the political situation, the transformation, what the Thakins were doing, and the intentions of the Japanese.

One day a friend came to show him a newly issued Japanese note he had received as change from a ferryman. After the guest left, Ko Ko came into our room looking upset.

"Do you have any British currency?" he asked me, and I said yes, I have some pounds I was keeping aside to donate when I turned forty, as well as the profits from our business. He said to keep them safe and not spend any if I could help it, as in the future only the British pound would be of any value. I stared at him, stunned.

He asked his friends to find him a car as he must go to Yangon urgently, saying that because of the new Japanese currency the country was heading straight for hell and that he must get to Yangon quickly. They got a car for him, and he left for Yangon that very night.

He came back after three days, looking very upset. As I was taking out fresh clothes for him to wear after his bath, he pulled out the administrative plans he had drawn and tore them to pieces. I grabbed them in alarm, but I was not quick enough and they fell in shreds to the floor.

"What are you doing, Ko Ko, what happened?"

"It's all useless ..."

"Why? How can you say that?"

"Because I know, Tin Lay, it's no use, it's really no use. The Japanese are never going to give us independence.[5] These plans are worthless ... they're useless."

"But whom did you see in Yangon?"

"I saw all of them, and I disagreed with all of them. I sensed that some of them did not like the fact that I am a mere writer and editor, and there I was, talking like a politician!"

"Why?!"

"Because I refuse to *be* a politician."

"But, Ko Ko, didn't you warn them about what it could mean with this currency being issued by the Japanese?"

"Of course I did, I even told Thakin Mya to ask the Japanese what value they place on the currency issued for Myanmar, and that we've got to clear up that issue immediately or else I'm not going to sit by and watch, I shall inform the public. I don't know if he did or not."

"Is it true that Thakin Aung San is the Chief of Staff and that Thakin Tun Oke is the head of administration?"

"Yes, it's true so far ..."

"And in the future ...?"

"If Dr. Ba Maw is still around, I am certain the Japanese will make him the head of administration."

---

[5] Japanese leaders and Burmese politicians, led by General Aung San, had agreed that the Japanese could invade Myanmar provided that Myanmar's independence would be the result.

"Is Yangon full of Japanese troops?"

"They're everywhere. Most are very vulgar, so uncivilized. They bathe or walk around naked or near naked. If they can't get anyone to do anything, they just take off their belts and hit them! All those chaps who went to Japan,[6] high ranking or low, all have to bow to them, even our Thakin Aung San and Thakin Mya. We were walking from Du Berne Court[7] to Kokine and ran into a Japanese soldier standing guard on the street, and he became angry when we didn't stop to bow to him, and at gun point he made us come back to bow. If you see all that, you'll really be upset, Tin Lay. It won't be long before we drive them out; Thakin Aung San wanted to do it now, but I told him it's too early."

"You mean we have to fight the Japanese, too?"

"Of course! If they stay any longer we'll all be in serious trouble. If it were up to me, I'd go to Mandalay and join up with the British forces and with their help drive out the Japanese, but I think Thakin Thein Pe will get to them somehow."[8]

"So, you mean to say the Thakins are no longer so friendly with the Japanese?"

"Well, there are some who already see the reality and some who can't. So right from the beginning, we're split in two. Let's go back to Yangon, Tin Lay, there's so much to do there."

"Ko Ko, just now when you said some of them thought you were a 'mere' writer, what did you mean by that?"

"Well, at weddings when the master of ceremonies reads out the verses about the groom, have you ever seen the groom himself write it? It's someone else who writes it, right?"

"Yes? So?"

"It was Thakin Tun Oke; this political leader asked me to write a speech for him, a speech that he's going to deliver at the Shwedagon platform!"[9]

He smiled and went into the bathroom. I followed him and, sitting on a stool at the bathroom entrance, continued with my barrage of questions.

"Did you see Ko Hla Pe?"

"Of course, I stayed at his place. He's really a true patriot, and he's farsighted. He'll never become famous, as there will always be someone standing in front of him. Don't think I'm the only person who wants the country to prosper no matter who gets the credit; Ko Hla Pe is like that, too. One day the country might turn lucky just because of him. His *nom de guerre* is Bo Let Yar,[10] and Thakin Aung San's is Bo Tay Za. Ko Hla Maung is Bo Zey Ya.[11] Young Thakin Aung Than, whom you like so much, is Bo Sekkya.[12] Doesn't the name just suit him?"

---

[6] A reference to the Thirty Comrades.

[7] Du Berne Court is now named Malikha Road.

[8] Thakin Thein Pe, who later became the famous writer Thein Pe Myint, walked into India through the mountain passes to talk to the British forces.

[9] A place where many political rallies were held.

[10] Bo Let Yar resigned from the AFPFL (Anti-Fascist People's Freedom League) government a few months after independence. He went underground in 1969, during the rule of General Ne Win, who was also a member of the Thirty Comrades. He was betrayed and killed in the jungle by the Karen rebels in 1978.

[11] Bo Zey Ya went underground in 1953 and later joined the Burma Communist Party. He fell in a battle with government troops in 1968.

[12] Bo Sekkya went into exile in 1965, during the rule of General Ne Win. He passed away of heart failure in 1969.

Soaping his face as he talked, he laughed aloud about young Bo Sekkya, got suds in his mouth, and began to sputter and blow them out.

"But didn't you tell Ko Hla Pe about the Japanese currency?"

"I warned him that it might be hard to deal with the Japanese, and when I asked whether the British would return, he said not for some time. Poor chap, he was feeling really down. I have faith in this guy, he'd be good for the country. I met Thakin Soe and had a talk with him, too. I think he'll go underground."

"What's going to happen now, Ko Ko ...?"

"Well, something none too good, I can tell you ..."

I finally left him to bathe in peace and came away.

When I asked him if we would continue to publish our journal after we got back to Yangon, he in turn asked if we could live on what we had for at least four or five years. I said we could, if we sold off my jewelry, the British currency, and the stock of paper. He said we could not publish until the Japanese were gone, so I decided to keep the pounds safe and sell off my jewelry and the stock of paper to live on.

He had known the dangers our town faced when the British left and so he had planned for our protection, but perhaps not more than five people in Bogalay knew of what he had done. After having achieved the safety of others and preserved the anonymity of his involvement, we returned to Yangon.

We carried back all our possessions, apart from the stock of paper, and settled into the house in Yegyaw. The Japanese came to ask his help to publish a magazine, so he gave them a vague plan to publish something called "Modern Magazine."

A few days later, Ko Ohn Myint came with the news that Thakin Nu had suggested to the Japanese that U Chit Maung be made an information officer.

"Don't do it," Ko Ohn Myint said, highly resentful that such an inferior post had been offered. Ko Ko replied, "Perhaps they think a journalist is only good enough for this. Don't worry, I won't accept this or any other post the Japanese have to offer."

That night he asked me if he should enter politics, and I urged him to do so. As I had noted some time ago in my diary that I wanted him to enter politics, here I saw before me a chance for him to do so. The next day he told me that when he told Bo Let Yar that he planned to enter politics, his friend had told him to wait and in the meanwhile do something else.

"Do what, Ko Ko?" I asked.

"Something secret."

"Now, is there anything you do already that people know of?"

"No, I mean, this work is really something no one must know."

"What sort of work ... can I help?"

"I am only telling you because I have to."

"Well, what is it, Ko Ko?"

"Undercover work."

CHAPTER 32

UNDERCOVER INTELLIGENCE

I took extra care so that no one would notice what U Chit Maung was doing. He handpicked men he could trust from all parts of society, and every day he was busy gathering information from them. Bo Let Yar gave him 1,500 kyat to put these men on the payroll. Among the Burmese working for the Kempetai[1] were some who knew and trusted Ko Ko, and they told him everything they learnt at their work. I told Ko Ko he needed a right-hand man he could really trust, so he had his younger brother, Ko Than Tun, join him in the work.

Every morning he would leave the house to sit at teashops where there were many customers, and there make contact with his men or gather information just by talking to various people who thought he was merely an interested observer. As soon as he got home, he did not even write down notes but would sit at his typewriter and type out all the news in English. When I wanted to copy something down into my diary, he would grab my pen, saying, "Don't do it, Tin Lay, don't play with fire ... aren't you afraid of getting burned?"

When he left in the morning, he would leave packages with me to hand over to someone who would drop by during the day. One day I asked him where all the information went. "Is it to Bo Let Yar?" I asked. He answered, "Not Bo Let Yar," and when I persisted, he said he had no idea where the information reached, finally.

Bo Let Yar did not tell him who received the information. Ko Ko told me that his friend had informed him he would not tell anyone about Ko Ko's involvement. Not only did Ko Ko pass on the information, but he would also write suggestions on the last page about how various departments could be improved. He wrote better in English than in Burmese, and he did not pause to think over his sentences when he sat down to type out his reports. Not many people knew this about him, as they only read what he had been writing in Burmese; probably only the top-ranking people knew that he wrote the reports.

If we had no occupation, the Japanese might get suspicious, so we opened a bookstore on the ground floor. When Myanmar Alin U Tin founded a peace organization with the support of the Japanese government, he asked Ko Ko to handle the information work. Ko Ko took on the task, as it would be a chance to show that he was employed, and, besides, the work was temporary.

When the Japanese were preparing to hand over the administration to the Burmese, Thakin Chit came to ask whom Ko Ko would recommend to be included. Ko Ko replied that he thought Thakin Than Tun was a capable person and had a realistic view of the political situation. When we heard that the Japanese had sent for Dr. Ba Maw, who came escorted with bodyguards, I thought how right Ko Ko had

---

[1] Kempeitai—the Japanese Military Intelligence office.

been when he had said to me that as long as Dr. Ba Maw was still around, he would be placed in a position of power.

I was certain that his prediction of the return of the British would also prove to be true, and from that day on I did not spend any of my British currency. I was determined to restart the newspaper business with my savings after the Japanese left. We had in our possession two or three thousand bales of paper, and a dealer from Chinatown came to offer Japanese currency to purchase it, equivalent to twenty-five kyat for each. I had bought the paper stock with English currency equivalent to seven-and-a-half kyat for each, so I told him that if he transported the paper from Bogalay at his own expense I would sell it to him.

That night when Ko Ko came home I told him about the deal, but he said that, although he had refused an editorial post with a newspaper to be issued by Dr. Ba Maw's government, he had promised to sell our stock of paper at cost to the government as a gesture of support. Ko Ko said he would not go back on his word, so I informed the man from Chinatown that our deal was off. We brought back our stock of paper from Bogalay in several batches, using sampans to transport the bales. When we arrived in the evening to hand over the paper, the people in charge of accepting the bales shouted at us to go away, that the office was closed.

I was furious that we had brought over the paper all the way from Bogalay to give away at cost, and struggled to move the paper through Yangon on hired hand-pushed carts while sirens wailed, and then found ourselves treated in this manner. I told Ko Ko I would not bring over a single packet more from Bogalay, and he tried to persuade me to be more patient with those people.

The day that bombs fell around us in Yegyaw, I gave birth prematurely, at seven months, to my youngest child, our son Moe Hein. Our friend U Ohn Khin advised us to come and live near them in Ahlone, as downtown Yangon was growing dangerous, and he said there was an empty house available not far from where he lived. I had never seen the house, but Ko Ko knew of it. He told me the house was good enough, but that the neighborhood was not too pleasant, and the houses were crowded together. I told him to find a house in a good residential area and to say to U Ohn Khin that the house he had suggested would be too small for us, giving this as a polite excuse.

We could not find a house, and allied bombs began to fall more heavily on Yangon. Then Bo Let Yar said he would be leaving for Pyinmana[2] and that we should move into his house in Golden Valley. Thakin Ba Hein was already staying in this house, and Thakin Than Tun lived nearby, and so it became more difficult to keep Ko Ko's work secret. To cover up the sound of the typewriter, Ko Ko hired a young man to copy out the financial column of the paper issued by the Japanese government and had him work the whole day at the typewriter, using the same paper Ko Ko used for his reports. When the young man was out to lunch, Ko Ko would lock the door and type his work. Ko Ba Hein asked what he was doing typing the whole day, and we replied that he was copying out articles from the newspaper for research.

The Japanese were not above torturing or putting to death people they suspected of subversive acts, so one might ask whether I was frightened. I must say that Ko Ko was very good at covering up his work, and even I, astute as I am, though at all times

---

[2] Pyinmana, a town in central Myanmar, served as headquarters for the Burma Defense Army. It is located near the present capital of Myanmar at Naypyitaw.

having him in my sight, had no idea about all that he was up to, so I had no fear at all of his work being found out.

When we moved to Golden Valley, we asked that government officials come and take away the stock of newsprint at our house that very same day and asked that they give us permission to sell it elsewhere if they could not take it away by evening. Someone promised to come by four in the afternoon, but by evening no one had arrived, so we left a man to manage the handover. Night fell, and still no one came, so the man we left in charge, afraid to stay on alone, went off to spend the night somewhere else. In the morning, it was discovered that every scrap of paper had been stolen during the night. The representatives of the government said they were "sorry," and I could not help but blame Ko Ko for getting us into such a mess.

We continued living in peace apart from that fiasco, selling off my jewelry bit by bit every month. Ko Ko continued with his undercover work, and the 1,500 kyat promised to serve as payment to his sources sometimes did not arrive in time, so I would often have to pay it out of my own pocket. One day a young man came, sent by Thakin Soe, or so he said, asking Ko Ko to head a Yangon-based force to drive out the Japanese, but we suspected this was a trap. One day Ko Ko discovered by chance that his reports were passing through our neighbor Thakin Than Tun's hands, but that he did not know it was Ko Ko who was sending them.

To make it easier to transport the bales of paper, we had repacked them, and so it was a simple matter to identify them. We reported the theft to the police with a description of how they were packed, and the bales were soon recovered. But as the deal had been made with the government, we now faced trial as defendants. After the paper had been sold at cost to the government, Ko Ko had not given another thought to the whole business, and so the trouble of unraveling the mess landed with me. I was furious that, not only had I missed selling the paper at a profit, but here I was now, facing more problems. Besides, Ko Ko was not taking anything for his own expenses out of the monthly payment of 1,500 kyat. When I complained, he would say, "Let's just help all the way if we want to help at all," and thus I found myself donating a fair bit to the undercover work as well.

When we were living at Bo Let Yar's house, Ko Ko felt sorry for Thakin Than Tun, who was at the time a bachelor[3] and living alone. Ko Ko would often tell me to "go look after his house, make it more comfortable," so in addition to handling my own housework, I had to go over to Thakin Than Tun's house and look after things.

When Bo Let Yar came back from Pyinmana, we moved to Kanbe,[4] where Su Su, a friend who was as close to me as a sister, lived with her mother. While putting up at her house, we looked for a place of our own in the area. I began to hate this life of moving from place to place. All the good houses had been taken over by the Japanese, so, knowing that finding one would be impossible, Ko Ko suggested getting a large plot of land and just putting up a bamboo shed to live in. I was so frustrated and exhausted with house hunting that, rather unfairly, I said to him that if I had half his abilities, I would kick the Japanese out of the governor's house and go live there.

My children had come into this world just before or during the war, and they had lived very little of their young lives in comfort and peace. I vowed that I would

---

[3] Thakin Than Tun later married Daw Khin Gyi, eldest sister to General Aung San's wife, Daw Khin Kyi.

[4] Kanbe is a suburb of Yangon, northeast of downtown.

never put them in a shed. Su Su's mother, whom I call Daw Daw, was just like me, a strong-minded and determined woman, and we were so much alike as to be mother and daughter. We went out together every day, tirelessly looking for a house.

Ko Ko, too, left the house every morning, by horse carriage if he could get one or else on foot for the five miles journey to town, carrying an umbrella. He would leave at nine o'clock every morning, not waiting for his meal to be ready, and would come home when it was almost dusk by trishaw, if he could find one, or more likely on foot. As soon as he got home, he would go straight to the typewriter to do his reports. He left them with me before leaving the next morning, to be picked up by someone.

Ko Ko was walking so much that a huge blister formed on his foot, but he did not complain about it. Every evening Daw Daw would wait for him to put some ointment on his blister; he kept on walking to town despite how painful it must have been, so that both Daw Daw and I were forced to nag him to rest. His health began to suffer; even as I looked after his health, he did nothing for it, so I had to tell him that I might be widowed young if he kept it up. As we were staying in Daw Daw's house and I trusted her completely, I felt obliged to tell her in part the true nature of Ko Ko's underground work.

Daw Daw cared so much for Ko Ko that in the mornings she would run after him crying shrilly, "U Chit Maung, please wait for a horse cart, I'm sure one will come soon, don't walk, it's too far, and the sun is so hot," etc. She made such a noise that all the neighbors came out of their houses to see what the commotion was about. I would look after my husband walking away in his black Yaw[5] *pasoe,* a jacket of brown homespun, and a big *lwe-eik*[6] on his shoulder, and tears would well up in my eyes.

All through the Japanese Occupation people saw him at teashops and thought he was idling away his time, but the teashops were his office and he gathered all his information there. Meanwhile, Daw Daw and I walked up and down many streets looking for a house. Feeling very dejected by our failure, we one day went to Thingangyun to attorney-at-law U Maung Gyi's house. When we got there, he told us that he owned two houses in a large garden near the Tamwe Race Course, not far from Kanbe, and that one house was rented by a Japanese and the other was available. Immediately Daw Daw and I went there and saw that both houses were empty, so we came back, and I rented one house for 500 a month. Such a strange fate brought me to this house that I wrote down all the details in my diary. The land had two ponds and many flowering shrubs and trees grew around the houses; it was truly a beautiful and pleasant place. We moved in at once.

We now lived in clean surroundings with fresh air, so all through the Japanese Occupation my children did not catch scabies or become ill as many others did. I had no need to worry about their health. I had two Karen girls to look after the house and children; finally, here, I could provide my family with all the comforts of a good home. As for the office furniture, we gave away some to the Burma Independence Army and sold off some. We only brought with us our personal belongings, the printing press, and typesetters' tables when we moved. We were living in an isolated area and, besides, it was far from town, so Ko Ko needed no strategy to hide the

---

[5] Yaw is a region in Upper Myanmar famous for its good quality cotton *longyi.*

[6] *Lwe-eik* is a cloth shoulder bag used to carry books by students and adults alike, especially the literati.

sound of his typing. As Bo Let Yar was back in Yangon from Pyinmana, whenever Ko Ko was asked to host dinners at which the political leaders could discuss their subterfuge plans, I would make sure to set a fine table in spite of the general shortage.

A businessman who had made his fortune in exports before the war happened to tell me how he was forced to keep his furniture in storage at a monastery, since he could not move it at present, and he mentioned that he wanted to sell it. So I bought all his things including a piano, a refrigerator, and good furniture. With all this, I was able to keep house in a grand style. Whenever our old friend Bo Let Yar came to visit, he would comment, "I cannot tell you how wonderful it feels to be here." I kept a very pleasant home so that my family and visitors could forget there was a war going on.

The compound was huge; the two ponds were the most beautiful of all, and the rows of roses and jasmine along their banks flowered profusely. In the early mornings, when I looked out from the upstairs balcony, I could see flocks of white paddy birds drinking at the ponds. On top of a hill in the distance, I could catch a glimpse of the Chauk-htut Kyee Pagoda. Every morning I would look out over this wonderful view from my balcony, watching frisky squirrels jumping from branch to branch in the mango and mayan[7] fruit trees. Sometimes I would even see rabbits scuttling around nervously among the flower bushes.

Before we married, Ko Ko had sent me a poem about Burmese tropical flowers, and here in our garden they bloomed so profusely that I was reminded of it. The yellowed summer leaves had fallen on the ground at the same time that flowers were bursting into bloom, and the breeze played through the small green buds just beginning to emerge on the boughs. Morning mists wrapped the scene in mystery, and even ascetics would feel an ache in their hearts to see such beauty.

Every morning I personally took care of cutting flowers from the garden to fill the vases for the household shrine as well as the vases in the parlor, the dining room, and the bedrooms. After my prayers, I would gather up my children and go out into the garden. While they played, I would walk on the banks of the ponds and softly recite the sutras of protection, sharing the merit with the guardian spirits of the earth and trees and asking their protection from all harm. I did all this without fail every day. Out of all the places I had lived in, none other offered me the sheer delight of living or the deep joy I found in religion as this house did. I often commented to Ko Ko during that time about the way one's surroundings have such strong effects on the mind.

As time passed, I could measure how Ko Ko's influence had changed and matured me since our marriage. He helped many people in his life, people of such diverse professions as artists, astrologers, writers, poets, artisans, etc., as he had a deep interest in and respect for any type of labor and learning.

Two of his friends lived with us in this house. The owner of the house had gone to considerable expense to build a very strong stone stairway up the front, and so we used it as a bomb shelter during air raids and did not bother to dig a shelter.

We were happily and most comfortably settled in this house. Then, one night a car drove up and someone rapped sharply on the front door. We opened it to find not friends, but strangers—Japanese men. They marched into the house, and one in a

---

[7] "Mayan" (canistel) is a small, sour fruit that ripens to an orange color, fruiting in the same season as mangos. Its tree is as tall as the mango's.

captain's uniform said harshly through the driver who interpreted, "We have come to take over this house. Move out by morning."

I told Ko Ko not to say a word. "I'll talk to them," I told him in Burmese.

Then I said to their interpreter, "Tell your officer we're not moving."

When my words were translated the captain was so furious that he lost his composure and, stalking through every room, said to us that tomorrow "the big master" would come and we had to be out by then; then he left abruptly.

I was furious that we were being ordered to vacate this house, a Burmese-owned house, not a British one. Ko Ko said we should find another house. When I told him there was no house to be found easily, he again repeated his suggestion that we buy a plot of land and build a bamboo shed. Retorting that I would never, ever live in a shed, I marched upstairs but could not sleep a wink that night.

The next morning, Ko Ko went out as usual to his teashop in Bahan, and soon after the Japanese arrived. One was in the uniform of a colonel in the Japanese Imperial Army, and the other two, presumably interpreters, were in mufti. As soon as the Japanese colonel saw us still quite settled at home, he raved in Japanese, making such a noise as to make my ears ache. One of the two Japanese in mufti, rather short of stature, interpreted what he said into excellent English, much to my surprise. I had never before met a Japanese who spoke English so well.

I said through the interpreter that as this house did not belong to their enemy, I would not leave and that, furthermore, we did not belong to the class of people who could pack up and leave at a moment's notice. The officer's moustache bristled and his eyes popped as he began shouting at me. The other gentleman in mufti, older than the interpreter and looking more like a tall European than a Japanese, said something to the colonel, who immediately calmed down and spoke more graciously. Later I learned the tall gentleman's name was Mr. Yoshida.

"It is the duty of the citizens to move when the army has need of a place to stay, and it is imperative that you move as soon as possible."

"So where are we supposed to live?"

"You can live in a shed that can easily be built with bamboo."

"It's not right for soldiers to live in a house like this, indeed, soldiers should be living in barracks. Civilians cannot live in huts or sheds."

"So move to another house, then."

"There's none available."

The interpreter said, "He's saying it's not his problem that there are no other houses. He said to move out tomorrow."

"And how are we to move, with all the stuff we have? No, we won't move. Unless I get a house to my liking, I'm staying right here."

"This is by military order!" The interpreter shouted the words in the same way his officer had. I was so furious I shouted louder at them: "You'll move into this house only over my dead body. So go ahead, shoot me!"

I had no idea what they were saying to each other at that point, but the house rang with their voices. I was past caring; I was determined to die to keep this house.

Mr. Yoshida, the tall Japanese civilian, stared grimly at my face and asked through the interpreter what my husband did and who he was. When I answered "U Chit Maung," it became apparent the sound "Chit" probably did not exist in their language, for they seemed to be having difficulty getting the name right. From a drawer I took out the recommendation that General Ida had signed for Ko Ko while he was temporarily employed at the peace organization and rapped on the signature for them to see. Mr. Yoshida bowed to the paper before reading it. It was crumpled from the way we had shoved it into the drawer, and he said through the interpreter that we should not keep it like this but to frame it. I was still so angry that I snatched it from him and tossed it on the sofa, saying "Useless" in English. Mr. Yoshida picked it up and told me to treat this paper with respect.

I said, "You treat someone who has a general's testimony like trash by ordering us to move out like this? Well, in that case there's no place in my house for this paper."

They again talked among themselves and then asked my permission to look over the house. They looked all over, and when they saw the thousands of books in the upstairs library, they looked astonished. No wonder! According to our list, Ko Ko had by then over ten thousand books. I explained that they were my husband's books and that he was a newspaper editor. Their faces changed somewhat, and they lost some of the stern look they had worn downstairs. After checking out every room, they commented that in the whole country they had not seen any house this clean and tidy. I retorted that if they had come before the war, they would have seen all houses in the same condition.

We came downstairs and again they asked me, in polite tones this time, to move. I noticed that the tall Japanese gentleman, Mr. Yoshida, was very gracious and did not speak much, but he stared thoughtfully at me the whole time. Finally they pleaded that they needed this location for their cavalry unit and that they would give me a house in Windermere that had once been owned by the British.

I asked Su Su's mother to come with me, and we went around, accompanied by the Japanese, to look at houses. The houses were already occupied by the military, and when the house was shabby, I would refuse to get down from the car. The area was often heavily bombed, so although I liked a few of the houses I grimly kept on saying no.

The Japanese soldiers arrived in droves to live in the garden, cutting down the old trees and building small huts to live in. I was determined to stay on until I found a place to my liking, but I was getting worried about living in close proximity to the military and wanted to move, so I secretly went out looking for houses. Every morning I recited sutras in the garden and begged the guardian spirits to help me out of this mess.

About twenty days after the Japanese cavalry set up quarters in my garden, Mr. Yoshida came to call one evening. He said he was not a military man but that he was a businessman trading in leather. On that first day we met, he had taken a lift from his friend the colonel. He said he did not like it that an editor's family should be treated so rudely and had urged the officers concerned not to force us out. If, however, we were feeling uncomfortable living with the Japanese soldiers around us, would we be willing to move to one of the two houses his company had taken over, in Baukhtaw?[8] He was offering us a house, he explained, for the good of Burmese–Japanese relations. Besides, he had asked around in town about my husband and had heard that he was a very patriotic man. Being one himself, he had deep respect for such a man. All this he said in fluent English, and I was surprised, as he had not let on he even knew the language the other day.

Living next door to a Japanese was not really a good idea, considering Ko Ko's work, but it seemed better than living surrounded by a horde of them, so we went to

---

[8] Baukhtaw is a suburb not far from Kanbe.

Baukhtaw to see the house, which was good enough. When I complained that it was dirty, Mr. Yoshida immediately said he respected people who liked cleanliness, and he promised to repaint, put in new plumbing, and clean up the place when we moved in. He gave the project of redoing the house to an Indian contractor, and so once again we moved.

We settled into the two-storey house next door to the bungalow where Mr. Yoshida lived with his Japanese household staff. My house was soon restored with new plumbing and fresh paint, and Ko Ko teased me that the spirits must be looking out for me after all, as I was getting help from this unexpected quarter—a Japanese no less. However, we warned each other to be more careful since we were living this close to a Japanese.

Every morning before he left for work and every evening when he came home, Mr. Yoshida came to our front door and would bow and speak to Ko Ko, asking if everything was all right and whether we needed anything. He treated us as if we were in Japan, and he our host. He would not allow any Japanese soldier to enter our compound, and I think he was trying his best to make up for the rudeness of the soldiers from his country, so that we would not think badly of his fellow citizens. He asked Ko Ko to write an article about why the Burmese resent the Japanese, and Ko Ko wrote one in English, listing examples of rudeness and cruelty at length. Mr. Yoshida was very shrewd; in the afternoons, while Ko Ko was not at home, he would come over to ask me what all the typing was about.

I showed him the pile of typed reports on the economy of East Asia copied from the newspapers, and he seemed very pleased to see it.

Politicians were, as usual, constantly in and out of our house, especially Bo Let Yar, and Mr. Yoshida came to ask me about why this particular man came so often. I said we were all interested in art and that he came to show us his painting and to look at the ones done by Ko Ko. I showed him some paintings, telling him that I had not yet had time to hang up their artwork on the newly painted walls and that my husband and his friend supported each other in their shared hobby.

Mr. Yoshida also asked where Ko Ko went every day from morning until dusk, and I replied airily that no man was as busy as my husband; why, he spent all his time on this welfare society or that, and he was constantly attending meetings to talk over such matters, aside from offering consultations to "government bodies."

Actually, Ko Ko *was* involved in such matters, advising Minister of Information Bandoola U Sein or attending meetings at Education Minister U Hla Min's office. If something were within his power, Ko Ko would do it himself, but if it would take someone of a minister's rank to get the task done, he would consult and support the ministers concerned with the project. He often gave talks on being a journalist at courses given to young men.

Once back home, and as soon as he finished his dinner, Ko Ko would sit at his desk to proofread the Burmese dictionary being prepared by U Aung Myat Tut and the Pyapon monks U Zaniya and U Awbatha. He would write a chapter or two for the *History of Burmese Culture,* to which such academics as Dr. Ba Han, Dr. Htin Aung, and U Pe Maung Tin also contributed, or else write up a report at the request of U Hla Min on an overall plan of administration for the country. Ko Ko sometimes wrote speeches for a friend who was a Member of Parliament, or at times continued working on his essay advising young men how they could work for the betterment of the country once we gained independence.

On top of all that, he had his intelligence work to type up, and sometimes he was interrupted by air raids, during which we all had to take shelter. Often he had to work until three or four in the morning. I would sit by him and nag him to go to bed, but mostly I would be so intrigued at what he was writing that I would forget myself and stay up as late.

To my surprise, as soon as we moved into this house Ko Ko began to keep a journal in a leather-bound ledger book. That, too, took up his precious time every evening. On the days that he stayed home, his brother Ko Than Tun sent men he trusted to bring the reports to him.

One day we had to take shelter for almost an hour, and it was three in the morning when the all-clear signal finally sounded. We went up to bed, but Ko Ko got up at once, saying he just remembered he had to write a report on military titles to give the next morning. After he had gone downstairs, I tiptoed after him and read over his shoulder. He was writing at a fast pace, line after line appearing on the page with lucidity and intelligence. I once asked him how he stored all this information in his brain, and he said, "I keep them in separate compartments."

The report he wrote that dawn was a proposal to use various Pali[9] names as titles for military personnel. It went as follows:

To
Lt. Col. Let Yar
Burma Defense Army
Dated 1306 Kason, 9th Waning Moon Day[10]

Dear Colonel,
I have here the list of titles by Pali names, and I will report on their ancient usage and meaning.
1. Maha Thurein
Maha means great, and Thurein means "one who could even swim the oceans dressed in armor, as well as being a leader and hero who with full confidence in himself would dare to go into battle alone." It is a better honor than Maha Thiha Thura: use it if you want to.
2. Zeya Pyanchi or Theinga Pyanchi
Pyanchi means a man without any fear, who is as swift as a bird and as agile. Zeya means victory, and Theinga means like a lion. So you can choose between two meanings, Theinga Pyanchi to compare to a lion, or Zeya Pyanchi to symbolize victory. Pyanchi has a deeper meaning, which suggests that the person is not only brave but has the ability to pierce into the enemy's ranks and "as an eagle, is able to claw away the crown on the enemy's head." Thiha Thura, on the other hand, also compares one to a lion, i.e., to be as brave as a lion, which is an ordinary title. For a title to mark individual bravery, I would prefer either Thiha Pyanchi or Theinga Pyanchi, take whichever you want. Personally I prefer Zeya Pyanchi.
3. Shwe Taung Akar

---

[9] Pali is the ancient language of the Buddhist scriptures; its relationship to modern Burmese can be compared to the relationship between Latin and English.

[10] May 4, 1944.

Instead of this I would prefer Thiha Yawda. Thiha means lion, of course, and Yawda means one who is skilled in warfare and has no fear. The Burmese kings would give the honor Thiha Yawda for Distinguished Conduct and Nanda Yawda for Meritorious Service. To combine both, they use the term Maha Yawda to mean Outstanding Bravery. I know you will notice the various differences.

4. Shwe Taung Akar or Ye Kyaw Swar

We have little record concerning the tradition of giving titles to those wounded in battle. The concept of a hero in our culture assumes that a brave or able fighter would not get wounded. Soldiers consider it a result of their weakness to be wounded and would go into battle determined to win or die. So, an honor to give to the wounded would be a new category for the country. Shwe Taung means the royal palace, or here, the State, and Akar means one who strives to serve with all his might. Ye Kyaw Swar, however, means one braver than others, and it might be at odds with our traditional concept of bravery, as I stated above.

5. Way Ya Kyaw Htin

There was a tradition in the old days of giving titles such as Way Ya Kyaw, Way Ya Kyaw Htin, or Theinkha Way Ya, etc. Way Ya means more than bravery, it means someone who tramples the enemy and one with a strong will. It means one who is brave and capable. It would be ideal for those rendering the best technical services. Way Ya in the old days was given to those who excelled in their professions.

I meant this to be a short explanation, but it seems to have grown lengthy. However, I wanted you to know the exact meanings of the titles you choose.

Chit Maung
Journal Kyaw

I never succeeded with my daily pleadings for him to rest for the day at home. Every day he had something new to do, and one day I wanted him to stay home to take a laxative, but he said he had to give a talk to the younger members of the Traders' Association, and off he went. I could only call out after him, "Your health will suffer one day, mark my words."

Everyone commented that U Chit Maung was doing nothing, and some politicians looked down on him. As he wrote in his diary once, this period of being at everyone's disposal involved not fewer responsibilities but more. He wrote that he did not wish to complain, but if he had more free time he could write more for the sake of the country's future. On the entry dated Tagu, 7th Waxing Moon Day,[11] he had written that he had become "everyone's slave," as he termed it, and so, I thought to myself, he was doing what he wanted: serving everyone for the sake of the country's political future.

When I saw him writing a finance and revenue plan for the country, I asked him who told him to do it. He said jokingly to me that he would use it when he became finance minister. I in turn teased him by asking whether he wanted it torn up the way another such plan had been torn up in Bogalay when the Japanese first invaded.

---

[11] March 19, 1945.

He knew finance and revenue were important for the country and studied it more than other subjects.

Bo Sekkya told Ko Ko that the Japanese wanted a report on the Thayarwaddy Rebellion led by Saya San, and that he, Bo Sekkya, had told them that only U Chit Maung could write it and would ask him to do so. Ko Ko wrote a report titled "The Real Origin and Causes of the Burmese Rebellion (1930–1932)."[12]

I watched and waited, vowing that one day I would stop Ko Ko from being "everyone's slave" and move him to take part openly in politics so that he might really do all he could for the country. Those who knew him closely during the Japanese Occupation already knew what a brilliant man he was, and there would be those who, like me, believed he could become a political force in building up the country with his talents and knowledge; there would also be people who disagreed with me. He was like the "drum that remained silent unless beaten," to repeat a Burmese idiom; he was not one to trumpet his own abilities.

I kept house in Baukhtaw the same way that I had in Tamwe, with well-polished floors and furniture and rooms filled with flowers. Whenever Mr. Yoshida came over to our house, he would not enter, using the excuse that his shoes were muddy, but instead would stand to talk at the front door. I had no work, so I became a proper housewife, with time to look after my household. I was busy from morning to night keeping things in order and trying out new ways to make our life more pleasant, so Ko Ko gave me a book and told me to write everything down.[13]

One day when he did not go to town we sat talking, and I persuaded him to publish a novelette written by Ko Saw Oo titled *We Don't Deserve This*, and so it was printed in a slim volume. After it came out, Ko Ko urged me to try my hand at writing a novel, and he was so insistent that I finally promised to do it. Even so, I had absolutely no idea what to write, and one day sat racking my brains at my desk, an empty page before me. Just then I heard the squeak of the back door as someone opened it and, finally inspired, wrote that down as the first sentence. I had no plans to publish it, I merely wrote it as a test to see if I could do it. After completing the novel, I gave it the title "A Hpyu" and handed it to Ko Ko. He read it and commented that it was too early to publish something like this.

We were not earning a cent and had been selling off my gold jewelry, and by now that was gone, so I was even beginning to sell off some of my diamonds. One morning before going out, Ko Ko said he wanted to talk and took me upstairs to our room.

"Tin Lay, can you give me about 4,500 kyat?"

"Oh, Ko Ko, didn't Bo Let Yar give you any money?"

"Yes he did, but not last month, so this month's payment is all gone now. I have to pay so many people that it's never enough."

"Then don't do this anymore, Ko Ko. To be responsible for such a huge thing and to have only 1,500 kyat to spend … you know how worthless Japanese currency is."

"I can't stop doing this, Tin Lay. Perhaps they haven't got much."

---

[12] See Appendix A.

[13] Journal Kyaw Ma Ma Lay's novel, *Thu Ma*, published in 1945, was based on this part of her life.

"It's not possible that they don't have enough, Ko Ko, this is the kind of work where people have to spend tens or hundreds of thousands, and to use only 1,500 on it sounds pretty sad to me. Can't you ask for more?"

"I don't want to ask … if I did maybe they would've given more. Anyway, they know how much I have to spend."

"You think they'd know? They might even be thinking they are also paying you out of this measly sum!"

"Bo Let Yar knows … he knows we're not surviving on this, and he knows I'm working for free."

"But Ko Ko, 4,500 is too much. I'm selling off something almost every day. Even your fare to go to town adds up, you know. You don't have to worry about a single thing concerning us and I don't think it's fair that you bother me like this. It's not fair."

"Please, Tin Lay, if you can please give me the money. Even if they don't keep their word, I must. *I* must."

"So, to save your honor I'm the one who's always forking out the money and would *they* know that?"

"Think of it as serving your country."

"I'm doing it not only for the country's sake, Ko Ko, it's so that you won't be compromised."

"I owe you so much already, Tin Lay. I hate to ask you like this, and I really feel bad about it."

He looked so unhappy I could not bear it anymore that someone like him should be in such a state of despair, and so the responsibility of selling off my stuff fell on my shoulders again.

Previously I had decided to use the valuable British currency I was keeping aside to publish our journal once the Japanese left. Then Su Su's mother, Daw Daw, happened to drop in at that moment. I explained things to her and asked her to change the money into Japanese currency. Daw Daw was appalled and scolded Ko Ko.

"U Chit Maung, I can't stand it that you walk to and fro from town every day without spending anything and then you have to use your own money, too. You are doing so much, and yet they ignore your needs … I feel so bitter when I think of it. If you are caught, the Japanese will kill you for sure, and yet your friends can't even arrange transportation for you. And they, they are all driving around in their own cars …"

"But Daw Daw, I am serving my country and doing all this for the people …"

I interrupted them, shoving the pound notes into Daw Daw's hands.

"Well, Daw Daw, consider yourself doing a service for the country and do please go and change the money for me."

Although I gave Ko Ko the money he needed, I thought all day about how he was being treated, and to soften my bitter feelings had to keep reciting sutras of Metta.[14]

Ko Ko was very gentle by nature, while I was hard-hearted, so he kept trying to teach me to have a softer heart. I was hard in the sense that if I were cheated, I would not look at that person again. For example, one of Ko Ko's friends cheated Daw Daw out of some money, and I was so angry that a man should do that to a woman that I

---

[14] A sutra of Loving Kindness in Buddhist thought.

did not even want to see his face, but Ko Ko spent hours persuading me to be more forgiving.

"Tin Lay, I would say that you have the heart of a good person when you say you never want to see the face of a cheat, but there is just one thing missing from that good heart. You know that according to the Mingala Sutra[15] it is correct to avoid bad people, but if you do that and keep strictly away from him, that person loses all chances of turning over a new leaf. Like you, I, too, hate to associate with sleazy people, however rich they might be or how wealthy their families, or if they are nobodies. I found that the more such people I met, the harder I became; I even felt less compassionate towards those who are truly in need. That is the beginning of a hardened heart. While having contempt for them, unknowingly anger and pride grow inside you, and so for me it became really hard to send Metta[16] to these people. So if we scorn them for being cheats, we, too, become bitter and angry at the same time. I remembered the Four Rules of Byamaso[17] that Buddha taught, and living by them I learned to deal with such people, but even then it was not easy to remove the pride and anger inside me. Previously I would have nothing to do with such people, but now I pity them and send them Metta as much as I can. What I mean to say is, I feel sorry for them and I pray I would not become like them and pray that they would change for the better. I must try to show them the right way to live. Because I am not cut from the same cloth as they are, at first I was loathe having to deal with them, and I must admit I remained proud. Then I noticed how much disgust I had in my heart and how much it influenced my writings, so it became clear I must also generate Metta towards myself to soften my pride. So, Tin Lay, can you, too, not forgive?"

As I listened to him, by the time he was halfway through I realized it was my pride that was hardening my heart. I forgave that man before Ko Ko finished talking and to this day bear no ill will against him.

Then once again the Japanese army wanted to commandeer our house in Baukhtaw and asked us to move out. I was getting sick and tired of the constant moving as well as the heavy expenses involved, so I begged Ko Ko to agree that we would just move to Bogalay, this time for good. He half joked that in his previous life he must have been a municipal tax collector if in this life he was being punished with the life of a gypsy. The military then ordered us to move within three days, this time it commanded not only us, but Mr. Yoshida as well. It was impossible to find any place big enough for our things within three days, and we were in despair.

Next door to Bo Let Yar, there was a house owned by some Burmese, and through Mr. Yoshida we asked the people who occupied it at the time, some Japanese, to move. They promised they would, but only in a month's time, so Mr. Yoshida said we could come and live with him in a house he had found on Pyay Road. The house was almost opposite the Teacher's Training College, and was a large house and compound, formerly owned by the McGregor Company.[18] We could

---

[15] The Sutra of Auspiciousness.

[16] The Buddhist way of generating loving feelings towards other people, even enemies, literally is called "to send Metta."

[17] The Four Rules of Byamaso are four cardinal virtues or sublime states of mind: Metta, loving kindness; Karuna, compassion; Mudita, happiness at others' good fortune; and Upyitkha, detachment.

[18] British timber merchants.

stay there until we were able to move next to Bo Let Yar. However, it was quite out of the question for us to live in the same house with a Japanese. Mr. Yoshida seemed to guess this and told us that if we came with him there would be no other Japanese in the house, apart from himself, and that his Japanese household staff would not rejoin him until after we had moved out, in a month's time.

We told ourselves it was only for a month and accepted his offer and went to see the house. As Mr. Yoshida was leaving his servants behind, I said I would give him his meals and have my staff look after his needs, and so we moved to Pyay Road and lived as if he were the guest in our home. After about ten days, Mr. Yoshida said he had to go to Singapore for two weeks, and so that we would not be alone, he left a very polite young Japanese man in his place. However, the young man only came every night to sleep downstairs and would leave for work the next morning.

For months, Ko Ko had been walking to town, so he asked Bo Let Yar to buy him a trishaw. Ko Ko hired someone trustworthy to pedal it for him, so he got at least this transportation to continue his work. If there were too many Japanese soldiers on the roads as he came and went, the trishaw would detour to avoid running into them.

Mr. Yoshida did not return within two weeks as he said he would, and so, as we could not leave his belongings unattended, we were stranded on Pyay Road. During that time, Ko Ko said he wanted to write a history book to be used in schools and began to write in his journal. For this project, his reference books in English and Burmese numbered nearly sixty. At the same time, he was writing something on the reconstruction of Myanmar after Independence, and so I asked him which book he thought would be finished first.

He joked, one or the other, for sure!

As there were so many rooms in the house, he said he wanted to use one to offer a free course on journalism to young men and asked me if I could give them lunch. I took joy in his generosity but thought to myself, "as if he hadn't enough to do!" In this period of scarcity, it was difficult enough to get food for ourselves so, regretfully, I could not feed the students and felt bad about it. While we were talking about journalism, he mentioned that I should read his favorite book, *Queed*. I said I had tried once but found it too difficult. He asked me where the book was, and I told him that it was in the cupboard in our bedroom, and so taking the key from me he went upstairs. Only a few minutes afterwards did I remember that this book was kept together with my diary and other reports, and I ran upstairs after him.

He was already reading my diary.[19]

"Don't read it now, Ko Ko, wait until it's in book form."

"Tin Lay, when did you write all this? Look, there are copies of my reports here, too, when I asked you to burn them. Don't you know how dangerous they are? Aren't you afraid, since we are living in the same house with the Japanese! Burn them all today without fail … it's too risky."

Suspicious that there might be more, he searched the cupboard thoroughly. I knew there was nothing I could do and sat silently on the bed, looking on. He took down the stack of dated envelopes and, seeing his hair clippings inside them, turned to me and said in English, "You are my perfect wife." He asked why I was keeping them, and I said I wanted to show his children how their father got grey hair so early in life. He looked over every page of my diary and asked how I would make use of

---

[19] It is normal practice for members of the immediate family to read each other's diaries.

it. I said I would write a book titled "My Husband," and he said he was already thinking of writing one called "My Wife."

"I have to write this book as payment for all that I owe you," he said.

"So, aren't you going to give any interest?"

"I'll give you the interest before I repay the debt ... come with me ... come ..."

He dragged me downstairs and, opening *Queed,* he proceeded to translate for me verbally. For the first few lines I heard nothing, as I was staring at him in amazement: he was translating from English, but it sounded as if he were reading the text in Burmese. Then I was caught up in the story, but I had things to attend to, and when I got up to do them Ko Ko followed me around, saying, "There's more, Tin Lay, come back."

I enjoyed the book so much that when he came home I would thrust it into his hands and ask him to read at once, and while he was away during the day I would simmer with impatience to hear more. It was a story of a brilliant and aloof man who met a woman of intelligence, one who dragged him into human society again, and of how he finally became a great editor. The twists and turns of the story were intriguing, and I was in awe of the main character but, at the same time, I was awed by Ko Ko's ability to translate like this, reading in English but smoothly and correctly turning the words into Burmese at almost the same speed. When I first tried to read *Queed,* I had to look up so many words in the dictionary that I had given up in despair, so I knew it was not an easy book to read. This little book, so long stored deep in my cupboard, now entered deep into my heart.

At night, we often had to go into the bomb shelter, and there I would listen to Ko Ko reading *Queed* until two or three in the morning. When he came to parts he had marked with a pencil, he would also read it in English to show me why he liked it. There were over four hundred pages of small print, and it took him about five days to read it out in Burmese. But these words in Burmese were unrecorded sounds that disappeared in the wind, and I was very annoyed with myself for not knowing shorthand. If I asked him to translate the book for publication, with his workload he would not get around to it for ten years. Now it had been read out in full to me in five days and if I had known shorthand I could have had the manuscript all ready by now. Out of a hundred readers, at least seventy-five would be inspired by *Queed,* and every time I thought about it, I felt that it was a great loss. This "interest" that he gave me not only covered all his "debts" but put me in *his* "debt of gratitude" twice over.

By then Mr. Yoshida had not returned for over five months, but we were not bothered by any Japanese, so we lived in peace. Every day Ko Ko's work began with typing reports as soon as he got up, then he would go to town, and at night he would continue writing his books. I loved and admired him more than ever; I made sure he had everything he needed and served him with all of the five wifely duties.[20] At night, I would sit up with him, and at that time I wrote a book titled *Thu Ma* (She),

---

[20] There are five duties of a husband and five of a wife, as stated in the old texts of correct behavior. The husband should: 1. not treat his wife with disrespect; 2. entrust his wife with his earnings; 3. be faithful to his wife and not enjoy the company of other women; 4. adorn his wife with jewels appropriate to her station; 5. be tender and loving towards his wife. The wife should: 1. be capable in managing household affairs; 2. be careful about how the earnings of her husband are spent; 3. be faithful to her husband and not enjoy the company of other men; 4. distribute the earnings to both her parents and parents-in-law equally; 5. rise from bed in the morning before her husband does and serve him faithfully.

and he wrote a preface for it under his pen name Shwe Lin Yone and had it printed by *Myanmar Alin*.

It would seem that we had a great deal in common, but actually, when I sat down to think it through, I realized we were very different from each other; he was a gentle-hearted person, while I was hot-tempered. He was humble, I was proud. He had patience, I had none. He acted with reason, while I was impulsive. He always spoke gently, while my words always came out strong. He was discreet, while I was frank. He would never let it show that he disliked someone, whereas if I did not like anyone there was no doubt about it. He was calm, I was a worrier. He was mature, and I was short tempered. He always kept his head down, while my head was always lifted high. He did not want to be out front, and I wanted to run ahead of the crowd.

One day Ko Ko came home while I was bathing; he rapped on the bathroom door and told me to come out quickly. I did, asking him why, and he told me to get his bedroll ready for him.

"Be quick, Tin Lay, they're coming to arrest me."

"Are the Japanese going to arrest you? Is the game up?"

"Not the Japanese, the Burmese government ... I found out they were going to arrest me today."

"Why!?"

"They thought I was agitating against them and will arrest me under the security law."

"Oh god, what a shameful thing for them to do ..."

I packed his bedroll while he packed books to read in prison. I knew that his arrest would reflect badly on the government and wondered how they could so underestimate the likely backlash against their action—arresting someone the public knew to be a good, patriotic man, even if none knew of his undercover work. I wondered if his close friends in government could ignore Dr. Ba Maw's order. I shuddered to think that someone like him could be put at risk by such a government.

I asked, "What should I do, Mr. Yoshida is not back yet? I think I'll send the children and all our things to Bogalay if you are in prison."

"Yes, do that. I'll send a note to Bo Let Yar, I'm certain he'll look after all of you. Don't worry."

Ko Ko wrote the note and had it sent quickly, and a reply came from Bo Let Yar at once, telling us not to worry and that he was doing what he could about the impending arrest. We waited in readiness, but no police came, not that day and not ever. We never found out who pulled what strings. However, Ko Ko's brother Ko Than Tun was arrested and kept at the Kamayut Police Station, where I sent meals to him every day. Ko Ko refused to ask anyone for his brother's release.

We had been in this house for about six months when there was a murder at the leather factory, and Mr. Yoshida came back from Singapore. The Japanese living next door to Bo Let Yar said they still could not move, so we had to try through Mr. Yoshida to have them vacate the premises; still, we could not move immediately. Mr. Yoshida would help as much as he could when I was busy with housework, and gradually I noticed that we became like father and daughter.

I remembered what Captain Cook, the son-in-law of Governor Sir Dorman-Smith, told Ko Ko before he left the country—that not all Japanese were cruel or rude. Mr. Yoshida was a true gentleman, considered a man of high principles not only by us, but also by the other Japanese. He knew I had no love for the Japanese and that I considered the independence they gave us to be a false one, but he often commented to me that my view reflected the true spirit of patriotism.

I had stubbornly refused to burn the reports I had saved that Ko Ko found with my diary, but with Mr. Yoshida back in the house, Ko Ko again insisted on it. I took the whole pile into an empty room and locked the door. Ko Ko would never know how wretched I felt. If I destroyed them all, it would fulfill his wish of not letting anyone credit him for such good work; but doing so would destroy my hope to have people know what kind of a person he was. To burn the proof of his contribution to our country, which he had accomplished at his own risk, was like burning my very soul. His wish was fulfilled, at last: all proof of his intelligence work turned into ashes.

A month after Mr. Yoshida came back, yet again the military wanted this house, and we were told to move out at once. I moaned and wondered what was so bad in our Karma that we were always being shuttled here and there. Ko Ko suggested I consult an astrologer, so we went to see U Hla Maung of Seitta Thukha Road, where Daw Daw took us. U Hla Maung checked Ko Ko's Zartar[21] and told him he would lose both his possessions and his life, and so I came back more despairing than before.

Ko Ko consoled me by saying that he did not believe everything the astrologers might say. "However, Tin Lay, I do not disrespect their knowledge, so we could ask others, too."

That he did, and to comfort me he told me that the other astrologers said his fate was at a low point now but that it would improve after his birthday. I prayed that I would die in his place.

We all moved to a house three doors down on Pyay Road and lived there with Mr. Yoshida, who was also trying his best to have the Japanese vacate the house we wanted. He complained to every Japanese officer he met that a Burmese editor's family was being forced to move repeatedly because the Japanese had originally requisitioned their house near the race course in Tamwe. Here, too, in the Pyay Road house, I kept things as clean as possible and installed Mr. Yoshida in one bedroom. I made things as comfortable as I could to make everything pleasant for all.

Every morning at five, I would prepare breakfast for Mr. Yoshida and for Ko Ko before he left for his undercover work. In the evenings, they would both return home at almost the same time. I would set the table first for Mr. Yoshida, and then Ko Ko and I would eat together. Mr. Yoshida appreciated the fact that he was looked after so well and kept comfortable without spending a cent for anything, and he never said a single word to upset me in the slightest. In this way, there was no problem living with a Japanese person; in fact, Mr. Yoshida's presence protected us from harassment. Mr. Yoshida considered us his family, and during air raids, when he would go into his own shelter, if we were not yet in ours he would come running up again to urge us to do so quickly. "It would be a loss for the country if you die, U Chit Maung, don't take risks," he would say, and he would make sure Ko Ko was safely installed in the shelter before running back into his. He often told me how much he liked and respected my husband.

Once, while we were walking in the garden, Mr. Yoshida asked me how we ever got married, seeing that in appearance we were so different. I merely said that a man

---

[21] A palm leaf packet containing astrological calculations made for a person at the time of his or her birth.

and woman could have different tastes in dress and left it at that. He said he had never met any couple anywhere who adored each other as much as we did.

One day Ko Ko told me that the Burma Defense Army would soon rise up against the Japanese, that he would have to go with Bo Let Yar, and that it would be best if the children and I moved to Bogalay before that happened. At the time, any boats on the rivers were being fired upon by machine guns from the banks, so I told him I would rather stay in Yangon and go live with Daw Daw.

The situation became worse day by day; all at once the Burmese were turning on the Japanese. During this dangerous period, Mr. Yoshida took better care of me than before. Ko Ko said that, once he left, I might be facing danger from the Japanese if I stayed on in Yangon, and he urged me to go to Bogalay. We asked one of Ko Ko's men, Ko Po Lu, to hire a sampan, and we planned to tell Mr. Yoshida when he returned that I must leave because my mother was ill in Bogalay.

Around one in the afternoon, air-raid sirens wailed, so Ko Ko and I took our children into the shelter and then sat at its mouth talking over things with Ko Po Lu. We went inside only when the planes passed right over our heads. We had suffered through many bombings living in Yangon, but this time was the worst. Bombs fell on the Teachers' Training College[22] across the road from us, and the sounds of the explosions were terrifying. Shrapnel kept flying into the shelter, and we covered the children with our bodies to protect them. The shelter was an old one, none too safe, but the new one we were building was not yet completed.

We heard bombs exploding all around us, and I thought that our house would be destroyed. The air inside the shelter became thick with black smoke so that we could not see each other. The earth heaved and rolled with each explosion, and it was as if we were being tossed like a ship in a storm. As the bombs continued to fall without letting up, Ko Ko began to recite the Sambuddhay verse and told the children to recite it as well. The children did so without any mistakes, not crying at all while black smoke rolled into the shelter. When we heard one heavy explosion very close to us, Ko Ko grabbed my hand and tenderly whispered, "Tin Lay..." I clasped his hand tight and replied that we might all die together. Even as I prayed for our safety, I was thinking that perhaps we would all of us together die a violent death.

When the sound of the planes faded into the distance, we could finally see each other in the light of the fires burning around our shelter. Before the all-clear sounded, Ko Ko told me to stay back, and he ran towards the house. He came back with what clothes he could find, and I had to beg him not to go again. It was about half past five by the time the all-clear sounded. When we came out of the shelter, we saw an unexploded bomb in our garden, and it frightened me a lot, not knowing where to run to be safe from it.

The houses all around us had been destroyed, and only ours was left standing, but the roof had fallen in and tiles were scattered everywhere. It seemed we could not live there anymore. Most of the diaries and files I had been keeping were destroyed: all the material that I had diligently written down with the intention of recording Ko Ko's life in a book one day. The roads were blocked in order for the dead bodies to be removed so we could not go anywhere, and there was this bomb

---

[22] At the time this was not a college; it housed the offices of the Home and Defense departments.

waiting to explode in our garden. I wondered wretchedly if the astrologer was not correct after all.

Mr. Yoshida came running back from his office and was very upset to see us like this. He told me not to despair, comforting us by saying that the bomb would not explode because we were meant to live. "One day you will enjoy great happiness," he consoled us. He arranged immediately to find a place for us.

Just as dusk was falling, a soldier came with the news that we could move into the downtown office once occupied by the Thomas Cook's Company. I said I would rather go to the countryside and not stay in Yangon anymore. Throughout the night, the air-raid sirens wailed and we moved in and out of the shelter. Since we could not light a lamp, in the dark we could not gather up our possessions. As soon as it was light enough, we raced to Thingangyun and made arrangements to hire a sampan to go across to Thein Chaung Village. From there we would try to make our way farther out into the countryside. By five that evening, we were ready to leave. I told Mr. Yoshida to keep our things at his office in Bahan for the time being and that I would send for them soon. Then we made our way to Thein Chaung Village.

We rented a house in Thein Chaung and sent word to Mr. Yoshida that we were settled in what lodgings we could find. The next day he wrote telling us "not to sit on the floor or eat sitting on the floor" and sent some furniture to us by sampan. He also packed up Ko Ko's books and hired a truck to send them on by sampan. We heard later that he had carried out the books himself. He also wrote me not to allow Ko Ko to come back to his side of the river and for me to come to see him as soon as possible at Daw Daw's house.

I went as he asked, and when I saw him he said to me, "The Japanese are waiting to arrest U Chit Maung. Don't let him come to Yangon, stay there. If the Japanese come to your village to arrest him, show them this." He showed me a document in Japanese signed by several Japanese officers, and he translated it for me; it said that U Chit Maung was a Japanese spy and not to harm him. In spite of all our troubles, I had to try hard to keep a straight face at this turn of events.

"As long as I am alive," he reassured me, "I will make sure no harm will come to U Chit Maung. Some Japanese may be cruel, but please remember always that I am good to the Burmese. Tell U Chit Maung that no Burmese has died at my hands. We Japanese respect those who love their country even if they were our enemies. Please make sure he does not come to Yangon."

He sent me away, and I hurried back to Thein Chaung, afraid that Ko Ko might have followed me. The next day a letter came from Mr. Yoshida saying that he would have to leave Myanmar in three days and that we should come for our things stored in his office in Bahan. We hired as many sampans as we could, and Ko Ko and his friend Ko Thein Maung left early the next day. I pleaded with him not to go and to send only Ko Thein Maung, but Ko Ko said the Japanese had all left.

"There's no one left to arrest me," he said, and off they went to Yangon. At dusk, they returned with a large dog trotting along at the end of a rope. I asked about our things, and Ko Ko shook out his fingers in a gesture meaning "nothing."

It turned out that Mr. Yoshida had had to leave the very day he had sent us the letter.[23] Before he left, he had repeatedly told his staff to give U Chit Maung his own

---

[23] Mr. Yoshida settled in Kobe with his wife, and Daw Ma Ma Lay visited him there when she went to Japan in 1958; she wrote a full account of this visit in her book *Myitta*. They remained as close as father and daughter until their deaths.

belongings as a gift and also to return U Chit Maung's things to him. However, when Ko Ko and Ko Thein Maung arrived, the young Japanese guarding the office had simply pointed to the things and then departed.

As there were no longer any Japanese left in this building, the people from neighboring streets rushed in and began to take away everything, ripping things apart and fighting over them with each other. When this happened, Ko Ko had simply warned the people not to rush or to fight and to take what they wanted in an orderly manner. He had sat watching as everything was taken. He closed the front doors when more people came, but they broke down the door.

I cannot begin to tell how it pierced my heart to lose all the things I had been saving and using for over eight years. More than that, I yearned for the files I had already lost in the bombing, and I was so ill with misery that I could not get out of bed. I became like an invalid, unresponsive no matter how hard Ko Ko tried to get me to eat or console me by saying, "What if your files were lost? We're still alive, aren't we? You can write it all again."

Material possessions could be bought again some day but not those daily accounts, the reports and files I had kept of Ko Ko's work and our life. I had vowed to write fully about him one day, to show the world what sort of a man he was, but now, all was lost. I knew he did not want any publicity, and I felt bitter that *his* wish about that seemed to be coming true, and I felt more desperate than ever.

Ko Ko had watched people taking away our possessions as if he were King Waythandara[24] giving a huge donation ceremony, and when everything was gone he had noticed a large dog wandering around. Taking pity on it, he had tied a rope around its neck and had brought it back all the way across the river to Thein Chaung.

Many of our friends still lived in Bahan near the office of Mr. Yoshida, and I thought that if I had gone instead of Ko Ko I could have arranged for our things to be stored safely. Ko Ko said to me that, while watching the people stealing our things, he had felt a deep despair to see people turn into thieves, losing all honor and decency.

Before the Allied forces arrived, Daw Daw sent word that there was an empty house next door to hers in Kanbe, so we moved there as quickly as we could. We came into a city that looked desolate, with ruined buildings and empty streets, a devastated city. The day after we arrived in Kanbe, Ko Ko went off to town on his political work, and I went with Daw Daw to Bahan to see if we could salvage anything.

As we entered the compound, my heart almost stopped when I saw shattered glass lying all around my cupboard, which had been battered to pieces. As we went upstairs, we saw some men using knives and axes trying to break open an iron trunk where I kept some odds and ends, and we came away, frightened. I managed to get in touch with Myanmar Alin U Tin and asked for help, so he came with his friends and the thieves ran away. We brought this trunk on bullock cart back to Kanbe, and Ko Ko was amazed I had done so. He laughed and said that when someday he wrote about me, he must be sure to include this story, and I retorted that if I had gone to Bahan instead of him the other day we would not have lost anything.

After our return to Yangon, the Japanese currency became absolutely worthless, so we had to use the British currency we had been saving for so long. I racked my

---

[24] In the Jataka stories, Waythandara, the Buddha-to-be, is a greatly charitable king.

brains all the time, trying to figure out how to set up and publish our newspaper again, now that everything we had was gone. Ko Ko went off every morning as usual, with his cloth bag slung from his shoulder, and came home at dusk. Downtown Yangon is about five miles from Kanbe, and if he were not careful of being on time for the rare bus, he would have to walk, so I decided to start the publishing business again as soon as we could and from that income buy him a car.

"This time don't do political work from behind the scenes ... do it openly. I will begin publishing our journal as soon as we can, so don't worry about our income," I told him.

I looked around every day to find where I could buy a press and stocks of paper. I strengthened my resolve by saying to myself that, no matter what fate might destroy, one needed only a strong spirit to succeed again. I was determined that I would simultaneously succeed in two goals I had set for myself long ago: to have Ko Ko established at the forefront of the country as a great political leader and to publish our own paper.

The fact that I could face every disaster with a strong will was also due to him; he once wrote out for me a poem titled "It is All in the State of Mind"[25] and told me to learn it by heart and keep it in my mind at all times.

---

[25] See Appendix B.

CHAPTER 33

AFPFL

As soon as the Allied troops entered Yangon, the military police came for Ko Ko. They asked him what he thought of the Burma White Paper,[1] and told him to write down his views. He wrote that he had no liking for it and gave a list of reasons. He was then interrogated and answered that as long as the British were not going to change their stance towards the Burmese, he could not treat them as allies. The next day, their detectives came in a jeep and took Ko Ko to Yangon Prison.[2] The detectives told me that he would be well looked after, and Ko Ko then said to me in English not to worry as he was going to be a special guest of His Majesty King George. The detectives reddened at that.

He was kept in prison for twenty-four hours and then released on condition that he not go out of the Yangon city limits. Ko Ko continued with his work of making plans on how to negotiate with the British.

Bo Let Yar, who had fled the country just before the Japanese left, came back, but before he met with the Allied Forces, he hid out in our house for a few days. He looked extremely tired. I had great admiration for someone who had risked so much for the sake of his country, and while he recuperated I made his stay as pleasant and comfortable as possible by giving him a woman's gentle care, which he so deserved, making sure he had good, nourishing food.

He and Ko Ko were alike in so many ways, as well as looking physically alike as if they were true brothers. Among Ko Ko's friends there was no one else as close to him. They were of the same age but treated each other warmly and respectfully like older and younger brothers. At every turn in the political situation, Bo Let Yar would come to talk to Ko Ko. Bo Let Yar said he did not like the administrative plan proposed by the British and asked Ko Ko what he should do to register a protest. "Burn the Union Jack," Ko Ko suggested, and said he would buy a flag for him. Off the two went to town to buy one at the Harter Company on Sule Pagoda Road. When the sales manager heard what they were going to do with it, he gave it to them for free.

I tried to buy up as much paper stock as I could, and when I got hold of some, Bo Let Yar himself carried the packets on his shoulders upstairs for me. He was that sort of a man, like Ko Ko, with true consideration for others and with the same *ah-nar* attitude. The two of them were busy with political activities while I was busy trying to republish the journal.

---

[1] The Burma White Paper of May 17, 1945, was issued by the British government. It proposed to restore the colony to its former status (i.e., limited self-governance) after seven years of direct rule under a British governor, who would have only an advisory body of Myanmar politicians to consult.

[2] The place where Yangon Prison once stood is now the site of the Nursing Institute on Bo Gyoke Aung San Road.

I was spending on things I needed for the office as well as on daily expenses, so I had soon used up about eight thousand kyat. In order to buy the presses, I planned to sell off some more diamonds. When Ko Ko heard of it, he begged me to open up the bag of savings I had started on our wedding day, but I did not want to, as I had vowed to do that only on my fortieth birthday. I had been putting in sometimes five or sometimes five hundred kyat, and I had no idea how much I had accumulated. I had even told Ko Ko that if I should die before the age of forty, he should continue saving money until my fortieth birthday came up. When he told me to open it and use these savings "just for the time being" I remained adamant, and although he even got Daw Daw to take his side, I refused and sold off some more jewelry to buy a printing press.

All the politicians arrived back in Yangon and held discussions about forming one strong party. Ko Ko came back from one meeting muttering about the casualness of the politicians, who had not cared that one letter from Major General Slim to Major General Aung San was not properly addressed. Ko Ko knew that such slights could not be considered minor details, especially when dealing with the British who are very precise in matters of protocol.

While I urged him to enter politics openly now, I also had to beg him for enough columns for the *Journal Kyaw*. It came out on 1307, Wagaung, 10th Waxing Moon Day,[3] with Ko Ko's name as Chief Editor and U Saw Oo's as Associate Chief Editor in the masthead. (Actually, at the time, we had no idea where our Associate Chief Editor was.) Ko Ko was writing every single column that was published in the weekly under different pseudonyms, in spite of his busy political schedule. The pieces ranged from "Why the *Journal Kyaw* Needed to Be Published Now," "Must Myanmar Be the Exception?" "Is the War Over?" "What Is Happening in the Countryside?" "The Many Deaths of Hitler," "We Want Dialogue with the British Government," "Excerpt from the Editorial of the *Myanmar Gazette*," "What the *Daily Worker* Said," "What the *Tribune Daily* Said," and "We Denounce These." Not only that, he even wrote fiction when he could not get anything from other writers.

I teased him that "editors are cheating the readers," while commenting on how he was filling the whole paper with columns under different names. He said to me, "In that case I must tell you what Sir Thomas Broune said, Tin Lay, that an ambassador goes abroad to tell lies for the sake of his country, and a journalist sits at home to tell lies for the sake of his purse. The journalists he was addressing did not deny the truth of his words, but retorted that the first are black lies and the second merely white lies. See, if readers know it's just one person writing all the columns, they would lose interest, and only when they see several names would they chose what they want to read."

Since the destruction of my diaries, I never wrote down anything more; I just kept his political opinions stored in my memory.

Every day I went to town looking for a place to set up my office and at the same time dealing with newsagents from out of town, so I barely saw Ko Ko during that time. One day he came back from a political meeting and said to me, "You'll be surprised, Tin Lay."

"Why? What's happening?" I asked.

---

[3] August 18, 1945.

"They're going to form the Anti-Fascist People's Freedom League [AFPFL]."[4]

"Really? What position will you hold there?"

"Nothing, they won't let me."

My temper flared at this as it had never done before. I walked up to him and demanded, "Who won't?"

"Thakin Soe."

I remembered the judge of the criminal court, U Mu, back in Bogalay, saying to my face that Ko Ko was doing nothing for the country and I was not very surprised. Apparently, Thakin Soe and others had been adamantly against Ko Ko taking a role in the AFPFL, saying he had done nothing concrete for the country and that it was they who had sacrificed a great deal. Thakin Soe even refused to be part of AFPFL if Ko Ko were included. Bo Let Yar listened to all that he had to say and then asked Thakin Soe where he thought he got the intelligence reports from all through the war years? Only then did Thakin Soe say that was an important job well done and nodded his head several times.

During the Japanese Occupation, Thakin Soe, Bo Gyoke Aung San, and Thakin Than Tun each headed different departments, and Ko Ko's reports had gone to each of them. If Bo Let Yar had not known or had said nothing, the politicians would have continued to consider Ko Ko superfluous to their war efforts. Ko Ko himself would not let on that he had done that job, not in this lifetime and not for ten lifetimes. Ko Ko became a member of the executive committee of the AFPFL, and the first statement issued by the league was written by him,[5] while he was sitting next to Bo Let Yar at his desk at the party headquarters.

Meanwhile I found two apartments on top of each other on Pansodan Street. Each morning I would leave for the office, and Ko Ko would go to AFPFL headquarters, and so we saw each other again only in the evening. The journal again became a huge success as I had hoped, but still we had no place to keep the presses, so while the office was on Pansodan Street, the presses were running at my house.

All the roads had been destroyed, and as I had to take a horse carriage to and from town, the shaking of the carriage rattled my bones so much that I would ache all over by the time I got home every evening, as if I had been beaten. Ko Ko finally bought a second-hand car for four thousand kyat, and although we spent another seven thousand on it, it refused to run and sat there in our garage. Ko Thein Pe returned from India, and we hosted a dinner in his honor with Bo Let Yar and Saw Kyar Doe as guests.

At this time, the communists were very strong and powerful, and they thought that Ko Ko, being a Buddhist, could not be a true believer in communism. It is true that he was a devout Buddhist, but at the same time he was a true believer in communism. When he was about eleven years old, a foreign circus troupe had come to Let Badan where he lived. Every evening he would visit the circus people and talk to one Russian clown. Even at such a young age he had been interested in international affairs and communism, and he had intrigued the Russian who tried to answer all his questions. When the clown returned to Russia, he sent many books to young Chit Maung and hid in those books pages of communist material on various

---

[4] AFPFL included the Burma Communist Party, led by Thakin Soe; the Socialist Party, formerly called the People's Revolutionary Party, led by U Nu; and the Burma National Army, led by Bo Gyoke Aung San.

[5] See Appendix C.

subjects. Thus Ko Ko had studied communism at a tender age, and he particularly liked the ideology that it should be flexible according to the situation.

Ko Ko was not a fanatic but was very realistic about his beliefs and believed that communism had similarities with Buddhism and that it was an admirable ideology. He wrote a long article about his beliefs under his pen name Shwe Lin Yone for a special edition of *Journal Kyaw*. In part, the article supported the communist party, and many came to believe in the ideology because of this article. He asked me to contribute one hundred kyat each month to the communist party, but I told him I would consider doing so later.

When Sir Dorman-Smith came back into power, Ko Ko wrote an editorial titled "The Governor Has Failed to Deliver the Goods," which was much appreciated by the readers and members of the AFPFL.

Inside the AFPFL, an argument broke out among those who wanted to accept government positions and those who, like Ko Ko, refused to do so. He kept insisting that they should go to London to fight against the White Paper, and he continued to submit proposals in the party for them to do so. When Bo Gyoke Aung San asked Ko Ko to withdraw his proposals, Ko Ko replied that, as nothing could be achieved by talking to the governor here, and as he believed that the matter should be addressed in London, he refused to withdraw his proposals.

One day, Ko Saw Oo (whom we finally found) and I were on our way back from town, and we dropped in at the AFPFL headquarters to pick up Ko Ko, but he said he could not leave.

"I've lost, Tin Lay," he told me. "Everyone has decided to accept positions. I alone cannot fight against them all. If they take the posts offered by Dorman-Smith, I see no way to strengthen the party. I'm going to try and persuade them to the last minute ... you go home, Tin Lay."

When he came back late that night, I greeted him with a smile and asked, "Did everything go well?"

"They all decided to take positions," Ko Ko complained. "I could not argue against Ko Thein Pe's arguments that they should, and anyway it was one against all. After they all decided, only then did I stand up to tell them that I did not believe anything could happen as a result of our dealing with the governor. I reminded them that I had suggested they should deal directly with the Home Office in London and that the posts they have accepted are not to their advantage ... it's like getting shoddy goods at a cut-rate price. I told them it was urgently necessary for them to insist privately and publicly, now and in the future, that the plans for the country as set out by the governor are not acceptable. They must make the people and the world know that they have accepted the positions reluctantly, as they have gained nothing.

"I suggested some things that, at the very least, they must get from the governor. I also told them that in accepting these posts they must make their positions clear before they accept. Then Bo Gyoke Aung San spoke up and said that the meeting had decided that party members would accept posts only on conditions and that he entrusted me with the task of setting out these conditions.

"And you know how shrewd U Ba Pe is, he knew exactly what I would do, that I would set out conditions that would be unacceptable to the British, and he suggested that Dr. U Sett and Ko Thein Pe should also work with me. It doesn't matter who works with me on this, I feel confident I'll win."

When Sir Dorman-Smith refused the conditions set by the AFPFL and gave the posts to Thakin Tun Oke's group, Ko Ko was overjoyed.

"See, the AFPFL may not be so strong now, but because it has refused the positions in the British government, in no time every household in the country will come to support it."

Ko Ko would often say that the British would keep on sending governors who were good at negotiating. "They'll keep on offering positions to the AFPFL leaders, mark my words. Unless we get the conditions we asked for, we must keep on refusing."

The AFPFL held many rallies to show their strength and to win more support. "I wish the government personnel would join us, Tin Lay. Then we could set up a parallel government, and we won't need to go to Britain, they'll come to us."

At all AFPFL meetings. Bo Gyoke Aung San would ask, "Does U Chit Maung agree?" before making any decisions. Also, Bo Gyoke and the other leaders would take Ko Ko's advice. As usual, the orders that he had suggested came out of the mouths of the leaders and not from him. The daily work he did for the party and the constant travel on bad roads in a horse carriage meant that he, too, suffered from aching bones as well as a new ailment—piles. He could not even sit when he got home and had to lie on his back.

One day when the AFPFL was holding a mass rally on the Shwedagon Pagoda platform, I left visiting newsagents at my desk and, taking along a clerk from my office, headed out to the Shwedagon. I waited midway up the stairs and sent the clerk up to find Ko Ko. He came down and said to me, "Tin Lay, why did you come here? Is anything wrong?"

I simply replied that I came to remind him of the promise I made long ago, swearing by the Iron Market that one day he would be on the political stage. He smiled and said in English, "Oh, Tin Lay, you are quite right."

On my way back to the office, I thought to myself that I had never been happier in my marriage. It is a joy to have an aim in life and great happiness when it is fulfilled. Later Ko Ko asked me why I did not stay to listen to the speeches at the Shwedagon, but I said I was too busy. I told him jokingly that I would come and listen when he gave a speech at Jubilee Hall,[6] and he said, "All right, just remember your promise."

One day I was so busy that I got home late to Kanbe. I saw Ko Ko and Bo Gyoke Aung San talking in the parlor. I went in silently and sat not far from them in the dining room, listening to their talk. Ko Ko said not a word but listened intently to Bo Gyoke. Bo Gyoke was a person who spoke rapidly and without pause, words coming out of his lips like machine gun fire. Earlier he was leaning back in his sofa, but by and by he came to lean forward, sitting on its edge. He was speaking all the time of U Saw: about his trip to Japan and his political record.

Just as Bo Gyoke was winding down and preparing to leave, Ko Ko said to him, "I know that we have announced AFPFL was formed to include many groups, but we cannot allow U Saw to join us. It's just not possible to have him with us."

Bo Gyoke nodded thoughtfully several times and was driven away in his car.

---

[6] Jubilee Hall is a British bastion built to mark Queen Victoria's diamond jubilee. Located on Shwedagon Pagoda Road, it stood where the Defense Services Tatmadaw Museum now stands.

CHAPTER 34

OUR CHILDREN

When the communist party split into two factions,[1] I remarked that politicians were beginning to get bad names for their involvement with women. Ko Ko himself was overly careful of his behavior with women, but he did not support what I said. He explained to me that it was a forgivable sin and not to attach too much blame to it.

"When I was studying history," Ko Ko related, "I read about a political leader from Ireland named Parnell[2] who really risked his life to bring about home rule for his country. However, he fell in love with a woman named Kitty O'Shea and there was a scandal, and he was removed as head of his movement and expelled from parliament. They had to begin all over again to try to get the Home Rule Bill passed. With his friends and the world against him, he went to live with the woman he loved and, not long after, died of heart trouble. What he said before he passed away should be remembered; on his deathbed, he had asked for his friends to come, and they did, knowing he was dying. He told them that they should elect a new leader and to try for home rule again and that to remember that he, too, was just a man and neither saint nor god. In working in an organization, it's important not to make too much of whether one man was right or wrong."

Because my husband was someone who lived without a blemish on his character regarding women, it might be difficult to understand his view on the matter, but it came clear to me that he could be highly objective because he himself was above it.

By now our daughter Khin Lay Myint was about seven, Maung Chit Shein nearly five, and Moe Hein almost four. Ko Ko would buy books for them even when they were so young that they tore out all the pages. When I protested at the waste, he said that at least they would learn to remember colors, know animals by names, and recognize letters. He told me to keep an eye on them to see which child liked to read. As he said, the children could name the colors correctly even when very young and, without being taught, knew their ABCs. Later they remembered the titles of his books and could fetch them correctly from the bookshelves. All three knew the books on and by Disraeli, Bernard Shaw, and Shakespeare, and knew about these men.

---

[1] This occurred around March 1946. Thakin Than Tun broke away from Thakin Soe, who was committing adultery with some wives of his junior members. Thakin Soe left the AFPFL and set up the "Red Flag" communist party, while Thakin Than Tun remained, with his "White Flag" faction. Thakin Than Tun went underground after Independence, and the Burma Communist Party he led fought against the Myanmar government until the BCP disbanded in 1989. Thakin Than Tun was assassinated in the jungle by one of his followers in 1968.

[2] Charles Stewart Parnell, born 1846, was an Irish nationalist leader who served as a member of the British parliament (1875–1891) and led Ireland's Home Rule Movement. He and Kitty O'Shea were charged with and found guilty of adultery.

Once when the children were eating their meal and Ko Ko was writing at the dining table, he looked over at Maung Chit Shein and said, "Hey, big boy, pick out that grain of paddy from your rice." I was sitting nearby so I pointed out the inedible grain to our son. The boy looked at both of us and putting the grain on his palm showed it to his father and said, "Pe Pe,[3] this is not a paddy grain."

"So what's that, then?" Ko Ko asked.

"It's a seed, Pe Pe, it's a seed to sow."

Ko Ko looked at me in delight, laughing until he cried.

"Mark my words, Tin Lay, this chap's going to be an editor."

The younger boy, Moe Hein, was not like his brother, but was quick, daring, and without fear of any kind, so Ko Ko said he would not become an editor but perhaps a doctor or a soldier.

One afternoon, while I was doing accounts, it was time for the children's nap but Moe Hein was refusing to get into bed, so I called to the boy while still at my desk. Ko Ko brought Moe Hein into the room and told the child to get into bed.

"It's time for your nap, Moe Hein, get into bed."

"Don't wanna."

"May May[4] said you must go to sleep … get in."

"Don't wanna sleep."

"What a difficult child you are … go to sleep, I'm telling you."

"Won't. Won't go to sleep."

"Tin Lay, if he doesn't want to sleep let's not force him …"

"Ko Ko, how can you say it in front of him? This is their nap time, he *must* sleep."

We were speaking to each other in English the whole time so that the child would not understand.

"But he's so stubborn! I can't do anything with him. You do it, Tin Lay."

"I can't do that, Ko Ko, you brought him in so you have to get him in bed or else they'll never learn to obey you."

"All right, Moe Hein, get into bed … go to sleep," Ko Ko tried again.

"Don't wanna sleep."

"I'm telling you, go to sleep."

"Moe Hein don't wanna *sleep*."

Ko Ko called to me: "See, Tin lay, what shall I do? He's said he doesn't want to … just let him be, shall we?"

Not looking up from my accounts, I merely said, "Get him to sleep."

"Hey, if you won't go to sleep, May May will spank you."

"How could you say something like that!" I yelled at him from my desk.

"But what should I say then?"

"Say you'll spank him."

"Right, then, Moe Hein, get into bed or I'll spank you."

"Moe Hein won't."

To me, "What shall I do, Tin Lay? He's still saying no."

"Show him a ruler, say you'll spank him with that."

"See here, Moe Hein, see this ruler? If you get into bed, Pe Pe won't spank you, if you don't Pe Pe will … see? So will you go to sleep nicely or not?"

---

[3] "Daddy."

[4] "Mommy."

"Won't"

To me, "See? I told you he won't go to sleep."

"Ko Ko you can't give in now, you'll have to get him in bed or he'll never respect you again. He's testing you, you can't give in."

"Moe Hein, get into bed, go to sleep, you hear?"

"Won't sleep"

"If you won't, Pe Pe is going to beat you."

"Won't."

"What shall I do now, Tin Lay?"

"Spank him then, Ko Ko."

"Right, I'm going to spank you right now, Moe Hein, are you getting into bed?"

"Moe Hein *won't*."

I knew Moe Hein would jump into bed instantly at a word from me, but I wanted Ko Ko to be able to handle this tiny tot all on his own, so I grimly sat on at my desk, saying nothing to the boy. Ko Ko began brandishing his little ruler but Moe Hein seemed completely unfazed by it, as he certainly would not be if he were to hear just one word from me.

"Well then, spank him on his bottom," I finally suggested.

"Can't I not do this, Tin Lay?"

"No, Ko Ko, it's the worst thing if you don't follow up on your word."

Ko Ko gave a slap on Moe Hein's bottom with his ruler, but as his father had never hit him before the boy got sulkier than ever and refused to budge.

"Let's let him be, Tin Lay, I spanked him but he's still not moving."

"If you give in now things will be worse later, I tell you, Ko Ko, spank him harder."

Ko Ko tried to hit harder but Moe Hein did not even glance at the bed let alone get on it. I called out to Ko Ko to spank harder and when he finally did, Moe Hein flopped into bed with his face down, sobbing his heart out. He was probably very hurt that his father who had never lifted a hand to him before had actually spanked him.

Ko Ko came over to me, wiping the sweat from his brow and arms, and said, "It's so exhausting, Tin Lay, I'm tired out just trying to steel myself to spank him. I feel so sorry for him."

He never spanked any of the children again but punished them in other ways if they misbehaved. Even then, they showed a healthy respect for him after this spanking fiasco. He said to me once that he wished the boys would grow up soon.

"Why, you want them to become editors?"

"No, I want to take them to the teashop, it's a good place to learn things."

CHAPTER 35

THE DIAMOND NECKLACE

As our associate chief editor, Ko Saw Oo, was back, Ko Ko no longer had to write everything himself but only handled the editorials and the columns for politics, namely, the "Views of Shwe Lin Yone" and "Gentle Words." Ko Saw Oo lived with us, as did artist Ko Ohn Lwin.

Each morning everyone went off to work, and we all met back at home in the evenings. After the dining table had been cleared, the men sat on to talk until one or two in the morning, and that was almost every day. Only when Ko Saw Oo and Ko Ohn Lwin went up to bed did Ko Ko sit down to write his columns, and that took him until three or four in the morning.

One day while I was doing accounts at my desk I heard Ko Ko say to Ko Saw Oo, "You know, I have never regretted getting married. Because I did, I got two blessings: the first is that I have great happiness and the second that I never have had any unhappiness."

As I knew there was no one else who nagged him as much as I did, I was doubtful if he was indeed that happy. I would nag him day in and day out to bathe and to relieve himself, and he would remark that I sounded like someone asking for a debt to be paid up rather than someone asking him to bathe.

When the AFPFL was holding their conference, he was so busy that he would not take a bath, and I marked down with a blue pencil on the calendar all the days he missed. After the sixth day I begged him to please bathe the next day and warned him that if he did not, I would do something to protest against him. He said not to worry and that he would, really, bathe the next day, and he even marked the date in red. The men in our household bathe in a space cleared for them not far from the well, under the big Jack Fruit tree,[1] and I asked the Indian gardener to fill the tank with water drawn from the well. But come the next evening, when I told Ko Ko his bath was ready, he said he had no time as he had to go somewhere with Thakin Mya and Ko Kyaw Nyein. He said he would bathe the next day, and off he went.

I was furious and carried out my protest: overturning the water tank and spilling all of it on the ground. Daw Daw walked over from next door, and when she saw my act of protest, sat herself down on the ground and laughed until she cried. I said to Daw Daw, going to sit by her, "You know the saying, Daw Daw, that one's efforts are lost 'as water poured on sand,' so isn't my protest just perfect?"

We both sat there and laughed.

The next morning I had to leave earlier than Ko Ko. When he was just about to get into the horse carriage, Daw Daw came running over and almost dragged him

---

[1] Men and women can bathe in the open as they wear waist garments while splashing water on the body with a bowl. Women in this case wear their waist garments pulled up over their breasts and tucked securely.

away to his bath. Afterwards he reportedly said to her, "Oh thank you, Daw Daw, now I feel so fresh!"

Just as Ko Ko had proposed, the AFPFL decided to send a delegation to London, and Bo Let Yar insisted that whoever was going, U Chit Maung must be one of them. When I said he must wear Western clothes if he went, as it was so cold there, he instead asked me to make him warm woolen underwear as well as shirts out of flannel, and said that he would wear Burmese dress over all this. When he got there, he said, he would try to contribute to the British papers and make sure the people become aware of our country's plight. If he got a chance, he would get in touch with a publisher to find out if his collected columns could be published. He thought it possible that someone would be interested in Myanmar.

When the governor's office said they could not give the AFPFL delegation the airfare, Ko Ko said even the long journey by ship was all right as it was urgent that the Burmese delegation get to London.

"Only there can we achieve our goals," he said, so I asked if we would get independence peacefully. He said, "If we are diplomatic and clever about it, now's the perfect time. You just need brains, you need to be capable, and you need to act."

The proposed trip fell through, but Ko Ko was certain delegates from the AFPFL would get to London one day.[2] He read out to me speeches made in the British Parliament, which he said he wanted to hear with his own ears. I said to him in English, "One day you will become a great man, definitely," and he said to me, "One day I will make you a great lady."

He continued with his AFPFL work, as well as his columns for the journal. One day he advertised a forthcoming book, titled *The Myanmar Monument*, and I asked whether he had the time to write one. He said that he needed to write just a few more articles like those he had written during the war years on the rebuilding of a new Myanmar, and then a compilation would be ready to be published under this title. However, he was so busy that he had no time to finish this project.

One evening he came home around five and showed me two pages of predictions written by astrologer Pyinmana U Than Maung, one for him and one for me. In his, the astrologer predicted a serious illness, and in mine, he saw death and advised me not to wear black.

"There's no need to consult an astrologer, Ko Ko," I said, "if you continue to disregard your kidney problems and your piles, they could really turn serious. I would die only out of misery that you're not taking care of your health."

"Don't say that, I promise I'll take care, and you, too, Tin Lay, promise me not to wear black ... not a single thing, you hear?"

"If I were to die as predicted, let me tell you in advance, Ko Ko, if I die don't remain alone ... get a nice woman who would look after you and marry her quickly. Otherwise I would not die easy, so please promise me, Ko Ko."

"There's no need to talk about that, at all."

"But what if there is? Aren't you going to promise me? Don't you want me not to worry?"

"If you ask me this, you, too, must promise, Tin Lay. If I promise to ease your mind you, too, must promise so that I won't die worrying about you."

"I'm to marry again?"

"But *you* asked *me* to marry again ... so, promise?"

---

[2] A delegation led by Bo Gyoke Aung San traveled to London in January 1947.

"You're not going to die, Ko Ko. The fortune-teller said only I would die. If I promise, would you? Then I do ... go on, promise me first."

"Sometimes I wonder if I'm worthy of your love, Tin Lay. If you want to make me happy, yes, I'll promise it to make you happy. But we can't say the predictions will all be true; we must take care and look after ourselves. You can't wear black, and you must do all the *yadayar*[3] he suggested. And don't dwell on his predictions."

I had no fear of what the astrologer said. Even when U Hla Maung had predicted Ko Ko's death, I had prayed that rather it would be I who died in his place. If I were to die first, my prayer would indeed come true, and I was only worried that he might be left alone.

In all parts of Myanmar, including Kanbe, there were so many crimes that Ko Ko said it was not safe to keep our valuables at home, including my jewelry and the bag in which I had been saving cash since my wedding day. Instead, Ko Ko suggested, we should keep them at the bank where I kept our money for our business. I refused, as I had vowed to keep the bag unopened until my fortieth birthday.

"I'm not asking you to use up the money, Tin Lay, just to keep it in the bank. If we were robbed it would be such a waste, after all these years. Do take it to the bank."

As I had vowed to put half the money in the bank for our old age when I opened the bag, I kept on refusing. He became so anxious that I finally opened the bag, counted the money, and took it to my office, where I locked it in a drawer. Ko Ko thought it was at the bank. I was so unhappy that I had to open the bag before its time, thinking it was a bad omen. Daw Daw, when she heard, said all I had done was open it, not use it, and that no harm could come from that. There was about seven thousand kyat in the bag.

I was paying 100 to 120 kyat for each packet of paper, and I was often short of money. One day Su Su from next door came to me with a diamond necklace, saying U Soe Tin of *Rangoon Spectacles* newspaper wanted her to sell it for him. The diamonds weighed a total of about twenty carats, and the price was eight thousand kyat. Ko Ko took the necklace from her and told me to buy it.

"What nonsense, Ko Ko, eight thousand is a lot of money, and I'd rather buy another press. I don't want a necklace," and saying that I took the necklace from his hands and gave it back to Su Su. As soon as Su Su left, he began the whole time to nag me to buy it, following me around the house.

"What's so important about a necklace, Ko Ko? I have no need for it. I don't want it."

"Please let me buy it for you, Tin Lay, please take it. Please, so that you'll always have this, something of value I bought for you."

"But eight thousand is a lot of money, and I don't want to wear anything this expensive. Why on earth are you being so insistent?"

"Have you forgotten, Tin Lay, the day we were to leave for Yangon after our wedding? I looked through the pages you had cut out from magazines, the ones with pictures of diamond necklaces. Then and there I decided that one day I would buy you one and place it around your neck with my own hands. I never told you, but I often remember my vow. Please let me buy it, Tin Lay, let me see you wear it ..."

Once he reminded me, I remembered that he had stared a long time at my face, and now I realized that, at the time, he was vowing to buy me a necklace. It was such

---

[3] The rituals suggested by fortune-tellers that their clients might perform to avoid bad luck.

a precious thought that I wanted to accept the gift, but it was so expensive that I had to beg him not to buy it now, but later, when things were better, and I tried to persuade him to this end. But he was adamant; he said if he bought it later I might be too old by then and that he wanted to see me wear it while I was still young. He bought it in spite of all my protests and placed it around my neck with his own hands on an evening when we went to Bo Let Yar's house for dinner.

I had also collected pages of pictures of grand houses, and Ko Ko said to me as he fastened the necklace that one day he would build me a house, too. As we sat around the table at Bo Let Yar's house, our host asked us to give a name to the portrait of his wife, Daw Khin Hla, painted by U Ngwe Gaing,[4] and Ko Ko said, "Emerald." Our hosts were delighted with the name.

Ko Ko told me one day that U Nu had asked him to accompany him to the Shan State. "He told me I have a sharp mind when observing politics and that it would be good to have me along when he talks to the Shan Saw Bwa,[5] and he repeatedly asked me to come along. They're going by car ... so I'll go with them, shall I?"

"But Ko Ko, you can't, you're not really healthy. Your piles give you so much trouble that you cannot even sit when you are home: you have to stand to eat and write; think how difficult it is for you. I couldn't stop you from going to the AFPFL headquarters, and that's why I didn't say anything, but a long trip by car is out of the question. You don't easily relieve yourself, you know that, and your health will get worse, Ko Ko. Please wait until you're better if you want to go."

"It doesn't matter, Tin Lay, it's only when I'm at the toilet that my piles hurt and as for the bleeding, I can wear thicker underpants. Ko Nu wants me to come along so much, so please let me go, Tin Lay, it won't look good if I refuse, and Ko Nu would be so disappointed."

"I beg you, Ko Ko, the roads are very bad, and it's a rough trip. If anything happens to you while you are on the way, it would be dangerous. Please get good treatment first and then you can go, but not now."

"Please let me go, Tin Lay, please ..."

"Not now, Ko Ko, please not now ..."

Ko Ko was miserable because I would not allow him to go, and I was terrified that he might leave anyway. I was unsuccessful in getting him to stay home and be properly treated by a doctor when his urine turned a dark color. If he went on a long trip by car, things could only get worse. He was not the type to relieve himself by the side of the road while they were driving through miles of deserted countryside. I knew this all too well, so I kept on begging him not to go.

Every time he begged me to let him go, I wished I could, but considering his health, I refused to agree. Ko Nu left for the Shan State without him.

---

[4] U Ngwe Gaing was a famous artist.

[5] Shan Saw Bwa are indigenous Shan rulers recognized by both the Burmese and British and considered to be feudal lords by left-wing nationalists.

CHAPTER 36

THE END OF HIS LIFE

As the end of March came near, Ko Ko planned to write every column in the journal slated for the week of Revolutionary Day, March 27, 1946. Apart from the short story, he wrote everything else and signed his name on the bottom of the last page. When I asked him why, as this unusual style attracted many comments, he only said that it was so that people would remember this particular issue. I did not make too much of it but reading over the journal I, too, thought it should be a memorable issue without knowing exactly why.

This edition came out on a Friday and, as I was preparing to leave for work the following Monday morning, Ko Ko said he would come to the office with me and that he need not go to the AFPFL headquarters today. When we arrived at the office, he said he had not been to the City Book Club bookshop for about two weeks and, saying he would like to see if any new books had arrived, went on to the bookshop; so I went alone into the office.

It was some time before he turned up, and when I complained about it, he said he had met Tetkatho Htin Gyi and Tetkatho Myo Thant[1] and had stopped to talk to them. They had asked him when he was going to publish a daily, and Ko Ko told them he would as soon as we found a place to keep the printing presses.

"I told them that we don't have a place yet, so we only have the name of the paper but cannot publish at present, and that if we did, we'd employ both of them, Tekatho Htin Gyi as a reporter and Tekatho Myo Thant as the translating editor. These chaps are good. As soon as we can move downtown, we'll publish two dailies, one in English and one in Burmese. I'll translate a lot of books and publish them, too. We need to open the eyes of the people, Tin Lay. I only need more free time and to have a place downtown. By the way, when are you going home today?"

"In the evening."

"Then I think I'll go home now. I don't feel too well."

"What do you mean, Ko Ko? How do you feel?"

"My heart's palpitating ... I should go home."

"Yes, go, Ko Ko. When you get home rest in bed, don't even read. Drink some milk. I'll come back early."

"Don't worry, I'm just tired. I'll be fine as soon as I have some rest. Don't worry, mind ... I'm off."

I got home earlier than usual that evening, at about four. As soon as I went into the bedroom, I saw him reading in bed. Saying, "I thought you said you were going to rest," I grabbed his book. His fingers felt fiery hot when I touched them, and I realized he had a fever. Hair stood up on my head in fear, and I became agitated, but

---

[1] Two young journalists.

he remained as calm as ever, lying back on the bed and stretching as if his limbs were aching.

I announced I was calling for the doctor, but he stopped me, saying he would be better the next morning and, as the doctor lived too far away, we should not bother him. Ko Ko only took some herbal medicine, and then called Ko Saw Oo to his bedside and told him what to do about the forthcoming Burmese New Year's issue, due in mid April.

During the next three days his high temperature did not fall, and small boils began to appear all over his body. By then he was being treated by his friend Dr. Aung Khin and, although I insisted at the onset that we consult Colonel Min Sein,[2] a senior physician, Ko Ko refused, saying he wanted to call Dr. Aung Khin first. Dr. Aung Khin thought the boils might be heat rash or measles, but he could not be sure at present and left him some medicine.

That evening, Bo Let Yar came over and, upon seeing Ko Ko ill in bed, went to fetch his younger brother, Dr. Hla Shwe, for a second opinion. Dr. Hla Shwe agreed with Dr. Aung Khin's prognosis that it might be heat rash or measles and approved of the pills prescribed by him.

I was afraid it might be small pox and, begging Ko Ko to excuse me, I opened his eyes and licked around them.[3] I longed to consult a Burmese traditional doctor and asked Ko Ko for permission to do so, but he refused not only to call one but even to take any traditional medicine.

"I'm being treated by a doctor," he said, "and during that time I must only take what he prescribes and nothing else."

At that time our presses ran at night. As I did not want Ko Ko to be disturbed by the sound, I told the printers to stop. When the sound ceased, Ko Ko asked immediately, "Tin Lay, why did the press stop?"

"So you can sleep."

"Tin Lay, please don't ever do that, the sound of the press does not bother me a bit even when I'm ill ... I've lived with this sound for ten or fifteen years by now and it's not at all noisy to my ears. I feel upset to have them stop, please let them run."

"I know it's all right when you are well, but when you are ill, let's stop the noise for the time being."

"No, let them run ... go tell them at once to keep on printing. I know whether it disturbs me or not. Go, tell them, or else the journal will not be ready in time."

"So what if it's late this time? Let's stop until you are well again."

"Come here, Tin Lay, listen, even if I die do not stop the press, never stop the press. Don't let anything stop this work I love so much. Go ... go ... tell them to start working."

He acted as if he would even get worse if the press were stopped, so, feeling miserable, I went to tell the printers to run the press again.

"Tin Lay, it makes me feel bad seeing you sit up by my side like this ... go to bed, you have to go to work in the morning."

"I won't be going to work, Ko Ko, not until you're better."

"I *am* better, I'll take a laxative tonight, and I'll be fine in the morning ... go to sleep."

---

[2] Dr. Min Sein was trained in Britain.

[3] According to Burmese medicine, a small-pox blister breaking out in the eyes can blind a person, and the ancient method of prevention is to lick around them.

"I wish you wouldn't take a laxative, we don't know what these boils are, and they might dry up."[4]

"I have to, my breath smells really foul, and I'm very constipated. I'm also having difficulty passing urine. A laxative would do me good, and you shouldn't worry yourself about something prescribed by a doctor, Tin Lay."

I gave him the laxative as he asked and brought in a chamber pot for his use and put it near the bed. I showed him where it was and pretended to sleep, as he would not allow me to sit up. I was in despair, unable to sleep.

At about two he sat up; I was startled and sat up, too.

"Tin Lay, go out of the room. I want to use the pot."

"Go ahead, Ko Ko, I can wait right here."

"No, don't, please, leave the room."

"Just in case you feel dizzy and fall, Ko Ko, I should be here."

"I'm fine, please just leave the room."

He was getting more and more upset at my anxiety to stay with him and, thinking I might be making him feel worse, I left the room reluctantly. That night he got up three times, and every time I, too, got up, and he would scold me for not sleeping, as well as make me leave the room. The night passed with frustrations for both of us.

In the morning when I washed his face, I noticed that all the little boils had disappeared, and I became alarmed. He, too, noticed, but tried to pretend he did not, so as not to worry me. With Dr. Aung Khin's agreement, we sent for a doctor from the Infectious Diseases Hospital. The doctor said he could not be sure whether it was small pox, as Ko Ko had had it in childhood already and, besides, he had been vaccinated against it. The doctor said it could well be measles and that if we wanted, Ko Ko could be admitted to his hospital. He left some pills and went away.

The whole day I sat by Ko Ko's bed writing the novel "A Woman Like Her." Ko Ko would ask me to read out each page as I finished. He complained about being idle in bed while there was so much to do at the AFPFL, that it was the most urgent time for the country's future, that his colleagues at the party would be missing him, and that he was failing in his duties. To keep his thoughts away from all that, I talked of all the happy things I could think of in the lively manner of my younger days.

I was trying to hide my fear from him, and in consideration for me, he, too, was pretending to be fooled, but both of us knew the seriousness of his illness.

I did all the *yadaya* rituals I could and made merit with donations and good deeds. I was not afraid he was going to die; I only wanted to ease his pain and make him well. I was happy to give him all the care he needed to make him comfortable, and I did not feel tired in the slightest. I was fresh and full of energy.

"The way you are caring for me, Tin Lay, is far better than a proper nurse could do. If you were a real nurse your patients would pretend not to get well just so that they could have you looking after them," he teased.

"So you're pretending to be ill, huh? Just let me feel your pulse!"

As if jokingly, I felt his feverishly hot hand and pretended with a smile as if nothing was wrong, but my heart was heavy with despair.

---

[4] Taking a laxative would ease the "heat" of the body and stop the boils from ripening. According to Burmese medical treatment, such boils must burst open and release their poison. If they dry up the poison would enter the bloodstream.

I sent the children off to Daw Daw's house next door and she, too, came to stay with me to care for Ko Ko. His fever did not abate. After the boils disappeared, his temperature climbed even higher. I began to think again of calling a Burmese traditional doctor, but as he himself had full confidence in Dr. Hla Shwe and Dr. Aung Khin, I could not persist. The pills prescribed by the doctors were good, but this illness was not a sudden thing; this was something that had been festering inside him for all those years when he sat for long hours, plus his disregard for regular bowel movements or passing urine.

His urine turned a dark color and smelt foul. He would not allow me to stay in the room while he relieved himself and, although I knew he did it out of consideration for me, I felt so unhappy about it that I burst into tears in Daw Daw's arms.

I wrote down the details every day in my diary. The entries beginning March 25, 1946, read as follows:

> 25 March, Monday: Today Ko Ko has a fever.
> 26 March, Tuesday: fever rose to 105 degrees.
> 27 March, Wednesday: small boils appeared.
> 28 March, Thursday: fever went down a bit; more boils.
> 29 March, Friday: boils dried up.

That evening, when Bo Let Yar came with Dr. Hla Shwe, Ko Ko admitted his mistakes to them. "I have been wrong; I have always been too shy, even as a child, and because of that I dared not even pass urine if I heard someone in the next room. I would keep forgetting to relieve myself if I'm reading or writing. Now I'm suffering for it ... I can't pass urine at all ... please give me something for it, doctor ..."

He smiled unhappily when Dr. Hla Shwe gave him some tablets, telling him, "Take these diuretics, U Chit Maung, it'll be fine, and take the MB tablets[5] regularly, too."

I was standing at the foot of his bed and reflecting on the fact that I had fallen in love with him with a determination to look after his health, and had all through our life nagged him constantly about relieving himself, and now I was seeing him like this as I had feared. I felt as if knives were piercing my heart.

Bo Let Yar, too, looked upset, and went out to slump on the sofa, his face black with gloom. Bo Let Yar and the doctor talked it over and decided that if Ko Ko were not better the next day, they would admit him to the Infectious Diseases Hospital. They went home late at night.

The next day, Saturday, Ko Ko called out: "Tin Lay, I'm burning hot, I can't pass urine, I can't see clearly," he said, and I informed the doctor immediately. When the doctor came, he gave Ko Ko some pills. We were planning to take him to the hospital the next day, and Ko Ko reminded me to send the papers concerning peasants' issues back to the party, to send a letter requesting leave, to give back Thakin Kodaw Hmaing's papers, and so on. To ease his mind, I showed all the papers to him and told him I would do everything.

He glanced from my face to Dr. Aung Khin's. As I turned away to put back some files into the cupboard, I heard him say slowly (in English), "All are miserable," so,

---

[5] Sulfa tablets.

dumping the files on a chair, I turned back quickly into the room. He seemed to be dozing.

The doctor told me we should let him sleep and took me out to the parlor. He warned me to eat and sleep enough so that I would not fall ill. After he left, I came back into our room and, seeing Ko Ko lying motionless in bed, placed my cheek next to his and listened to his breathing, feeling his fingers and then his feet, unable to be calm in my anxiety. After nearly an hour, I called him softly, and when he did not reply, realized he must be unconscious. He tossed about as if in pain the entire day.

Bo Let Yar came that evening and sent for Dr. Hla Shwe, who gave Ko Ko an injection. Bo Let Yar, too, was extremely worried that night, at the same time telling me not to worry. I had no desire to tell anyone what was happening and felt a misery so deep that I could never tell it to anyone. It was true what Ko Ko had last said, that everything was miserable. Bo Let Yar and Dr. Hla Shwe did not leave till three in the morning. Dr. Aung Khin and I sat by Ko Ko all night.

31 March, Sunday: In the early light I waited for the ambulance that Dr. Hla Shwe had said would be sent from the hospital. Ko Ko was still unconscious. The printers begged me to send for a Burmese traditional doctor, but I feared that if I could not find a good one, Ko Ko would die and I would be responsible. There were a few good traditional doctors, but many more were quacks, and at this point I dared not risk looking for one I could trust. I deeply regretted the fact that I had not been in contact with a reputable one, just in case. I felt like breaking into wild sobs or screaming my head off and had to keep a tight control over myself.

When the ambulance came, and he was lifted onto the stretcher, Ko Ko had a fit. His arms twisted and thrashed, and foamy saliva fell from of his lips. Everyone stood in shock, and someone ran to fetch Colonel Min Sein at my urging. In the hour before the doctor came, sweat poured from Ko Ko's face, and he began to choke, the whites of his eyes turning up as if in death throes. The household staff could not bear to watch and quietly went out of the room. There were also Ko Than Tun (Ko Ko's brother), Saya Sein, and Zawanna[6] present, and they, too, went out of the room.

I kept reciting fiercely to myself that he must not die, he must not die, and with my nerves straining to breaking point, I bent to hold him as close to my heart as possible and began reciting the sutras with force and energy as if I were a Zawgyi[7] commanding a dead body to come to life again. I was amazed at myself that I could believe so much in the sutras to keep him alive.

Nearly an hour later, Bo Let Yar arrived, soon followed by a leading doctor in the country, Colonel Min Sein. The physician was calm and collected as he examined Ko Ko, and I felt a deep admiration for him in spite of all my fears. When the doctor told us to give Ko Ko a sponge bath, I did so, and when he recommended an enema, we performed it as well. I was saddened to see my husband, someone so shy of his bodily functions, reduced to this. I will tell him about it when he is well, I thought to myself. I felt no distaste at any of the things I had to do for him then, although I was normally extremely sensitive, and I never knew how my sensitivity vanished so totally.

Ko Ko was still on the stretcher, his arms flailing, his eyes rolling in their sockets, and foam dribbling out of his mouth. Colonel Min Sein said he could not be sure

---

[6] Zawanna was a well-known writer.

[7] "Zawgyi" is a mythical magician healer who lives in the jungle and is able to even cure death.

whether it was small pox and that it could well be a neurology problem. Before he left, he said he would need to check whether blood was flowing to Ko Ko's brain, and as this could not be done at the Infectious Diseases Hospital, he told us to have Ko Ko sent to the Rangoon General Hospital.

We drove Ko Ko to the RGH in the ambulance, but his condition was unchanged. I firmly tried to ignore the thought that he might die in the hospital. To believe that he would be cured in the hospital was also an illusion in which I could not entirely find faith. At the reception counter, we had to wait a long time with his stretcher on the floor. There was no empty bed available in the wards, so he was first kept in the corridor. I spent the whole of that day and night sitting by him and wiping away his dribble. He was in a coma.

The next day he was taken to a small room, and his condition remained the same. Colonel Min Sein came by at nine while doing his morning rounds, and the whole day the nurses and doctors did everything recommended by him. I opened my diary and wrote down that he suffered great pain and then lost consciousness at 2:00 PM on March 31, 1946, Saturday.

> 1 April, Monday: Ko Ko calmed down a bit. Myanmar Alin U Tin and his wife came. Dr. Hla Shwe's wife came and took me home, so I went with her for a while.

That day, seeing Ko Ko lying so still on the bed, my tears flowed freely, and the doctor told me to keep optimistic. I looked out of the window and saw his friend Ko Thinkha waiting out front. He asked me how Ko Ko was, he was very worried, and I told him Ko Ko had calmed down. Rather tactlessly, he mentioned the fact that Saya Gyi P. Monin had died while in the hospital, although he said he was much relieved to hear Ko Ko was calmer. He left after saying he would come again in the evening. I looked after him and fear rose to clutch my heart, and I said to myself, Ko Ko must not die ... not like Saya Gyi, he must not die. I recited sutras the whole day and night.

> 2 April, Tuesday: Ko Ko regained consciousness! Ko Ko, at around two in the morning, you regained consciousness! Your jaw seemed heavy, and you could not say anything, but you could nod and shake your head, and your Tin Lay was so happy! I could not describe how happy I was. Yesterday evening your breathing became labored, as if you were dying, and I rushed to inform Colonel Min Sein, and he had you injected with penicillin. Ko Ko, remember how you once said penicillin is a miracle drug? It saved your life last night! Everyone said you would recover ... all your friends came, and Bo Let Yar was overjoyed. Out of all your political colleagues, only he seemed to care.

I wrote the above entry in the evening when all visitors had left. I felt my aching heart being soothed to peace when I saw him nod when I called his name. I was deeply happy. I thought to myself that when he reads this entry later, he will surely smile.

Dr. Hla Shwe arrived around eight that night and told me that only penicillin could save him now. He said the penicillin injected today had just arrived by plane, so it was fresh. It was to be injected every three hours, and after each shot—at nine that night, midnight, three, and six—Ko Ko should be able to talk, he said.

But I only learned late at night that there was no more of this drug to be had after the dose scheduled for nine o'clock. My younger brother and Ko Ko's protégé, Maung Thein Pe, were the only two at the hospital with me, and I had to send them out to see if they could find more penicillin anywhere. Actually, they were not supposed to stay the night, but I had sneaked them in; if I had not, there would have been nobody I could have sent.

During the night, Dr. Hla Shwe had the nurse feed Ko Ko milk through a nose pipe, and he choked so much at first that they had to do it slowly. Ko Ko was breathless as if exhausted, and the doctor said it was only because of the forced-feeding and to call him when the penicillin arrived; and then he went home. I was alone in the room with my husband. There was a patient in the next room in a fit, struggling the same way as Ko Ko had, and I went over to see him. The nurse told me they needed ice for him, so I gave them the money to buy some.

By ten o'clock that evening, the men who had gone out looking for penicillin had not come back. There was no electricity at night in the hospital, and I sat by the light of a candle watching over my husband.

"Ko Ko, do you feel bad? You'll be fine soon, you'll get the injection soon ..."

Ko Ko was breathing heavily, his chin jerking and his eyes wide open. He could not speak, but I believed he could hear me, so I continued to comfort him. I could see the dying patient in the next room, which filled me with fear. Right in front of my eyes was my husband, apparently not aware of anything and almost like one dead, struggling to breathe. I felt very alone.

Only when it was half past ten did the men come back with the drug. They had to go from shop to shop and said they could not be sure if the drug was still fresh, and my heart fell upon hearing that. I was further upset when the doctor came to give the injection, and he injected it into the arm, although Colonel Min Sein had written on the chart that it was to be in the buttocks.

By two in the morning, my eyelids began to droop in spite of trying my hardest to keep them open. From the day that Ko Ko fell ill, I had not slept and had never felt the need to, but strangely enough, that night I felt so sleepy that I had to keep rubbing my eyes. My brother and Maung Thein Pe told me to doze a bit and said that they would wake me up for the next injection at three. So I closed my eyes, confident that I would be up by then. When I opened my eyes again it was light and, looking at my watch, I saw it was nearly five. Ko Ko was breathing with so much difficulty he was almost choking.

"Look, it's nearly five, why didn't you wake me up at three for the injection?" I asked my brother.

"No one came, not one doctor. We went to look for nurses, but they said the doctors have all gone home."

"Oh dear, you should have woken me!"

I rushed out while still saying these words and ran frantically all over the wards looking for a doctor. I did not see a single one, and the nurses I saw told me that only the doctor assigned to the particular case would give the injection, and no one else. In the midst of this emergency they were being finicky about rules, and I wanted to burst out crying then and there.

At six o'clock, a Sikh doctor came to give the injection. Ko Ko's eyes were no longer rolling but were fixed and staring at a point, and he was breathing heavily. I asked this doctor to do something and he said Colonel Min Sein would arrive at nine for his morning rounds.

I sent my brother to inform the family in Kanbe. That day, too, I was alone with Ko Ko. When he seemed to take a turn for the worse, I worried that he would pass away even before the physician got there. The thought suddenly came into my head that if Ko Ko were worried about me, he would not pass easily into his next existence. Feeling much alarmed at this, unthinkingly I ran out to lean against the corridor wall. I suddenly remembered that when we went to see Saya Gyi P. Monin in the hospital, Ko Ko had gone to fetch a monk from another ward and had requested him to recite sutras for the dying writer. I ran back into the room and, placing my hand on Ko Ko's heaving chest, began to recite in a soft voice.

Zawana and Ko Ohn Myint came and stood by, looking on. I could not say a word to them but continued with my recitation. They left after a while. Daw Daw came from Kanbe and could only exclaim in pain when she saw us. She had brought some jasmine flowers that she placed near Ko Ko's nostrils for him to breathe in some refreshing scent.

I was reciting softly, not in the fierce way I had done just before we brought Ko Ko here. I recited in a cool, calm voice, as if I were praying in front of a shrine, so that he could listen to the words of the Buddhist texts with a peaceful mind. I held my face close to his and, although I could see him struggling to breathe, I was so intent on his passing peacefully that my voice did not falter, tremble, or break, and I made no mistakes.

Ko Ko suddenly shook his head violently and coughed, so I put my palm under his lips and a pile of mucus, hot as if boiling, dropped from his mouth into my hand; it was as if even at the very end he was teaching me about the impermanence of the human body. Just as I was coming to the end of the Dhamma Sekya[8] text, he coughed again, and this time his spirit passed out with his breath.

All the nerves that I had controlled rigidly for those days broke the moment I knew he was dead, and such a deep pain pierced my heart that I fell face down on his chest. I felt the monument of my dreams for our future crumble and break all around and on me, pinning me down with its weight. I struggled to lift up my face and saw Myanmar Alin U Tin and Thakin Nu coming into the room. As soon as I saw Thakin Nu, I remembered how Ko Ko had wanted so much to go to the Shan State, and I felt choked at the thought that I had denied this to him, so choked that I could not shed a single tear. If I had been able to cry at that moment, I might have cried my very life out of my body. I knelt down on the floor to *kadaw* his body three times and came away with Dr. Hla Shwe's wife to her house.

"Cry, Ma Tin Hlaing, let it out. Don't sit there like that, cry, cry out loud," Ma Khin Yi kept urging me. She had no idea what it was that was choking back my tears, and when Dr. Hla Shwe came home, he, too, told me not to keep it in but to release my mind with a good cry. They were afraid something would happen to me, and the kind couple led me tenderly to their own bed to lie down. To please them, I did lie down, and to please them I drank some coffee that they brought. Dr. Hla Shwe told me that others would take care of the body and prepare it for the funeral, so I nodded my head. Ma Khin Yi had such heartfelt sympathy for a bereaved woman that she treated me with utmost tenderness and, apart from my inability to cry, I gratefully rested under her care.

---

[8] The "Wheel of Dhamma" sermon, the first one given by Buddha after his enlightenment.

I was told that the body had been laid out in the Satu Ditha Zayat,[9] at the foot of the Shwedagon Pagoda, and I went there. When I arrived, Thakin Than Tun handed me the letter of condolence from the AFPFL, and I felt such a pain as if I were being cut up to bits, and tears began to well up in my eyes. But when I saw Bo Let Yar, my dam of tears broke and he, too, went behind a pillar to sit and sob his heart out.

When my children were brought to the Zayat, I looked at them and at the body, fully aware that I was now a widow and they fatherless, and my heart fluttered painfully as if it would break to pieces. Bo Let Yar would not allow me to remain at the rest house and forcefully made us go home. When we arrived at Kanbe, I did not go into my house but went to stay at Daw Daw's next door.

From there I could hear the sound of the press running, and at once I felt bitterness well up in me. I thought I would stop the press, but remembering Ko Ko's injunction never to let it stop, even if he were dead, I suffered the noise with an aching heart. I could not rest the whole night due to hearing the press, and I got up often to rub my aching chest and to drink glass after glass of water ... I felt such a burning inside me. I never suffered so much from the noise of the press as that night. Memories that stretched from the time of our first meeting at the Indo Burma Clinic until his death in the hospital kept haunting me, and my mind played tricks to make me think that he was still near me. None of my thoughts gave me any peace.

Ko Ko had been too busy to write the books he wanted, and I felt it was a great pity that his wishes were not fulfilled. I remembered what he had written in his diary on his birthday.

> *1306, 13 Waxing Moon Day of Pya Tho*[10]
>
> *Today I am 32 years old. As I look back, I can see nothing much that I have done to my satisfaction. It is the halfway mark of a lifetime, and yet I have many more things to accomplish.*
>
> *These are not personal: they are more about what I want to do for my country. What you do for your country benefits yourself, for if the country prospers, you prosper. If the country is poor and you prosper, this is not true prosperity.*
>
> *One day while we were chatting, Mr. Yoshida told me to stop reading and to write more. It is something I should consider. Since I was young, I have longed to serve my country and to that end have relentlessly studied and read and never considered that I knew enough. But maybe it is time to use whatever knowledge I have gained for the good of the country.*
>
> *If that is so, it seems that I must first strive to become known to be able to do something. In our country, one needs to be famous before one can achieve anything, and to work towards fame is something I am loathe to do. In this society, where writers are not considered men of ability and only demagogues are considered to be so, it is difficult for men of the pen to get anywhere in politics. But I believe my desire to do good will not be wasted, and if I cannot do all I want now, like the waxing moon I will slowly give forth some light.*

I tried to console myself that if he had not married me, he would probably have died much younger, given the way he had been living, and I tried to feel happy that

---

[9] Zayat is a rest house used for funerals or sermons, and where travelers may stay the night.
[10] December 26, 1944.

he managed do some things at least. At the same time, I was disappointed that all his aims had not been achieved. Before the morning, I had to decide how I would live on as a widow. I thought about what he had wanted to do and before dawn I had made up my mind: I would continue publishing *Journal Kyaw*.[11]

At Dr. Hla Shwe's house the previous day, I had told them I would use up my bag of savings for the funeral expenses. They both pleaded with me to keep it until my fortieth birthday as I had planned, to leave something for the children's future. I had no desire to keep or save the money any longer without him in my life. Daw Daw was very upset about this, too.

I wrote in the diary for 3 April: *A great loss for the whole country.*

---

[11] Ma Ma Lay did as she vowed, and U Saw Oo stayed on as chief editor. Bo Gyoke Aung San was assassinated by U Saw on July 19, 1947, along with members of his cabinet, and Myanmar gained its independence on January 4, 1948. In March 1948, while U Nu was prime minister of a democratic Myanmar, a scandal concerning one AFPFL "Thakin" of the Socialist faction was reported by three newspapers, including *Journal Kyaw*. The person who had been exposed sent a group of thugs under the banner of "Peasants and Farmers," led by a few members of the Socialist faction of AFPFL, to destroy the three publishing houses. This plan was unknown to Premier U Nu, but carried out with the knowledge of many AFPFL members. When he learned of the destruction, U Nu was appalled that such an atrocity had been committed in this new period of democracy. The government offered a loan, but no outright compensation, to the destroyed publishing houses. *Journal Kyaw* never recovered from this blow.

CHAPTER 37

A MAN LIKE HIM

Ko Ko's body was laid out for three days and the funeral expenses were borne by the AFPFL, so in the end he did not even burden me with that expense. I took all the cash from my savings bag and used it to do acts of merit on his behalf. The money I had planned to use at age forty was all gone at the age of twenty-nine, but as it was used for him, I was well satisfied.

On April, 5, 1946, we offered Soon and other offerings to thirty-five monks to mark Ko Ko's age,[1] and after the Tharanagon ritual at death and sharing merit with the deceased, we carried his coffin to Kyandaw Cemetery. A large crowd, including young children, walked all the way from the rest house at the foot of the Shwedagon Pagoda to the cemetery. I walked close behind his coffin. I told myself that in the life I would live without him by my side, I needed to be strong to face whatever fate brought me.

Bo Gyoke Aung San gave a speech in front of Ko Ko's open coffin. He said that this great man died "because unlike those in independent countries, our medical facilities are undeveloped." Poor Bo Gyoke did not know that actually there were *no* facilities at all at the hospital. As Bo Gyoke spoke, I reflected on all that I owed my husband and honored him repeatedly in my heart.

People knew Journal Kyaw U Chit Maung as an editor and, as such, he had the ability to learn from the past and to spotlight the situations of the present and future when writing for his readers. During the Japanese Occupation, he served his country in a vital role. His character was as solid as if hewn from unblemished rock, while his writings led others to believe in the same principles. He allowed others to pick his brains, willingly sharing what he knew with anyone and at anytime. He sowed the seeds of independence with whatever means he could. He worked hard but not for personal gain, and he was contented with little.

He was one who acted upon his words: there was no duality in him. He worked like a machine, an irreplaceable machine, for his country. Among men of whom one could say "he was such a man," he, too, could be said to be one ... "a man like him."

In the last satirical verse he wrote, he poked fun at the arrogance of those with power who cared naught for ordinary people. He said that, in such cases, the people can only suffer while they witness liars and frauds reveling in fame and glory. Any objections would be crushed, so those of pure heart who wished to speak out, he warned, would be silenced.

Indeed, he, too, has been silenced, as he wrote, silenced forever.

He was buried next to Bo Aung Kyaw.[2] At Bo Aung Kyaw's funeral, I had not been able to get through the crowds to see his resting place. Now, in burying my

---

[1] A person's years are marked not exactly, but with at least one year added.

[2] Journal Kyaw Ma Ma Lay passed away on April 6, 1982, and was also buried at Kyandaw Cemetery, but in a different section, as there is no tradition of reserving plots. In 1990, when

husband, I was standing right beside Bo Aung Kyaw's tomb. If I were any less strong, I would have fallen in a faint just thinking about it. They did not know each other well when alive, but in death they had come together.

Sad music was played, and the coffin opened for the last time as I knelt to *kadaw* my husband. After the coffin was closed and lowered into the grave, people saw me dropping lumps of earth into it. They would have no idea that to me they were not lumps of earth but lumps of love and my faith in him. Then I turned away and, not looking at anyone, left the cemetery and went straight home.

And from that day we were forever parted.

Journal Kyaw Ma Ma Lay

Kyandaw Cemetery was cleared, Daw Ma Ma Lay and U Chit Maung's remains were moved to Ye Way Cemetery and reburied side by side.

THE REAL ORIGIN AND CAUSES OF THE BURMA REBELLION (1930–32)[1]

I

To a casual observer the qualifying word may appear quite unnecessary. But to those who are already acquainted with the Blue book—the one and only on the subject—or, even less, with the bare title alone, the word "real" will be realized as one of absolute necessity.

For "The Origin and Causes of the Burma Rebellion (1930–32)," published under the orders and by the authority of the Government of Burma in the year 1934, has already broached the subject and branded it as a "carefully planned rebellion ... undoubtedly organized to overthrow the existing Government by force of arms" by Saya San, who "sincerely believed that he was destined to be a king."

We are not dismissing the findings of the Government as fully documented in that Report as wholly untrue. Far from that. The Report, be it said in all fairness, quite comprehensively and judiciously attempted to explain in its own inimitable way the Origin and Causes of the Burma Rebellion as the Government found them. It expressed the Truth—it did—though not the whole of it. It approached the subject from just one of the many angles—that of vindicating the character of the Government—and left it at a point where it had satisfied itself that the rebellion was the work of a man [Saya San] whose one motive and one object was hatred of the Government and intention to destroy it.

As we have observed earlier, the Blue book did speak the truth, though not the whole of it. And it has fallen to us now to start at the point where the Government decided conveniently to leave off, satisfied, and to explore far enough to get to the real origin and causes of the Rebellion of 1930, causes that lay behind those which the Blue book has found to be quite sufficient enough to serve its purpose. Hence the need of the qualifying word "real" in the title of this little essay.

II

The Government Report was cleverly built up. It had to prove that the persistent suggestions both inside and outside the Burma Legislative Council of the day to the effect that the prevailing economic depression and particularly the catastrophic fall in the price of paddy resulting in shortage of money, want, and starvation, were the main causes of the Rebellion of 1930 were not at all correct. It had to circumvent far beyond these reasons which politicians were quick to provide and people no less

---

[1] Mentioned in Chapter 32. A report written in English by U Chit Maung in early 1945 for the Japanese, at the request of Bo Sekkya.

slow in accepting. And it went just far enough to find evidence which "rapidly accumulated that although the rebellion was aggravated by, just as in its turn it proceeded to aggravate, economic stress, it was almost entirely political in origin." Then it went on to speak of Saya San, who "was a native of the Shwebo district in Upper Burma the district which furnished most of the recruits to the army of the Burmese kings and which was well known as the home of pretenders and leaders of rebellions, had been in turn, a *phongyi*,[2] a quack doctor, and a fortune teller, was first a member of the Chit Hlaing GCBA [General Council of Buddhists Associations] and subsequently transferred his allegiance to the So Thein GCBA, and apparently conceived the idea of a rebellion as far back as 1928, and was the actual leader of the rebellion in 1930."

If it could not prove all that, or if it failed to find that evidence which exposed Saya San as having exploited the prevailing economic and political situation, and engineered a nefarious plot to overthrow the authority and Government of the King-Emperor of India by himself proclaiming Thupannaka Galuna Raja, it would have been a very hard day for the government. For the whole world had been taken by surprise with the sudden outbreak of rebellion in Burma and it was wondering who was at fault—the Rebels or the Government? The rebels had to prove their case to the Government at special tribunals when once they were taken, and whatever it was, it was enough if and when the Government had heard it. But the Government had to prove its case to the world and show that it was not the offender but the offended. And it proved it so ably and successfully that it was able to carry on with its system of administration, without a single change for the better, of the people whom it ruled, and whom it found writhing in painful agony after, as indeed before, the Rebellion.

When all is considered, it had been the question of one Man or group of men against one set system, the Man with his mission to get rid of an Alien Government which was reducing his people to abject poverty amidst plenty which all the non-Burman were partaking themselves of in abundant munificence and the System with its policy to serve the higher interests of a large empire to the exclusion of everything else. And in a struggle of this kind, it was the weaker that must go down, and Saya San was no objection [*sic*. Probably should read "exception."] He fought like a fanatic and he fought like a brigand but he was fighting against overwhelming odds which an Empire in no time could and did, actually, place before him. And he went down and so swung for it.

III

The Report was ingenious enough not to rule out the economic stress of the time as having nothing to do with the Rebellion. To do that would be too absurd. So it very wisely set out to show that it was but one cause which Saya San exploited in order to raise the countryside in open rebellion. "But," it summed up, "there is not a scintilla of evidence in support of the thesis developed in some quarters that the rebellion was purely an economic rising, that it was the spontaneous revolt of an ignorant peasantry impoverished by the slump in paddy prices and maddened by harsh taxation, that it was chiefly due to oppression on the part of tax collectors, and that it was precipitated by a statement made in Tharrawaddy by His Excellency the Acting Governor on the 21st December 1930."

---

[2] A monk.

We who knew what there was to know knew for a fact that, whatever the Report might have said to the contrary, the Rebellion was motivated by an economic force and so was fundamentally an economic rising with, of course, a political coloring which simply could not be helped, that it was the spontaneous revolt of an angered if ignorant peasantry impoverished by the slump in paddy prices and maddened by harsh taxation, that it was indeed precipitated by a statement made in Tharrawaddy by His Excellency the Acting Governor on the 21st December 1930. And then, of course, there were other reasons.

IV

It is quite true that Saya San conceived the idea of a rebellion as far back as 1928. He was a very staunch Wunthanu (Nationalist) and there were hundreds of thousands like him who were finding it increasingly difficult to live in peace and contentment under a Government which was alien. The Burmese in their own country were beginning to find that the rulers did not mean to do much to improve their lot or to apportion an appreciable share of the country's vast wealth to them. There was not only no means of obtaining larger incomes but also no means of preserving what little they already owned in the teeth of increasing Indian and Chinese competition, which was already beginning to suffocate them. That foreigners, whoever they were and whatever they were, should be managing the country's resources only to fatten themselves and their folks at home and their folks' relatives and the relatives of their folks' relatives, while the sons and daughters of the soil had to toil and toil and toil endlessly just for the sake of living from hand to mouth on the barest minimum, was somehow evil and unnatural, and the irony of it was mocking them day and night. Their embittered minds were hardening, their tempers on edge. And that was only the economic aspect of the situation. On the political side, was it any better? There was a Legislative council which pretended without any great success to carry on the business of the Government in the name of the People: there as everywhere it was the dominating British and their underlings whose word was law. Look where they might, there was no hope of relief much less of salvation. Political parties there were, of which his own party was one, ranged as they were against the Government, but Saya San found that they were more or less impotent to check the latter from always having its own way.

The notorious Boolinger Pool, a private British combine which was responsible for the ever-lowering of the Burma rice market, was still in its prime, and the poor Burmese producers were reeling under the blows it was dealing. The world economic crisis, then in its earliest throes of pain, was stealthily beginning to tell on Burma's already bad conditions, and the people were in an acute state of distress and dismay. The rice market, which to the Burmese was as a first-aid ship, was fast floundering. The whole population knew that it was ruined. And if the British and Indians were equally or even more adversely affected, there was no sign of it anywhere for the Burmese to see. For they were as usual enjoying the best salt of the Burmese earth and were showing that they could take it.

All the politicians save those who happened to be holding office knew how hard things were going for the people; they saw that their incomes were diminishing and what little business they had was fast shriveling up, though the British and the Indians and the Chinese were still simply rolling in gold. Crops had not been good and their outturn was getting poorer and poorer. They could not keep pace with the cost of living, which somehow seemed to be going up and up. The people and more particularly the peasantry found that they were against the wall—dead stuck.

And January came and then February. The Government began to collect the Thathameda and Capitation taxes. It was the practice of the Government to collect taxes in earnest at this time of the year as paddy began to leave for the markets and people were supposed to have some money in hand. But the market was nowhere, it was nothing to the cost of production and the means of livelihood. People felt that it was clearly the duty of the Government to improve their sad plight, and as far as they knew no serious attempt whatsoever had been made in that direction. Then, why, why, argued they, should they pay their taxes, and how, to such a Government? The political creed of the day not to pay taxes was beginning now, as never before, to exert its whole force, and people found that they were subscribing to it anyhow.

They wanted to pay, but there was no means to pay. And when the tax collectors of the Government came they did not pay. The Government, affording to lose neither its face nor its fees, set wheels in motion, turned the lash of authority on the poor defaulters, and exacted the dues at any price. And what was the price? Hearths and homes, cattle and farm, the only belongings the poor people had in all the rich, rich land that was Burma, were either auctioned at ridiculous prices or razed to the ground. It cut the people's minds to the quick, but the Government had its collection all done with perhaps just a little more trouble than ordinarily necessary.

Such a state of things had been existing for more than one season now, and the Government became harsher and harsher each year. The impoverishment of the people was genuine and complete, but it was determined to have its dues, and where stubbornness was suspected, thither was dispatched promptly the Burma Military Police, composed largely of Punjabis and Gurkhas, who would destroy entire villages for a couple of rupees. Nor was that all. Property was looted and cattle slaughtered indiscriminately. Wives and village maidens were raped openly and in a beastly manner. Husbands were shot when they were not cruelly tortured in the presence of all. The Sanctity of religion was sacrileged, pagodas and *kyaungs*,[3] sacred places to the people, were raided and sacked, images decapitated, and *phongyis*, who attempted to intercede, thrashed.

The excesses of the Burma Military Police only increased with each year … they were most rampant in Tharrawaddy District, a place which was noted for its antipathy to pay taxes and its contempt of authority … and they reached to such an extent that the So Thein GCBA began to feel that something ought to be done. It could no longer look on. It had to do something, and before determining on its line of action, it would be necessary to know to the fullest extent where the people stood with a Government which was taking from them more than it was prepared to give. Saya San was accordingly chosen to go about the country on a fact-finding commission. He went as Chairman and toured the whole country, his heart hardening as he went on hearing tale after tale of the grossest excesses of the Burma Military Police. What second-hand information he formerly obtained of the real plight of the people starving and suffering so in their home of plenty was now conclusively confirmed by the statements he had straight from the horse's mouth and by the heart-rending sights he personally saw, the unmistakable signs of woe and misery, dire want and destitution.

---

[3] *Kyaungs* are monasteries.

He was now quite firmly convinced that the people living in such conditions, and as long as they were to continue to live in such conditions, could never be able to afford to pay their taxes: that the laws of the land were oppressive to the sons of the soil, for they permitted, if at all, little or no scope for satisfaction of one's bare needs. He came back from the country with a report in which he found it proved that "illegal acts and excesses had been committed by the authorities; ... it was necessary to protect villagers against a repetition of the aforesaid illegal acts and excesses by the formation of *athins*[4] for the resistance of forcible collection of the aforesaid two taxes."

He pleaded strongly with the principal chiefs of the So Thein GCBA (i) to resist the forcible collection of the capitation and Thathameda taxes, and (ii) to offer civil resistance against oppressive forest laws which deprived villagers of the free use of bamboo and timber for domestic purposes. That would mean open rebellion, and the GCBA was not prepared to go so far as that. A section was for supporting Saya San but it happened to be in such a minority that he thought it useless to press his points home. He saw now that he must act alone, all alone. He resigned from the GCBA and formed a Sandati Galon Association with the avowed purpose of carrying out the two proposals he had put forward. He could not run his party as a GCBA—there were too many of them already—and so he had to think of something original which would commend itself to the public and command a faithful and ardent following. He knew he would have to wage war against the British Government. He knew that it was no small affair. He must have as large a following in the country as possible. How could he raise it? Where and how soon?

The urban population was also badly hit, but he doubted if it would rally to his cause. It formed the lower middle class and was living on crumbs which the British, the Indians, and the Chinese let fall. So long as there was bread and so long as there was that eating, there would always be crumbs for them, however few they might be getting. He saw that he must go to the villages which were ruined already. And to go there as an ordinary leader would yield only ordinary results. His was going to be a very big fight, and preparations had to be correspondingly big. And that in Burma meant one thing and only one. He must make himself a really Big person. And were not the people in their acute distress prayerfully hoping that a Burmese King would return and drive all these aliens away and restore the natural resources to where they belonged? He must bank everything on that hope of theirs. He decided to go to them in exactly the same way as they wanted their deliverer to come. So he came to the resolution of going as a King, no less, and accordingly went about making preparations to rise against the British in right royal fashion. That, as far as he could see, was the easiest, quickest, and surest way, and he fell on it without any qualms.

V

But it was not until 1929–1930 that he proclaimed himself king with the title of Thupannaka Galuna Raja for the first time. It shows that Saya San was not eager to assume the title until it became absolutely necessary. At first he went about as merely President of the Galon[5] association collecting Strength. Only on the 13th December 1930 did he openly declare to his delegates from various parts of the country his intention to rebel and outline his plan for the rebellion. Until then he did

---

[4] *Athins* are organizations.

[5] Garuda Bird.

not speak of rebelling. He just went about his business. And had things improved, he would have abandoned the project, but the callous neglect and the cold attitude of the Government only made matters worse. In 1929 things reached such a peak that it was no longer possible to trust oneself to Fate. And to make matters far worse, still darker clouds were gathering on the horizon. Seventeen days later everyone knew that the British were openly trying to force separation of Burma from India on the people and to men of Saya San's School who were led to believe that the tying of Burma to the apron strings of India would bring Independence sooner than otherwise it was the grossest crime which Britain could ever contemplate.

Burma's constitutional status after the separation was uncertain, but the British Government in Burma had recommended separation and a certain type of constitution which smelled of inferiority. People were getting very fidgety, and the Government possessed no clue to the way in which their aroused spirit might manifest itself. It was common knowledge that Sir Charles Innes, Governor of Burma, was drafting a constitution of a separated Burma which not only fell far short of the aspirations of the people but also would be much inferior to that proposed by Parliament for India. It, so everyone believed, was for turning Burma into a Crown Colony, a trading preserve exclusively allotted to foreign capitalists, and for perpetuating the economic subservience of the Burmese people to these foreign exploiters.

Already there was one law for the white and another for the brown, and people feared that if Burma were to be separated from India, she would be left alone to carry on her struggle for independence which would never come. Combining forces with India, she had, they verily believed, a better chance of attaining her goal sooner. And as if to lend support to their fears, a case had occurred on 4th November 1929 in which one white man aided and abetted by another threw a brown man from a second story—threw him to his death—and yet at the inquest, the verdict had been "suicide"! Only the great indignation that was accordingly aroused and the drafting of certain questions on the case by certain members of the Legislature led to an open prosecution. And a fair measure of justice was meted out to the offending white man.

The year 1930 saw no change in official attitude. The Government seemed more than ever determined to have its pound of flesh while people found themselves stuck at a dead end. The peasantry were the hardest hit, and the fear of again losing their all, of again being slapped, thrashed, or chopped off at will by the Military Police, of again seeing their earthly possessions wantonly destroyed, and the fear of witnessing mutely their own daughters and sisters and even wives ruthlessly raped and ravished, began to haunt their minds afresh. They shuddered to think of it all, but they knew that they could not escape from that fate which had now become a persistent factor in their doomed lives. And as they thought, so did events happen, so many villages were burnt, so much modesty and sanctity outraged, and so little sympathy shown ...

Then came Sen Gupta with his gospel of freedom from the British yoke which he said would only come if the Burmese remained by India. He warned the Burmese "of the danger they ran by cutting themselves off from the great India paladins who were strong enough to stand up to the British." He said "he was certain that the British Government would cheat them if it possibly could." It was during the last week of February. On 17th March he again returned to Rangoon from Calcutta, a prisoner come to face the Rangoon District Magistrate to account for his February speeches, which were looked upon by the authorities as being highly seditious and inflammatory. His trial attracted even greater attention and created a lasting impression. A huge crowd of Indians had come to hear the proceedings, and one of them was parading with a banner. A mounted policeman came up—he was a Britisher—and attempted to interfere with the parade of the banner. This aroused the anger of the mob, which pulled the police off his pony at once: a scuffle ensued, a volley of bricks was thrown, and for one whole hour the crowd and the police had a real fight, which when brought to a close ended in eighty casualties.

That was the first attempt of the year 1930 to exhibit public dissatisfaction when the authorities were challenged with the only weapons that were at hand, bricks and missiles, though on that occasion the public was not only not large but not representative in that it was wholly Indian.

On the afternoon of 5 May, Mahatma Gandhi was arrested in India, and when news of it was received a few hours after in Rangoon, the Indians at once observed a *hartal*.[6] The Burmese did not do anything but looked on. But another event was to take place a couple of hours later which shook Burma to the very foundations. It was the big earthquake at 8:15 in the evening and many in Rangoon were injured and killed, many buildings toppled down into dust, and even the jeweled finial of the great Shwedagon came down with a crash. Pegu was almost completely destroyed, and casualties were heaviest there. The great Shwemawdaw Pagoda was rent into two, a larger part tumbling down in ruins.

The Indians interpreted this earthquake as a sign of victory to their Mahatma, but the Burmese did not think so. Surely an earthquake which was responsible for so much devastation of sacred structures could or should by no means be interpreted as being auspicious in any way. It could only mean one thing, and that was evil. Even the most optimistic among them took it to be a prelude to a still greater event which boded evil and which must certainly come.

Each to his interpretation, thus. But the Burmese hid it in their heads, while the Indians in their new found strength made a great show of it. Too great a show of it, so that on May 26, at about 10:00 AM, when a communal riot suddenly broke out, the Burmese found that they were heartily cracking, hacking, and thwacking one another's heads and limbs with comparative ease and skill. The Indians thus engaged were dock labourers, and the Burmese were poor people who had been driven by force of circumstances to look as a last resort for a job—the Indians' job at the docks. It would not be out of place to quote a Magistrate of the time, who in his famous book *Trials in Burma* wrote: "It seemed that the fight at the docks, which had started the conflagration, had followed an action on the part of a British firm of stevedores, which ordinarily employed hundreds of Indian labourers to stow and unload cargo in the port. There had been an Indian strike, and the firm had taken on Burmese labour to break it. (As a rule Burmans were not employed by stevedores, as they were disinclined to do that kind of work.) The strike had been settled the previous evening, and that morning, when the Burmans arrived to work, they were told that their services were no longer required. A number of Burmese women were there with their husbands' breakfasts in baskets. All of them walked in a long distance. The sudden news that they were not wanted was an irritation. They felt that they had been made a convenience of by the stevedores. Having broken the strike, they could now clear out."

---

[6] A sit-down strike.

At this touchy juncture the Indians committed the grave indiscretion of laughing at the Burmese in front of their women. As the Burmese regarded the Indians as little better than rats, which had swarmed into the country to the detriment of the working classes of the native population, they were disinclined to tolerate any hilarity at a moment when they found themselves in a humiliating position. A preliminary blow or two was struck, which the Indians were foolish enough to return, with the result that within half an hour at least two hundred Indians were cut down or flung into the river. The news was through the city in a flash. Some Indian reprisals were probably taken at this point, and the story of the mutilation of a Burmese woman was carried into the suburbs. Hundreds of Burmans then hurried to town. There developed a civil commotion on a grand scale which threatened to spread to the villages and lead to the death of the numerous Indians scattered over the country.

The poorer classes of the Burmese living in Rangoon, finding themselves up against a wall, without any outlet for their natural gifts and talents, deprived of every means of livelihood in their own homeland, had solved the problem in the only way they could. They saw the Indians reaping and growing fat on rich harvests which ought to be theirs by natural rights; they found that the Indians were everywhere taking the whole of the place, particularly in the field of labour, a portion of which at least ought to have been allotted to them; they realized that they had not even the dog's chance to work and live. If they who lived in Rangoon, the capital city, were in such straits, what would be the lot of those who worked the land—the Burmese proletariat that hoped to live decently on it, but that was every year deprived of its income by various factors which were getting farther and farther beyond their grasp, what with Indian capitalism on the one hand and British Imperialism on the other?

The subservience of the Burmese in their own country and the Government's indifferent attitude were responsible, more than most other causes, for the riots in Rangoon and later for the Rebellion itself.

VI

In the districts, in the year 1930, people were battling uselessly if bravely with economic laws which conspired to starve them all. Paddy markets had taken a downward flight, and the slump was getting abnormal. And another dreadful tax-collecting season was fast approaching when, alas, the usual round of excesses wantonly indulged by the Military Police would again arrive.

Sir Charles Innes had gone to England on four months' sick leave; he left Burma on August 12, having handed over the Governorship to Sir J. A. Maung Gyi a distinguished Burmese gentleman who served the government well. Sir Charles' absence, however short the duration, was a tremendous relief to the country, and the appointment of a Burmese senior in the gubernatorial office was for a while welcome news to all sections of the Burmese public. Sir J. A.'s own supporters hailed his appointment so enthusiastically that they led the ignorant to believe thereby that a Burman had actually become king of Burma and that Burma might now be governed wisely and well by this great Burman. The politicians did not think much of the appointment or at any rate they did not care much. Their minds were wholly occupied with the uncertainty of Burma's political future. A Round Table Conference in London of representatives from Burma to determine it was long mentioned, but still no invitation was issued from Whitehall. If the people were profoundly dissatisfied, so were politicians.

But Sir J. A.'s appointment as Acting Governor, so highly played up by a section of the Press which was supporting him, was serving as a ray of light to the dismayed and depressed whose hearts began to beat again in ardent anticipation. Perhaps he would ameliorate their conditions and restore them to their normal position.

They began quite eagerly to rely on him. They did not know that a Governor under existing laws could not do much, however well meaning he might be, much less a Burmese Governor hedged in as he was between very experienced British officials of the highest standing and craftiest intellect. He could do nothing even if he were so inclined. He was only a puppet, the strings were in British hands.

But who of the long suffering public would know? A Burman was occupying the greatest office in the country, and that was enough. They banked great and high hopes on him. He would come to the country's rescue. He would sympathetically hear their pleas. He was their last, their very last hope.

Then came newspaper announcements that His Excellency would be touring the country. He was scheduled to arrive at Tharrawaddy, that hotbed, on 1 December, when a *durbar*[7] was to be held. And in the mountain fastnesses, Saya San was fast maturing his plans ... his followers were getting ready ...

The 21st of December came and with it the Acting Governor. The *durbar* was fully attended, and one would quite honestly think that the audience had come to pay homage to a son of the soil at the height of his glory and in the topmost pinnacle of political fortune. Nobody except the parties themselves knew that in their midst were men whom Saya San had deputed to attend. It was arranged at the *durbar* to petition the Government for the reduction of taxes and postponement of their collection; Saya San had sent them to hear His Excellency's reply to it.

And what could the Acting Governor do? He quite honestly and promptly informed the audience that the petition could not be granted. He unfortunately did not explain the why and the how. Had he done that, he might have stayed Saya San's hand at least for some while. Even then it was doubtful, for the merciless truth had been dinned into the people's ears. His Excellency thought that he had said enough. He could not expose the fact that, though a Governor, he could not do anything of the nature without due consultations. To do that would be virtually admitting his anomalous position and his being no better than a puppet in the dexterous hands of British masters.

If His Excellency thought that he had said enough, Saya San's men thought that they too had on their part heard enough. For them, it was the last straw ...

VII

They were beside themselves with rage. They were faced with the blunt, painful truth that they had nobody else to appeal to, and no more to hope for. They cried for deliverance, they had sent out their SOS, but the highest person, the acting Lord of Burma, had decreed in their face that deliverance could not be. If such as he could not save them from their plight, how could those others? The representatives of the people, so called, who had pledged themselves at the election to roar and fight like

---

[7] A *durbar* may be either an official council for administering a state's affairs or a purely ceremonial gathering.

lions, and who ever since they were returned to the Legislative Council were braying and behaving just like asses?

Where, then, was help to come [from]? What way was there to take them out of the sea of distress whose hungry waves were already swallowing them up in their eternal fury?

Memories of the sad Past and the realization of the utter helplessness and hopelessness of the Present forced their way in and haunted their troubled minds afresh. And the vision of an empty Future with its regular features of oppression in the name of law arose, in all its irony and melancholy, in their eyes, which were getting dimmer and dimmer. What was left for them to do, aye, what?

There was a sound of approaching footsteps. A couple of men were coming up their way. Who was that man at the top who was coming on with light steps and a happy look as if the whole world had become his? Ah! Was he not the Headman of Seinza whom they had seen at the *durbar* receiving awards from His Excellency? Now why did he get such rewards, why? Was it not because he had served the Government well? And did not serving the Government well mean exhorting us folks to bleed white until the last *anna* or *pie*[8] was forcibly taken from us? Was it not he and his like who were directly oppressing us for the sake of those cursed rewards? Well, he would be a good riddance anyway, so let's finish him! Let us finish every damned agent of this accursed Government …

If their fleeting thoughts were dark, as indeed they were, their hands raised in desperation were defter. A scuffle ensued, just a scuffle, and the man with the rewards went down like a dog, and Saya San's man, collecting the arms and ammunition found in the possession of the fallen man and his party, made quickly for the hills, where their Master was waiting impatiently for their return.

The Tharrawaddy Rebellion, father of several risings that were soon to spread all the country over in those troubled times, had started!

VIII

In the above little essay I have attempted to parade the real origin and causes of the Burma Rebellion (1930–32) as I came to discover them. My capacity as a newspaper Editor has enabled me to make an independent inquiry into the events of those troubled years, and I have spared no pains or resources to obtain all the facts bearing on the question. And when in 1934 the Government Report came out as it did, I was tempted to challenge some of the conclusions it thought fit to draw, but conditions prevailing then and long afterwards have not been favourable. Through all those years, I have found that the whole truth would be regarded as gall and wormwood and that it would in no case be permitted to break the bonds of silence. For the Government had said its say and closed the chapter with perhaps a sigh. It had washed its hands of the affair. Falling into oblivion was the order of the day.

The above is a tragic story. It is the story of a peasant revolt in ancient style, à la Birmanie.[9] But is that all? No, it is more than a peasants' revolt. It is an open rebellion against an open conspiracy, the conspiracy being that of the British to keep the Burmese as their own slaves of labour, enjoying nothing of the country's riches which may be had in abundance, and it has been the most adversely affected section of the population that has taken up arms against authority. And there is one other

---

[8] Small denominations of coins.

[9] Birmanie: "Burma" in French.

reason which has goaded the poor people into rising, and that is the forcible collection of taxes which have never been popular in the country under British rule. A student of politics will realize that the system of taxation which was finding favour with the Government of the day has been too ill adjusted to the ever varying and unequal incomes of the people. Nor has it been fair. People feel that they are wronged. And when the Government goes in for forcibly collecting them and for harshly treating the defaulters, well, it would, anywhere and in any case and at any time, mean trouble. In December of the year 1930, when the poverty stricken peasants of Burma were asking the Governor for the reduction in and postponement of collection of taxes, they were asking not for more time to make effective preparations to rise against authority but for more time and opportunity to obtain a means of paying them. They were trying even at that moment to drive away the nightmare of the excesses of the Military Police, who would certainly come if they could not pay. But none understood their harrowing experiences, none knew of their fluttering hearts and their feverish hopes.

IX

It would not be irrelevant here to quote at length what a British, a flesh of their flesh, had to say on the subject. He is Maurice Collis, who has already been quoted above. He wrote:

"The rebellion, which at close quarters had been just another revolt in a year of revolts, now loomed up for what it was, a shocking tragedy. Why had the farmers and field labourers of Lower Burma, peasants whom generations of English writers had praised for their gentle religion and manners, their charity and high spirits, flung themselves with desperation in front of our machine guns? What had broken their hearts in 1930, making even death seem preferable to longer submission? These were not easy questions to answer, but my experiences had given me some clue to their answer.

"It seemed to me that during our occupation of Burma we had done two things there, which we ought not to have done. In spite of declarations to the contrary, we had placed English interests first, and we had treated the Burmans not as fellow creatures, but as inferior beings.

"... The Burmese lacked the capital and the knowledge to develop their mineral and forest wealth. We therefore let in capital from outside. Englishmen, Indians, and Chinese bought concessions and created great industries ... in the long run it came to this, that nearly all the rich people in the country were foreigners and that the Burmese, from being poor in a poor country, had become the poor in a rich one, a very different state of affairs, which meant that, relatively and from every psychological and human point of view, they were worse off than they were before. All sorts of foreigners lorded it over them, and had little opinion of them because they were poor.

"This is no place to suggest how the Government could have secured to the Burmans a part, at least, of the exploitation of the forest and mineral wealth of their country. It might not have been easy to fit the Burmans for modern commerce and industry, but if they have learned to become judges of the High court and Members of Council, it is fantastic to argue that they could not also have managed commercial undertakings. However, it was much simpler—and, of course, much more directly lucrative for us—to allow private enterprise, in the form of foreign capital, to do the work. This policy was also a stupid policy—we did not think of the Burmese first.

Many of our Civilians have lived lives of great devotion. But they could not redress the results of the invasion of foreign capital and of the crowds of Indian labourers who followed in its wake. The Burman became steadily less important industrially in his own country. In the capital, Rangoon, he was nobody. The stigma of poverty beat him down. The merchants treated him like an office boy, and the army in its ignorance thought of him only as a happy-go-lucky scamp.

"It was all this which was at the back of the peasants revolt. The situation in 1930 was enough to make any Burman doubt the good intentions of England. The constitutional agitation in India had ensured that Indians should get a liberal measure of self government. The Burmese felt that they had not succeeded in capturing the ear of Parliament. The desire of their leaders was to get to London and explain their case, but in 1930 it was uncertain whether a delegation from Burma, representing all interests, would be summoned to London. Impatient, desperate, deluded by prophecy and by the promises of magic, the least instructed part of the electorate broke out."

X

Thus concluded Maurice Collis who, had he desired, could, in keeping with all the Britishers of the land, easily have fallen in with the views of the Government as laid down in the Blue book and remained silent. But his thirst of knowledge, like ours, has probed deeper and found the real causes. How do they compare with those provided by the Government? And for that matter, with those furnished by us? It must be left to the reader to judge for himself.

IT IS ALL IN THE STATE OF MIND[1]

If you think you are beaten, you are;
If you think that you dare not, you don't;
If you'd like to win, but you think you can't
It's almost a cinch you won't.
If you think you'll lose, you're lost
For out in the world you'll find
Success begins with a fellow's will;
It's all in the state of mind.

Full many a race is lost
Ere even a step is run,
And many a coward fails
Ere even his works, begun.
Think big, and your deeds will grow,
Think small and you will fall behind.
Think that you CAN and you WILL;
It is all in the state of mind.

If you think you're outclassed, you are:
You've got to think high to rise;
You've got to be sure of yourself before
You can ever win a prize.
Life's battles don't always go
To the stronger or faster man.
But soon or late the man who wins
Is the fellow who thinks he can.

---

[1] Mentioned at the end of Chapter 32, this is the poem U Chit Maung recited to Daw Ma Ma Lay. Author unknown.

APPENDIX C

ANTI-FASCIST PEOPLE'S FREEDOM LEAGUE STATEMENT[1]

As soon as Militarist Fascism came to Burma to implant itself, the strain of its iron heels was such that the peoples of Burma found it utterly impossible to submit to it for any length of time. The Burma Army, the Communist Party, the People's Revolutionary Party, the East Asiatic Youth League, and a considerable section of the Mahabama, the Myochit Party, the Fabian Party, the Thakin Party, the Sanghas' Asi-ayone, and of the Karen, Shan, Kachin, Chin, Chinese, and Indian communities, began to strive each in its own way to struggle themselves free from Fascist oppression. In August 1944 it became possible to coordinate all the above-mentioned groups into one whole organization under the name of the Anti-Fascist People's Freedom League. When the League was thus founded, a great deal more of others from the vast public fervently sought its membership or alliance and from that moment on, the anti-Fascist activities which hitherto were carried on sporadically became much more centralized, systematized, and concentrated.

The League's primary objectives are:
- to drive Fascism out of the country until it is completely smashed in its homeland with, or even without, outside help, and
- to see that Burma positively attains her cherished goal of independence. The League rightly counted on all the freedom-loving peoples of Burma to give what aid they could in the event of an open struggle against Fascism taking place anywhere and at any time. The Burmese Army quite naturally was to lead the fight, with the people acting as active supporters in the rear. And in order to give utmost effect in the event of armed uprising, members of the League were recruited to undergo intensive political and military training.

The first task before the League, as has already been mentioned, was to rid the country of the Japanese. And as events have shown, it may say with justification that it has fairly accomplished it. No doubt there are still some Japanese divisions scattered all over Burma which remain to be wiped out. The League is confident that its fighting forces will do their best to accomplish this task in the quickest possible time. No quarter will be given to the Fascists wherever they may be. The League shall see that Fascism no more exists in this country in any form, nor for that matter in any part of the world.

The second objective still remains to be achieved. And the League is confident that the British Government as well as the Governments of the United Nations

---

[1] Mentioned in Chapter 33. This statement was written in English by U Chit Maung sometime in 1945.

already fully realize our political aspirations and that they will know how to honor a nation that has proved its worth by serving the cause of the Allies in a way which would have seemed quite unthinkable and impossible. For all the world knows that to defeat tens of thousands of Japanese at their own game—and in so short a time—was no easy task for an ill-equipped and oppressed nation such as ours to accomplish. It is no exaggeration to say that the Burmese have not only faced but also conquered overwhelming odds.

The League wishes to emphasize its political faith by reiterating the fact that, short of complete independence, no other form of Government will satisfy the people. The League wishes also to mention a simple but rather important fact, which should not be overlooked or underrated, that the Burmese during the past three or four years have undergone such a tremendous change in thought and outlook that they could no more be pushed back to the spiritual or political level of 1941. If anybody thinks that all that Burma wants now in the year of 1945 is supplies of food and clothing and materials for reconstruction purposes—these and these alone—he will be greatly mistaken. Burma does not want charity, though she would indeed be only too glad to accept the whole-hearted and honest cooperation and support of any or all of the free nations of the world in establishing herself in the world family of democratic nations. Burma only aspires to be completely independent—nothing more, nothing less. And she expects every honorable nation on the face of this earth to uphold her in this respect.

The League thinks it only fair to remind powers that be that the above-mentioned facts are not lost sight of in determining the future of Burma. The League declares solemnly that this and this alone is Burma's case and that there is none other.

Burma wants complete independence. Burma wants her constitution to be framed by a Constituent Assembly elected on the basis of universal adult suffrage as soon as war conditions in Burma permit. All her actions in the remote as well as in the recent past, all her actions at the present moment, should bear ample testimony to this fact.

Burma will not rest until she is free. And in a world just about to be free from the throes of a most deadly struggle for freedom from Fascist domination, Burma expects quite rightly that she will not be denied her Freedom. Were that to happen, which Heaven forbid, it would be tantamount to admitting that only a couple of Fascist powers have gone down in this deadly struggle and that Fascism still remains to keep smaller nations in subjugation. That would be losing the Peace. That would be War again, and the League fervently hopes that the Frankenstein monster of Fascism is finally nailed in its coffin and that no Phoenix of disguised or unadulterated Fascism may ever rise again from the ashes.

SOUTHEAST ASIA PROGRAM PUBLICATIONS

Cornell University

Studies on Southeast Asia

Number 47   *A Man Like Him: Portrait of the Burmese Journalist, Journal Kyaw U Chit Maung*, Journal Kyaw Ma Ma Lay, trans. Ma Thanegi, 2008. ISBN 978-0-87727-747-7 (pb.)

Number 46   *At the Edge of the Forest: Essays on Cambodia, History, and Narrative in Honor of David Chandler*, ed. Anne Ruth Hansen and Judy Ledgerwood. 2008. ISBN 978-0-87727-746-0 (pb).

Number 45   *Conflict, Violence, and Displacement in Indonesia*, ed. Eva-Lotta E. Hedman. 2008. ISBN 978-0-87727-745-3 (pb).

Number 44   *Friends and Exiles: A Memoir of the Nutmeg Isles and the Indonesian Nationalist Movement*, Des Alwi, ed. Barbara S. Harvey. 2008. ISBN 978-0-877277-44-6 (pb).

Number 43   *Early Southeast Asia: Selected Essays*, O. W. Wolters, ed. Craig J. Reynolds. 2008. 255 pp. ISBN 978-0-877277-43-9 (pb).

Number 42   *Thailand: The Politics of Despotic Paternalism* (revised edition), Thak Chaloemtiarana. 2007. 284 pp. ISBN 0-8772-7742-7 (pb).

Number 41   *Views of Seventeenth-Century Vietnam: Christoforo Borri on Cochinchina and Samuel Baron on Tonkin*, ed. Olga Dror and K. W. Taylor. 2006. 290 pp. ISBN 0-8772-7741-9 (pb).

Number 40   *Laskar Jihad: Islam, Militancy, and the Quest for Identity in Post-New Order Indonesia*, Noorhaidi Hasan. 2006. 266 pp. ISBN 0-877277-40-0 (pb).

Number 39   *The Indonesian Supreme Court: A Study of Institutional Collapse*, Sebastiaan Pompe. 2005. 494 pp. ISBN 0-877277-38-9 (pb).

Number 38   *Spirited Politics: Religion and Public Life in Contemporary Southeast Asia*, ed. Andrew C. Willford and Kenneth M. George. 2005. 210 pp. ISBN 0-87727-737-0.

Number 37   *Sumatran Sultanate and Colonial State: Jambi and the Rise of Dutch Imperialism, 1830-1907*, Elsbeth Locher-Scholten, trans. Beverley Jackson. 2004. 332 pp. ISBN 0-87727-736-2.

Number 36   *Southeast Asia over Three Generations: Essays Presented to Benedict R. O'G. Anderson*, ed. James T. Siegel and Audrey R. Kahin. 2003. 398 pp. ISBN 0-87727-735-4.

Number 35   *Nationalism and Revolution in Indonesia*, George McTurnan Kahin, intro. Benedict R. O'G. Anderson (reprinted from 1952 edition, Cornell University Press, with permission). 2003. 530 pp. ISBN 0-87727-734-6.

Number 34   *Golddiggers, Farmers, and Traders in the "Chinese Districts" of West Kalimantan, Indonesia*, Mary Somers Heidhues. 2003. 316 pp. ISBN 0-87727-733-8.

Number 33   *Opusculum de Sectis apud Sinenses et Tunkinenses (A Small Treatise on the Sects among the Chinese and Tonkinese): A Study of Religion in China and North Vietnam in the Eighteenth Century*, Father Adriano de St. Thecla, trans. Olga Dror, with Mariya Berezovska. 2002. 363 pp. ISBN 0-87727-732-X.

Number 12   *Fields from the Sea: Chinese Junk Trade with Siam during the Late Eighteenth and Early Nineteenth Centuries,* Jennifer Cushman. 1993. 206 pp. ISBN 0-87727-711-7.

Number 11   *Money, Markets, and Trade in Early Southeast Asia: The Development of Indigenous Monetary Systems to AD 1400,* Robert S. Wicks. 1992. 2nd printing 1996. 354 pp., 78 tables, illus., maps. ISBN 0-87727-710-9.

Number 10   *Tai Ahoms and the Stars: Three Ritual Texts to Ward Off Danger,* trans., ed. B. J. Terwiel, Ranoo Wichasin. 1992. 170 pp. ISBN 0-87727-709-5.

Number 9   *Southeast Asian Capitalists,* ed. Ruth McVey. 1992. 2nd printing 1993. 220 pp. ISBN 0-87727-708-7.

Number 8   *The Politics of Colonial Exploitation: Java, the Dutch, and the Cultivation System,* Cornelis Fasseur, ed. R. E. Elson, trans. R. E. Elson, Ary Kraal. 1992. 2nd printing 1994. 266 pp. ISBN 0-87727-707-9.

Number 7   *A Malay Frontier: Unity and Duality in a Sumatran Kingdom,* Jane Drakard. 1990. 2nd printing 2003. 215 pp. ISBN 0-87727-706-0.

Number 6   *Trends in Khmer Art,* Jean Boisselier, ed. Natasha Eilenberg, trans. Natasha Eilenberg, Melvin Elliott. 1989. 124 pp., 24 plates. ISBN 0-87727-705-2.

Number 5   *Southeast Asian Ephemeris: Solar and Planetary Positions, A.D. 638–2000,* J. C. Eade. 1989. 175 pp. ISBN 0-87727-704-4.

Number 3   *Thai Radical Discourse: The Real Face of Thai Feudalism Today,* Craig J. Reynolds. 1987. 2nd printing 1994. 186 pp. ISBN 0-87727-702-8.

Number 1   *The Symbolism of the Stupa,* Adrian Snodgrass. 1985. Revised with index, 1988. 3rd printing 1998. 469 pp. ISBN 0-87727-700-1.

SEAP Series

Number 23   *Possessed by the Spirits: Mediumship in Contemporary Vietnamese Communities.* 2006. 186 pp. ISBN 0-877271-41-0 (pb).

Number 22   *The Industry of Marrying Europeans,* Vũ Trọng Phụng, trans. Thúy Tranviet. 2006. 66 pp. ISBN 0-877271-40-2 (pb).

Number 21   *Securing a Place: Small-Scale Artisans in Modern Indonesia,* Elizabeth Morrell. 2005. 220 pp. ISBN 0-877271-39-9.

Number 20   *Southern Vietnam under the Reign of Minh Mạng (1820-1841): Central Policies and Local Response,* Choi Byung Wook. 2004. 226pp. ISBN 0-0-877271-40-2.

Number 19   *Gender, Household, State: Đổi Mới in Việt Nam,* ed. Jayne Werner and Danièle Bélanger. 2002. 151 pp. ISBN 0-87727-137-2.

Number 18   *Culture and Power in Traditional Siamese Government,* Neil A. Englehart. 2001. 130 pp. ISBN 0-87727-135-6.

Number 17   *Gangsters, Democracy, and the State,* ed. Carl A. Trocki. 1998. Second printing, 2002. 94 pp. ISBN 0-87727-134-8.

Number 16   *Cutting across the Lands: An Annotated Bibliography on Natural Resource Management and Community Development in Indonesia, the Philippines, and Malaysia,* ed. Eveline Ferretti. 1997. 329 pp. ISBN 0-87727-133-X.

Number 15   *The Revolution Falters: The Left in Philippine Politics after 1986*, ed. Patricio N. Abinales. 1996. Second printing, 2002. 182 pp. ISBN 0-87727-132-1.

Number 14   *Being Kammu: My Village, My Life*, Damrong Tayanin. 1994. 138 pp., 22 tables, illus., maps. ISBN 0-87727-130-5.

Number 13   *The American War in Vietnam*, ed. Jayne Werner, David Hunt. 1993. 132 pp. ISBN 0-87727-131-3.

Number 12   *The Voice of Young Burma*, Aye Kyaw. 1993. 92 pp. ISBN 0-87727-129-1.

Number 11   *The Political Legacy of Aung San*, ed. Josef Silverstein. Revised edition 1993. 169 pp. ISBN 0-87727-128-3.

Number 10   *Studies on Vietnamese Language and Literature: A Preliminary Bibliography*, Nguyen Dinh Tham. 1992. 227 pp. ISBN 0-87727-127-5.

Number 8   *From PKI to the Comintern, 1924–1941: The Apprenticeship of the Malayan Communist Party*, Cheah Boon Kheng. 1992. 147 pp. ISBN 0-87727-125-9.

Number 7   *Intellectual Property and US Relations with Indonesia, Malaysia, Singapore, and Thailand*, Elisabeth Uphoff. 1991. 67 pp. ISBN 0-87727-124-0.

Number 6   *The Rise and Fall of the Communist Party of Burma (CPB)*, Bertil Lintner. 1990. 124 pp. 26 illus., 14 maps. ISBN 0-87727-123-2.

Number 5   *Japanese Relations with Vietnam: 1951–1987*, Masaya Shiraishi. 1990. 174 pp. ISBN 0-87727-122-4.

Number 3   *Postwar Vietnam: Dilemmas in Socialist Development*, ed. Christine White, David Marr. 1988. 2nd printing 1993. 260 pp. ISBN 0-87727-120-8.

Number 2   *The Dobama Movement in Burma (1930–1938)*, Khin Yi. 1988. 160 pp. ISBN 0-87727-118-6.

Cornell Modern Indonesia Project Publications

Number 75   *A Tour of Duty: Changing Patterns of Military Politics in Indonesia in the 1990s*. Douglas Kammen and Siddharth Chandra. 1999. 99 pp. ISBN 0-87763-049-6.

Number 74   *The Roots of Acehnese Rebellion 1989–1992*, Tim Kell. 1995. 103 pp. ISBN 0-87763-040-2.

Number 73   *"White Book" on the 1992 General Election in Indonesia*, trans. Dwight King. 1994. 72 pp. ISBN 0-87763-039-9.

Number 72   *Popular Indonesian Literature of the Qur'an*, Howard M. Federspiel. 1994. 170 pp. ISBN 0-87763-038-0.

Number 71   *A Javanese Memoir of Sumatra, 1945–1946: Love and Hatred in the Liberation War*, Takao Fusayama. 1993. 150 pp. ISBN 0-87763-037-2.

Number 70   *East Kalimantan: The Decline of a Commercial Aristocracy*, Burhan Magenda. 1991. 120 pp. ISBN 0-87763-036-4.

Number 69   *The Road to Madiun: The Indonesian Communist Uprising of 1948*, Elizabeth Ann Swift. 1989. 120 pp. ISBN 0-87763-035-6.

Number 68   *Intellectuals and Nationalism in Indonesia: A Study of the Following Recruited by Sutan Sjahrir in Occupation Jakarta*, J. D. Legge. 1988. 159 pp. ISBN 0-87763-034-8.

Number 67   *Indonesia Free: A Biography of Mohammad Hatta*, Mavis Rose. 1987. 252 pp. ISBN 0-87763-033-X.

Number 66   *Prisoners at Kota Cane*, Leon Salim, trans. Audrey Kahin. 1986. 112 pp. ISBN 0-87763-032-1.

Number 65   *The Kenpeitai in Java and Sumatra*, trans. Barbara G. Shimer, Guy Hobbs, intro. Theodore Friend. 1986. 80 pp. ISBN 0-87763-031-3.

Number 64   *Suharto and His Generals: Indonesia's Military Politics, 1975–1983*, David Jenkins. 1984. 4th printing 1997. 300 pp. ISBN 0-87763-030-5.

Number 62   *Interpreting Indonesian Politics: Thirteen Contributions to the Debate, 1964– 1981*, ed. Benedict Anderson, Audrey Kahin, intro. Daniel S. Lev. 1982. 3rd printing 1991. 172 pp. ISBN 0-87763-028-3.

Number 60   *The Minangkabau Response to Dutch Colonial Rule in the Nineteenth Century*, Elizabeth E. Graves. 1981. 157 pp. ISBN 0-87763-000-3.

Number 59   *Breaking the Chains of Oppression of the Indonesian People: Defense Statement at His Trial on Charges of Insulting the Head of State, Bandung, June 7–10, 1979*, Heri Akhmadi. 1981. 201 pp. ISBN 0-87763-001-1.

Number 57   *Permesta: Half a Rebellion*, Barbara S. Harvey. 1977. 174 pp. ISBN 0-87763-003-8.

Number 55   *Report from Banaran: The Story of the Experiences of a Soldier during the War of Independence*, Maj. Gen. T. B. Simatupang. 1972. 186 pp. ISBN 0-87763-005-4.

Number 52   *A Preliminary Analysis of the October 1 1965, Coup in Indonesia (Prepared in January 1966)*, Benedict R. Anderson, Ruth T. McVey, assist. Frederick P. Bunnell. 1971. 3rd printing 1990. 174 pp. ISBN 0-87763-008-9.

Number 51   *The Putera Reports: Problems in Indonesian-Japanese War-Time Cooperation*, Mohammad Hatta, trans., intro. William H. Frederick. 1971. 114 pp. ISBN 0-87763-009-7.

Number 50   *Schools and Politics: The Kaum Muda Movement in West Sumatra (1927– 1933)*, Taufik Abdullah. 1971. 257 pp. ISBN 0-87763-010-0.

Number 49   *The Foundation of the Partai Muslimin Indonesia*, K. E. Ward. 1970. 75 pp. ISBN 0-87763-011-9.

Number 48   *Nationalism, Islam and Marxism*, Soekarno, intro. Ruth T. McVey. 1970. 2nd printing 1984. 62 pp. ISBN 0-87763-012-7.

Number 43   *State and Statecraft in Old Java: A Study of the Later Mataram Period, 16th to 19th Century*, Soemarsaid Moertono. Revised edition 1981. 180 pp. ISBN 0-87763-017-8.

Number 39   Preliminary Checklist of Indonesian Imprints (1945-1949), John M. Echols. 186 pp. ISBN 0-87763-025-9.

Number 37   *Mythology and the Tolerance of the Javanese*, Benedict R. O'G. Anderson. 2nd edition, 1996. Reprinted 2004. 104 pp., 65 illus. ISBN 0-87763-041-0.

Number 25   *The Communist Uprisings of 1926–1927 in Indonesia: Key Documents*, ed., intro. Harry J. Benda, Ruth T. McVey. 1960. 2nd printing 1969. 177 pp. ISBN 0-87763-024-0.

Number 7   *The Soviet View of the Indonesian Revolution*, Ruth T. McVey. 1957. 3rd printing 1969. 90 pp. ISBN 0-87763-018-6.

Number 6   *The Indonesian Elections of 1955,* Herbert Feith. 1957. 2nd printing 1971. 91 pp. ISBN 0-87763-020-8.

Translation Series

Volume 4   *Approaching Suharto's Indonesia from the Margins,* ed. Takashi Shiraishi. 1994. 153 pp. ISBN 0-87727-403-7.

Volume 3   *The Japanese in Colonial Southeast Asia,* ed. Saya Shiraishi, Takashi Shiraishi. 1993. 172 pp. ISBN 0-87727-402-9.

Volume 2   *Indochina in the 1940s and 1950s,* ed. Takashi Shiraishi, Motoo Furuta. 1992. 196 pp. ISBN 0-87727-401-0.

Volume 1   *Reading Southeast Asia,* ed. Takashi Shiraishi. 1990. 188 pp.
ISBN 0-87727-400-2.

Language Texts

INDONESIAN

Beginning Indonesian through Self-Instruction, John U. Wolff, Dédé Oetomo, Daniel Fietkiewicz. 3rd revised edition 1992. Vol. 1. 115 pp. ISBN 0-87727-529-7. Vol. 2. 434 pp. ISBN 0-87727-530-0. Vol. 3. 473 pp. ISBN 0-87727-531-9.

Indonesian Readings, John U. Wolff. 1978. 4th printing 1992. 480 pp.
ISBN 0-87727-517-3

Indonesian Conversations, John U. Wolff. 1978. 3rd printing 1991. 297 pp.
ISBN 0-87727-516-5

Formal Indonesian, John U. Wolff. 2nd revised edition 1986. 446 pp.
ISBN 0-87727-515-7

TAGALOG

Pilipino through Self-Instruction, John U. Wolff, Maria Theresa C. Centeno, Der-Hwa V. Rau. 1991. Vol. 1. 342 pp. ISBN 0-87727—525-4. Vol. 2., revised 2005, 378 pp. ISBN 0-87727-526-2. Vol 3., revised 2005, 431 pp. ISBN 0-87727-527-0. Vol. 4. 306 pp. ISBN 0-87727-528-9.

THAI

A. U. A. Language Center Thai Course, J. Marvin Brown. Originally published by the American University Alumni Association Language Center, 1974. Reissued by Cornell Southeast Asia Program, 1991, 1992. Book 1. 267 pp. ISBN 0-87727-506-8. Book 2. 288 pp. ISBN 0-87727-507-6. Book 3. 247 pp. ISBN 0-87727-508-4.

A. U. A. Language Center Thai Course, Reading and Writing Text (mostly reading), 1979. Reissued 1997. 164 pp. ISBN 0-87727-511-4.

A. U. A. Language Center Thai Course, Reading and Writing Workbook (mostly writing), 1979. Reissued 1997. 99 pp. ISBN 0-87727-512-2.

KHMER

Cambodian System of Writing and Beginning Reader, Franklin E. Huffman. Originally published by Yale University Press, 1970. Reissued by Cornell Southeast Asia Program, 4th printing 2002. 365 pp. ISBN 0-300-01314-0.

Modern Spoken Cambodian, Franklin E. Huffman, assist. Charan Promchan, Chhom-Rak Thong Lambert. Originally published by Yale University Press, 1970.

Reissued by Cornell Southeast Asia Program, 3rd printing 1991. 451 pp. ISBN 0-300-01316-7.

Intermediate Cambodian Reader, ed. Franklin E. Huffman, assist. Im Proum. Originally published by Yale University Press, 1972. Reissued by Cornell Southeast Asia Program, 1988. 499 pp. ISBN 0-300-01552-6.

Cambodian Literary Reader and Glossary, Franklin E. Huffman, Im Proum. Originally published by Yale University Press, 1977. Reissued by Cornell Southeast Asia Program, 1988. 494 pp. ISBN 0-300-02069-4.

HMONG

White Hmong-English Dictionary, Ernest E. Heimbach. 1969. 8th printing, 2002. 523 pp. ISBN 0-87727-075-9.

VIETNAMESE

Intermediate Spoken Vietnamese, Franklin E. Huffman, Tran Trong Hai. 1980. 3rd printing 1994. ISBN 0-87727-500-9.

* * *

Southeast Asian Studies: Reorientations. Craig J. Reynolds and Ruth McVey. Frank H. Golay Lectures 2 & 3. 70 pp. ISBN 0-87727-301-4.

Javanese Literature in Surakarta Manuscripts, Nancy K. Florida. Vol. 1, *Introduction and Manuscripts of the Karaton Surakarta*. 1993. 410 pp. Frontispiece, illustrations. Hard cover, ISBN 0-87727-602-1, Paperback, ISBN 0-87727-603-X. Vol. 2, *Manuscripts of the Mangkunagaran Palace*. 2000. 576 pp. Frontispiece, illustrations. Paperback, ISBN 0-87727-604-8.

Sbek Thom: Khmer Shadow Theater. Pech Tum Kravel, trans. Sos Kem, ed. Thavro Phim, Sos Kem, Martin Hatch. 1996. 363 pp., 153 photographs. ISBN 0-87727-620-X.

In the Mirror: Literature and Politics in Siam in the American Era, ed. Benedict R. O'G. Anderson, trans. Benedict R. O'G. Anderson, Ruchira Mendiones. 1985. 2nd printing 1991. 303 pp. Paperback. ISBN 974-210-380-1.

To order, please contact:
Mail:
Cornell University Press Services
750 Cascadilla Street
PO Box 6525
Ithaca, NY 14851 USA

E-mail: orderbook@cupserv.org

Phone/Fax, Monday–Friday, 8 am – 5 pm (Eastern US):
Phone: 607 277 2211 or 800 666 2211 (US, Canada)
Fax: 607 277 6292 or 800 688 2877 (US, Canada)

Order through our online bookstore at:
www.einaudi.cornell.edu/southeastasia/publications/

www.ingramcontent.com/pod-product-compliance
Ingram Content Group UK Ltd.
Pitfield, Milton Keynes, MK11 3LW, UK
UKHW012252060225
454777UK00009B/768